Stones of Contention

Stones
of
Contention

Timothy H. Ives

Published by New English Review Press
a subsidiary of World Encounter Institute
PO Box 158397
Nashville, Tennessee 37215
&
27 Old Gloucester Street
London, England, WC1N 3AX

Cover Art and Design by Kendra Mallock

ISBN: 978-1-943003-54-9

First Edition

NEW ENGLISH REVIEW PRESS
newenglishreview.org

To the memory of Roger Williams, an individual who championed freedom of thought, created a haven for political and religious dissidents, was part of a movement that succeeded in briefly outlawing slavery, spoke out to defend indigenous land rights, and published a compassionate portrait of Narragansett Indian language and culture that remains nothing less than a national treasure. And he pursued these projects with little regard for his own safety, holding a critical mirror to the prevailing prejudices of his day.

CONTENTS

AUTHOR'S NOTE   9

INTRODUCTION: WELCOME TO THE LAND OF STEADY
HABITS   13

1 - ON THE ZEITGEIST OF RACIAL DYSPHORIA, REPARATIONS,
AND DECOLONIZATION   18

2 - PLOTTING A COURSE FOR CEREMONIAL STONE
LANDSCAPES   31

3 - ON SEEING BEYOND VISIONS   37

   PART ONE: THE RISE OF CEREMONIAL STONE
   LANDSCAPE ACTIVISM   43

4 - BROMANCING THE STONES   45

5 - A MODEST CULT FOLLOWING   52

6 - CARLISLE EPISODE I: A RAINCHECK FOR WHITE
VISIONARIES   56

7 - CONVERTING "THE INDIANS" BACK   61

8 - CARLISLE EPISODE II: WE HAVE "THE INDIANS"   66

9 - A WONDERFUL WEAPON   71

10 - INDIGENIZING THE MOVEMENT   75

11 - ANTIQUARIANSGONEWILD.COM   82

PART TWO: INCONVENIENT INFORMATION   87

12 - WAYSIDE MEMORIES   89

13 - FORGOTTEN FARMS   100

14 - ARCHAEOLOGICAL EVIDENCE   115

PART THREE: STONES OF CONTENTION   125

15 - ROOTS AND BRANCHES OF RACIAL PARANOIA   127

16 - THE GRAFT OF WHITE SETTLER COLONIAL GUILT   141

17 - THE WRONG SIDE OF HISTORY   147

18 - ANATOMY OF A RACIAL BARGAIN   153

19 - A "GOOD GUYS VERSUS BAD GUYS" MINDSET   163

20 - THE ACADEMIC SWAMP   166

21 - THE HUNT FOR REDNECK ARCHAEOLOGY   171

22 - THE NEW ANTI-RACIST FACE OF NIMBYISM   181

23 - A STORM GATHERS   186

24 - PEACE, BALANCE, AND HARMONY COME TO TOWN   189

CONCLUSION: EXITS ARE LOCATED ON EITHER SIDE OF THE THEATRE   199

25 - THE THEORY THAT DARE NOT SPEAK ITS NAME   201

26 - BALDWIN WAS RIGHT   210

BIBLIOGRAPHY   213

AUTHOR'S NOTE

THIS BOOK DID NOT find its way into your hands easily. It was originally accepted for publication in the controversial "Problems of Anti-Colonialism" book series, which aimed to critically examine anti-colonial history, scholarship, and politics under the assumption that appraising their benefits *and* costs to humanity at large makes sense. Rowman & Littlefield, who originally committed to publishing this series, dropped it in October of 2020 after receiving a Change.org petition signed by leftist academics accusing the series of being a "white nationalist" project. The fact that one of the two co-editors, Dr. Eric Louw, is a former United Democratic Front activist who put his very life on the line pursuing the defeat of South Africa's apartheid regime was, apparently, irrelevant. The series was subsequently taken on by Anthem Press, who dropped it in March of 2021 after a leftist academic Twitter mob made similar objections without acknowledging that the series' growing international editorial board had been joined by Drs. Fouad Mami and Wanjiru Njoya. With the series frozen in leftist carbonite, publishing this book independently with a smaller and braver outfit presented the next logical option. Rebecca Bynum, editor of New English Review Press, agreed to take on this manuscript and see it through publication. Of course, I surveyed this publisher's diverse catalog of book titles and descriptions before signing the contract. Some looked amusing, others thought-provoking, and yet others alarming. The scene reminded me of large family gatherings during the holidays, where heated arguments concerning politics, religion, and culture constantly erupt over appetizers and dinner but have never prevented any of us from meeting again at the same time next year, always with new ideas and viewpoints to share. I am grateful to have been welcomed to the table of New English Review Press.

Note that I have not written this book in my capacity as Rhode Island's state archaeologist. This has not been authorized, endorsed, or even so much as previewed by my employer, the Rhode Island Historical Preservation and Heritage Commission, so it should not be presumed to represent the views or opinions of that agency. Nonetheless, my workplace experiences have proven so integral to my understanding of the topic of ceremonial stone landscapes that any attempt to filter them out of this book would significantly diminish the breadth and efficacy of its analysis. Accordingly, I afford the lessons of personal memoir equal standing to those of archaeology, history, journalism, and social criticism, combining them in a literary excavation broad enough to expose its object from many angles.

Essentially, this book combines a series of journal articles that I have published concerning historical stone heaping practices and the Ceremonial Stone Landscape Movement with some additional context and commentary. Scattered throughout Part 1 are passages from my 2015 article in the *Bulletin of the Archaeological Society of Connecticut* titled "Romance, Redemption, and Ceremonial Stone Landscapes." Most of Chapter 12 consists of sections from my 2013 article in *Northeast Anthropology* titled "Remembering Stone Piles in New England," while Chapter 13 is largely a reproduction of my forthcoming article in *Northeast Historical Archaeology* titled "Historical Accounts of Forgotten Stone Heaping Practices on Nineteenth Century Hill Farms." Portions of Chapter 14 were adapted from my 2014 article in *Archaeology of Eastern North America* titled "Cairnfields in New England's Forgotten Pastures," while numerous passages from my 2018 article in *Northeast Anthropology* titled "The Hunt for Redneck Archaeology" appear in Part 3. These materials are all used with permission.

I commend the politically neutral reporting of Massachusetts-based journalist Mary Serreze, who has allowed me to reproduce photographs she took when covering the ceremonial stone landscape preservation campaign discussed in Chapter 24. Otherwise, know that I have written this book in virtual solitude, disregarding any possibility of assistance from friends or colleagues to insulate them from any associated controversy. And I would never have written this book without the interest and encouragement of perhaps the least insulated scholar of our time, Dr. Bruce Gilley.

You may be struck by the total absence of doe-eyed idealism in my writing, which reflects a major shift in perspective that I experienced in recent years that has left me, in some ways, almost unrecognizable to my former self. And that former self was quite the doe-eyed idealist. I could never forget how excited I felt, as a student of archaeology in the early 1990s, to be entering a field that promised to mitigate racism in America. I fantasized about working alongside Indians to pursue deeper understandings of our colonial-era pasts as we gleefully dismantled whatever ideological machinery prevented us from truly seeing one another in the present. It was a noble and poetic vision which carried a generic promise of "making a difference" in the world. What I failed to foresee was that ideological machinery being ironically maintained by a morally elite stratum of antiquarians, archaeologists, and Indians in the twenty-first century. But this century is young, and I would like to believe that if we can harness enough courage and humility to allow our visions to pass into, rather than replace, history, social progress may become free to resume.

Lastly, I wish to address those readers who count themselves among New England's Indians. Over much of my adulthood, I have had the great privilege of learning from many of you. And one thing I have begun to understand is the depth of adversity that many of your ancestors negotiated for centuries under the cruel and shifting pressures of colonialism. I have heard family stories of racism and abuse so extreme that they have made me feel sick in body and spirit. And I have become convinced that on the stage of world history, the survival of your people through such conditions demonstrates the resilience, pragmatism, and strength of the human spirit on the highest order imaginable. Arguably, one of colonial society's greatest offenses was its radical break from reality, denying many of your ancestors their full humanity and even inventing histories to erase their very identities. Fortunately, that house of cards has finally collapsed. Unfortunately, the collapse itself has stirred up such a cloud of shame and racial anxiety that it has become difficult for anyone to see clearly, or to move on.

Out of respect for these truths, I do not trivialize or romanticize your pasts, sugar-coat your contemporary challenges, or cast myself as your advocate. As you must already realize, many of your fellow citizens, specifically those who think of themselves as white settler colonists, have become almost desperate to be publicly seen as your special allies, if not champions. I invite you to consider the possibility that their interests in you and your Indian identity are often objectifying and self-serving, and that their pursuit may represent the very last gasp of colonialism's racialized mentality.

INTRODUCTION:
WELCOME TO THE LAND OF
STEADY HABITS

GREETINGS FROM A SETTLER COLONIST

F OR RHODE ISLAND CITIZENS who know that they are served by a
state archeologist, I fill any number of roles. Every October, I
organize and promote the Rhode Island Archaeology Month program,
which offers free public lectures and walking tours led by local archaeologists. That role is, by far, the most personally gratifying, the one least
likely to attract negative attention.

On the other hand, developers know me as a bureaucratic pen-push-
er who might call for their construction projects to be preceded by an
archaeological survey, at their expense, to comply with state and/or federal regulations. And, in a handful of instances, I have felt like a social
worker for citizens who grew outraged when I attempted to explain that
the stones they discovered, which they insisted bore ancient inscrip-
tions, display no signs of human modification. On other fronts, independent researchers unsuccessfully imploring me to join their crusades
to uncover "the truth" about Rhode Island history, which inevitably
concerns Vikings or the Knights Templar, insinuate that I must be part
of a government conspiracy to keep "the truth" under wraps. Aside from
the fact that government institutions such as mine are hardly capable of
implementing grand historical conspiracies, if I had a mere handful of
evidence that those independent researchers were right, I would gleefully retire today and establish my own donor-funded institution to study
such phenomena.

Yet, there is another role I play. Calling it settler colonial agent is not far off the mark seeing that I operate at the often-contentious inter-section of state power, neotribal politics, and cultural patrimony. First, I am relieved that the name of my employer, the State of Rhode Island and Providence Plantations, got abridged in 2020, the year I wrote this book. Those last three words offend many local Indians (also known as American Indians, Native Americans, or indigenous peoples) and blacks (a.k.a. African Americans), a considerable number of whom carry the surnames of the British colonial "planters" for whom their eighteenth-century ancestors toiled on South County's sandy flats. In mid-June of 2020, Governor Gina Raimondo acknowledged a petition to remove "and Providence Plantations" from the state's name (Streich 2020), suggesting it should be decided through a statewide ballot. A few days later, she got ahead of direct democracy by ordering those words to be struck from official state correspondences, tweeting: "I am fully com-mitted to continuing to work alongside the community in stamping out individual and institutional racism in our state" (Baffoni 2020). With the COVID-19 crisis underway and a capitol city recently shaken by protes-tors and rioters on the heels of George Floyd's killing, not to mention political ambitions pointing toward the White House, she needed to get ahead of any fires that could further destabilize her state. It was decided by statewide ballot in November that the state's name would henceforth be abridged to the "State of Rhode Island," officially putting Raimondo on "the right side of history."

So I have decided to spare my defense, throw down my hand, and self-identify as a settler colonist inhabiting and working for the settler colonial state for most of this book, which should appease the prefer-ences of many local academics. An undeniably white archaeologist, also carrying a British colonial surname, I am charged with representing my particular state's interests in indigenous archaeological objects and sites under its jurisdiction.

It should come as no surprise that many local Indians harbor a deep distrust of archaeologists, according to our discipline's history of un-earthing the bones of their ancestors, with little to no regard for the interests of the living. Unlike dirt, such a stain does not easily wash off. While many of the region's professional and academic archaeologists have the luxury of avoiding such matters altogether, my involvement with Indian ancestral remains is inevitable. When unmarked Indian burials are inadvertently torn open during construction, state law di-rects me to visit, consult with tribal representatives as the next of kin, and offer advice on how to proceed.

And, some non-burial-related archaeological site investigations requiring my office's oversight are in locations that two or more tribes treat as part of their ancestral territory. As one might guess, opportunities to gain new insights into past lifeways can be pushed onto the back burner when tribal entities engage in territorial negotiations. Seventeenth-century settler colonial administrators could not ignore the complicated realities of indigenous tribalism any more than I can today.

So it seems all too fitting that my office is located within the imposing walls of a former Rhode Island state house, notably, the one where the Rhode Island Colony's General Assembly renounced loyalty to King George III in 1776. If you visit, by all means read the historical plaques hanging about, though the darker recesses of this building's memory are not fully spelled out. If they were, I imagine many of the radical leftist visitors would conclude that this building represents little more than a historical front row seat to white supremacy.

If I loitered by this building's west windows in September of 1831, I would have seen smoke billow from the nearby, but since vanished, neighborhood known as Snowtown. In decrying the shooting death of a white sailor, a local white mob justified its descent on this emergent interracial neighborhood in the heart of Providence, destroying the homes of black residents who had nothing to do with the offense (Melish 2016). In 2019, Providence hosted a number of archaeological presentations and community history conversations concerning this understudied historical neighborhood, which led to the establishment of the Snowtown Project, which aims to generate collaborative research opportunities and public programming. A ceremony was held at the nearby Center for Reconciliation in January of 2020 to launch a new self-guided Early Black History Tour of Providence that featured Snowtown. Among the guests of honor was the city's Mayor, Jorge Elorza, who declared, "I believe that mankind is made better when we afford ourselves the opportunity to publicly reflect on our shared history, including moments of shame" (Tomison 2020). One of the organizers solemnly read aloud the names of Snowtown's historic residents, as gleaned from archival sources, in a cadence broken by sobs.

If I continued loitering through 1844, I would have overheard the trial and conviction of John Gordon, an Irish immigrant charged with murdering a member of a prominent Yankee family the previous year. Though contemporary Irish Americans are popularly presumed to have always been part of America's white socioracial class, they were historically regarded as sub-human upon arrival (e.g. Victorian-period cartoons commonly depicted them as fully clothed apes) and were certainly not beneficiaries of the institution leftist scholars call "white privilege." Otherwise, Gordon would not have met death at the end of a rope. Despite the blatant racial bias of Gordon's trial, and the surfacing of exonerating evidence in the meantime, he was executed by the state in 1845 nonetheless, to the satisfaction of an anti-Irish-Catholic establishment (Caranci 2013). In 2011, Rhode Island Governor Lincoln Chaffee returned to these halls to sign a long overdue pardon for Gordon, acknowledging his trial and execution as a "dark spot" in state history (Niedowski 2011). A state congressman added that "an innocent man was forced to suffer the terror, despair and humiliation of a public execution and that society and government will remain complicit if the record of that travesty of Rhode Island history is not corrected" (Schieldrop 2011).

And if I remained through 1880, I would have witnessed the state's declaration that the Narragansett Indian Tribe no longer existed. It was a legal machination intended to dissolve tribal landholdings and political authority. Today, the tribe is both state and federally recognized, and is in possession of 1,800 acres of reservation lands. According to the tribe's hereditary Medicine Man, his people have been at war with the State of Rhode Island since the seventeenth century and have no intentions of changing course (Brown III and Robinson 2006). In this new millennium, his people also appear to be at war with each other, with over 100 members being purged from tribal roles (Henry 2007), a standoff between factions to control tribal headquarters that required federal intervention (Mulvaney 2017), and, eventually, suspension of tribal meetings "in the interest of public safety" in response to a proliferation of what the current Chief Sachem calls "splinter groups" (Stanton 2019).

As unsettling as the Narragansett Indian Tribe's political situation may sound, the situation across the greater U.S. is much the same. Splinter groups, purges, standoffs between factions, and battles to control headquarters – welcome to the tribalized nation of twenty-first-century America. It seems as if history is calling out to each and every one of us now, usually through our ironically-named "smartphones," but not to whisper its nuanced wisdom or counsel us regarding growing threats to our democracy at large. Its voice has become megaphonic and darkly efficient, telling us exactly what we want to hear about the past without any potentially confusing details. Then it directs us into camps, inflames our spirits, and tells us who and what to tear down, promising us that justice and equality will rise from the ashes. What history is not telling us (rather, the lessons we are refusing to learn from the past 200 years of world history) is that when such conditions develop in multicultural nation-states, they tend not to be followed by conditions of justice or equality, but by ethnic Balkanization and conflict.

And if we scroll down to New England's intermediate scale, the signs are equally ominous.

CHAPTER ONE

ON THE ZEITGEIST OF RACIAL DYSPHORIA, REPARATIONS, AND DECOLONIZATION

The only thing that's on the ballot this year is to get rid of 'Plantation.' That's not good enough for us. We should have demanded that they get rid of all of this systemic racism that is holding us back, that is killing our people, that is oppressing our people ... Now we are running thin because that is what they do. They send people in with purpose, to fragment us, to burn us out, to tire us, so that we are not united as one. (From a speech by Narragansett Indian tribal member Bella Noka at the Rhode Island State House on Indigenous People's Day, October 12, 2020, transcribed from a video posted in Ahlquist 2020.)

N EW ENGLAND'S INDIAN people must be more oppressed today than ever before, because they have never been so openly and extensively aggrieved. This is an entirely reasonable conclusion to reach if one's perspective is distilled from popular sources. Though a broad spectrum of Indian issues doubtlessly exists, the media's interests are overwhelmingly cynical. Racism, casino politics, and tribal scandals comprise their chief interests which, presumably, satisfy the appetites of their readership. But at least the media serves three areas of interest.

Indian spokespeople are often even more limited in focus, decrying racism, be it personal, systemic, or institutional, as the underlying cause of nearly any problem that deprives their people of the "peace, balance, and harmony" that is otherwise presumed to naturally prevail. Racial dysphoria appears to have become a defining feature, if not the defining feature, of popular Indian identity region-wide. Certainly not every Indian has a deep personal investment in this zeitgeist. Many do not seem to make cultivating a sense of racial victimhood a special priority in their daily lives. But rarely do any publically voice criticisms of those who do.

Of course, tribal leaders and spokespeople stand ready to undercut the political legitimacy of tribal competitors and/or decry the advantages they have gained in the presumed interests of their respective groups (e.g., Narragansett versus Pokanoket [Kuffner 2017], Pokanoket versus Mashpee and Aquinnah Wampanoag [Hays 2017], Aquinnah versus Mashpee Wampanoag [Conneller 2019], Mattakeeset Massachuset versus Mashpee Wampanoag [Marcelo 2020]). Such is the nature of tribalism.

However, the notion of any tribal constituent proclaiming herself to be a timeless victim of settler colonialism has become as publically incontestable as a prayer. And the voicing of that prayer mobilizes an ideological unity that may effectively elevate the authority of the Indian racial identity over various tribal identities in popular contemporary politics. Or, think of it this way. Representatives of particular tribes have, for centuries, been cleverly evaded by settler colonial politicians on jurisdictional grounds. But today, politicians who evade representatives of races do so at their own peril. This marks the expansion of a call to power that operates beyond the political limits of long-established tribal groups.

In dramatic contrast to the 80.7% registered as white, the U.S. Census Bureau registered 0.3% of the region's population as Native American in 2018 (American Community Survey, 2018). They appear to be distributed among dozens of tribal groups that occupy varying positions within a political legitimacy hierarchy in relation to the settler colonial state. At the top are federally recognized tribes, some of whom have casinos, and others who have tried or are trying to get them. Next are state recognized tribes, some of whom failed to achieve federal recognition and others who only briefly achieved it. And several of the federally and state recognized tribes have one or more related versions by a similar name—in some cases a long-standing band functioning as an independent political entity, and in others a faction that split off of the parent tribe in the late twentieth century under the intense pressure of federal recognition politics. This political re-tribalization of New England over the last half-century harnessed the ethnic pride of the Civil Rights-Era "Red Power" movement, gained political traction under President Richard Nixon's ostensibly pro-tribal-sovereignty policies, was bureaucratically guided by a process established by the Bureau of Indian Affairs in 1978, and economically incentivized by the passage of the Federal Indian Gaming Regulatory Authority Act of 1988. So while most tribes falling into the aforementioned categories may have existed since "time immemorial," many, if not most, have also been considerably tumbled, broken, and redeposited in fierce political currents of the past half-century. But there are yet more Indians to be found.

Some local tribal communities, often consisting of little more than extended families with a common ethnic background, have continued existing quietly under the majority society's radar without attracting political attention. Others, for whom no direct political precedent is plainly evident, appear to have formed since the advent of the internet. There are also numerous sub-regional Indian councils and associations that do not require their constituents to hold particular tribal memberships. And, of course, there are members of tribes from distant parts of the country and from even more distant parts of the Western hemisphere who live locally as well. Furthermore, because many of the region's colleges and universities have generated a strong demand for students bearing Indian identities, one would assume that demand is being fulfilled, in part, by young pragmatists who recently started identifying as Indian, justified by the results of commercially available genetic testing and/or genealogical information, or have amplified their pre-existing Indian identity. So the next time you hear someone trumpeting a blanket concern for the rights, welfare, or sovereignty of New England's Indians, consider asking them to be more specific, if only to solicit a potentially interesting and productive conversation. Indian Country holds remarkable diversity—economically, intellectually, politically, and socially. But a general public steeped in simplistic race rhetoric could hardly be expected to understand this.

The relative demographic scarcity of contemporary Indians seems to be compensated by their appointed (and sometimes self-appointed) spokespeople, who routinely notify and re-notify society at large that Indians are "still here" and that it is high time to publicly recognize and honor them. Their rhetoric may encourage fellow Indians to strike a defiant pose, announce grievances, and make demands—preferably, not overlapping ones. Their ideological tool kit typically includes a license to assume that racist intentionality is at play in any situation involving outsiders. And today's race-obsessed media validates that license on demand.

As American economist and social theorist Dr. Thomas Sowell famously remarked, "The word 'racism' is like ketchup. It can be put on practically anything." This statement certainly applies to New England's Indian political theater, where racism provides a simple and publically viable answer to otherwise complicated questions. For instance, why would residents of Taunton, Massachusetts, oppose the Mashpee Wampanoag Tribe's plans to build a casino in their town? According to a 2017 statement by the tribe's chairman, Cedric Cromwell, those townspeople are "very anti-tribe," "very hostile negative people" who "are racist" (Winokoor 2017). It is difficult to imagine his allegation improving his tribe's chances of winning over those locals, who had already been down this road. It was only in 2013 at a public meeting in Taunton that the tribe's vice chairwoman Jessie "Little Doe" Baird warned federal officials to anticipate written objections to the tribe's proposed Taunton casino from "xenophobes, skinheads" and "NIMBYs," (short for "not-in-my-backyard") later clarifying that she did not mean to offend "casino opponents, the people of Taunton, or city officials" (Tuoti 2013).

Another question that would seem to demand a robustly informed answer: why has environmental activism in Rhode Island failed to make greater progress to date? An answer is offered in an article published by a journal dedicated to "Environmental News for Southern New England." The article is titled, "Green New Deal and RI Climate Efforts Lack Color." Disregarding any consideration of benchmarks against which environmental progress might be measured, Bella Noka insists that Rhode Island's environmental movement lags because society ignores the wisdom of indigenous people and refuses to "follow their lead when it comes to protecting – working in harmony with – the environment" (Carini 2020). Her associate, Michael Roles, a "white activist working with Rhode Island's indigenous population," adds that "People who lead institutions and people who are white need to step outside comfort zones…They need to meet people where they live and work."

Or, why would the State of Rhode Island refuse to transfer to the Narragansett Indian Tribe additional land in their ancestral territory after planning to for years? The tribe's hereditary Medicine Man points to racist intentionality on behalf of the governor's legal counsel. As quoted in a media report, he stated: "I know that she has a high dislike and a great disrespect for Indian People…I could not guess the machinations that are in that person's mind, but I can tell you they are troubling at this day in age" (Lin-Sommer 2016). As to whether compelling facts and context were supplied to the reporter running the story remains unknown to the readership that was, ultimately, supplied with little more than an allegation of racism.

Unbridled defiance toward the greater society by Indians has never been more fashionable or more popularly applauded, and may yield any number of returns, including land rights. Such was the case for the Pokanoket Tribe, who occupied the Mount Hope property in Bristol, Rhode Island, in the summer of 2017. Decrying the land's ritualized seizure by seventeenth-century settler colonists, the Pokanokets decided to take the land back through an occupation led by "Po Wauipi Neimpaug, William Winds of Thunder Guy, Sagamore of the Pokanoket Nation," (Haueisen 2019) and "tenth generation descendent of Massasoit" (Sowamsheritagearea.org 2017). Following a month of tribally-sympathetic media scrutiny, the property owner, Brown University, signed an agreement with the tribe, beginning a process to formalize their land use-rights (Brown University 2017; Faulkner 2017).

It is not surprising that Brown University administrators, who must be keenly aware of their ever-deepening moral authority crisis, acquiesced to Guy's demands. In recent years, the university's public image has been engulfed by an ideological conflagration fanned by its overwhelmingly left-leaning series of visiting speakers (Shultz 2019) and fueled by many of its own morally outraged professors and students. Among them is Ruth Scott Miller, who identifies as part Dena'ina Athabaskan (McDonald 2019). In her 2019 graduating senior commencement speech, she declared that Brown University stands "on the occupied territory of the Wampanoag and Narragansett peoples" and praised "we who are the dissidents" who "fight to improve" the university "often in spite of the institution itself." Or consider the case of Assistant Professor of American Studies Dr. "Adrienne J. Keene, Cherokee Nation (enrolled)." Triggered by criticisms that she was under-supportive of the Pokanoket's Mount Hope occupation, she felt compelled to clarify to the world that she was not a "sell out" or "complicit in the colonial education system" (Keene 2017). So she took to social media to sell out someone else in her place, her employer. She cast herself as an indigenous underdog struggling against overwhelming odds to reform a white supremacist institution that is so sinister as to provide her with an office and perhaps a six-digit salary:

> I'm a midwife engaged in harm reduction. I'm not going to fix a university that has been open for hundreds of years, I'm not going to single handedly tear down a colonial educational system that has helped to destroy our

cultures, but I can make it better for the students who are on campus right now... I can also engage in settler harm reduction, the process of conscientization settlers need to undertake to understand their role and complicity in settler colonialism... I can do research and teach courses that disrupt the status quo, I can bring voices and perspectives into spaces where we haven't been heard. I can mentor and support Native students... Are these moments going to end white supremacy and settler colonialism? No. But they matter deeply. (Keene 2017)

All of this prompts the question of why such professors and students seek to inhabit an elite institution that they claim to resent so deeply. But land claims and the indulgence of platinum-card levels of moral indignation are not the only apparent motives for public performances of racial dysphoria.

Money may be a relevant factor to consider, as in the case of the Mashapaug Nahaganset Tribe. Reportedly "reestablished in 2009 as descendants sought to reconnect with their heritage," this tribe made its public debut by announcing a lawsuit against the State of Rhode Island and the United States government (Faulkner 2016). The tribe, comprised of "some 100 members living in the Providence area," sought roughly $200 million in compensation for historical grievances. If divided evenly, that comes out to some $2 million per member. As Raymond "Two Hawks" Watson, the Pomham Sachem (Sachem = tribal chief) of the Historic Mashapaug Nahaganset Tribe since its founding in 2009 (Watson 2015), Sunnadin Sachem of the Nehantick-Nahaganset Nation (Watson 2019), former spokesperson for the Pokanoket Nation (Kuffner 2017), War Chief of the Northern Narragansett Indian Tribe from 2008-2009 (Watson 2015), and self-described "Black Indian" and "Aboriginal Warrior Activist" explains:

> The overall case is environmental racism and that's doing things to denigrate my natural inhabitation specifically because of who I was. Basically, the first argument is that you took my land and it's not yours. It's mine... It's about the fact that you did something wrong and you need to make amends for it, we can't move forward collectively... unless we address what the wrongs in the past were. (Faulkner 2016)

Watson could not have laid out the prevailing logic of reparations more efficiently, and we should expect no less, seeing that he was awarded a $300K, no-strings-attached "genius" grant from the Rhode Island Foundation only a few months before issuing this statement to pursue "cultural equity" in Providence (Borg 2016) and was suggested as a candidate for Rhode Island Historian Laureate by a local freelance journalist (Eil 2020). Watson's charge that local lands once controlled exclusively by Indians are currently controlled by many non-Indian people is historically verifiable. Nonetheless, the idea that he and the membership of any group for which he speaks should be compensated in cash requires society at large to hold faith in a matrix of intertemporal abstractions.

Watson seems to transubstantiate past injustices suffered by his ancestors into present injustices suffered by himself, because of "who I was," as if he was someone before he was born. He finds non-Indian people, presumably those falling within the historically predominant White Anglo-Saxon Protestant (WASP) demographic, guilty of something "you did wrong," before they were born. He insists that it is possible to "address what the wrongs in the past were" through a contemporary bulk transfer of funds from state and federal governments. Of course, governments do not spend or give away their own money. Their money is sourced from taxpayers, most of whom will never be so fortunate as to receive a no-strings-attached "genius grant."

Like most reparationists, Watson does not address how other ethnic minorities, and even non-WASP whites, such as recent Albanian, Croatian, and Ukranian refugees, who also comprise the fabric of America's settler colonial society, would be exempted from the initial costs of such a transfer or insulated from its second-order effects. Those nations provide particularly ironic examples because they rank 5, 8, and 7, respectively, on the Global Slavery Index for Europe and Central Asia (Walk Free Foundation 2018:93), which informs a combined estimate of their modern slave population at 331,000, and because they were historically culled for slaves by the Ottoman Empire. (Note: the Foundation defines modern slavery more broadly than chattel slavery.) Yet, recent arrivals from these nations are, by skin color alone, automatically folded into the historical slave-owner identity of American whiteness by a general public that is undereducated in world history and cultures. Such complications aside, it is tempting to imagine that if Watson's demand were satisfied, the psychosocial encumbrances of historical injustices upon his tribe would be lifted, allowing members to more freely and independently "move forward" with their windfall. It might. And a rapidly expanding constellation of groups competing with one another to achieve similar results would follow.

And if Watson were compensated in state and/or federal tax dollars for historical injustices correlating to the Indian dimension(s) of his identity, his municipal residency status might add a complicating layer. Watson is a resident of Providence (Borg 2016), the mayor of which recently signed an order to pursue a "Truth-Telling, Reconciliation and Municipal Reparations Process" to "correct the wrongs of the past," specifically for residents of black and Indian heritage (List 2020). If such a course were decided, would Watson qualify for municipally-based programmatic benefits specifically according to the black dimension of his identity? Furthermore, if the colonial institution known as indentured servitude qualifies as a form of slavery, as Watson himself recently insisted (GoLocalProvNewsTeam 2020), Providence's attempt to "correct the wrongs of the past" would categorically dismiss the interests of contemporary whites whose impoverished and legally bound ancestors also survived that institution's abuses, deprivations, and indignities.

It is not that I oppose social programs aimed at addressing societal disparities according to race. Contemporary racial disparities in healthcare, housing, income, and education have become nothing less than a national scandal. It is that I feel morally obligated to remain aware that such programs too often benefit a handful of intellectuals and politicians while damaging the very populations they claim to assist. As Milton Friedman once insisted: "one of the great mistakes is to judge policies and programs by their intentions rather than by their results." Arguing to this point, if the domestic programs of Lyndon B. Johnson's Great Society had worked, the well-being of blacks would not have declined across so many major metrics over the past half century. If this sounds like brand new information, explore the writings of non-leftist black intellectuals such as Glenn Loury, John McWhorter, Jason Riley, Thomas Sowell, Shelby Steele, and Walter Williams.

As noble as the vision of reparations may appear, it is remarkably slippery, dodging the complexities of history and rushing past messy social realities that otherwise threaten to break its spell. As scholars and journalists have already observed (e.g., Frum 2014; Steele 2006; Sowell 2018; Williams 2019), this vision insists that qualities such as guilt and innocence, or criminality and victimhood, are like metaphysical substances that can be exclusively and broadly passed through the core membership of socioracial groups for centuries, and that these groups can resolve these cosmic "imbalances" through bulk transfers of capital at any point down the road. Of course, this vision demands that we downplay, if not disregard, centuries of cultural and biological admixture involving multiple streams of immigrants from various districts of the planet, ignoring an ever-broadening and complicated continuum of commonality between members of colonial-era descent groups.

Incredibly, Americans at large have already forgotten that only two decades ago they had engaged in a vigorous and thoughtful national conversation about reparations for slavery, which was "soundly defeated as a viable notion" (McWhorter 2020b). For many today, the only relevant message standing is that the descendants of historical perpetrators of racial oppression have never been satisfactorily prompted into a full public accountability to the descendants of historical victims, and that until such a reckoning occurs, social progress cannot resume. Unfortunately, social progress has not remained a stationary hostage. It is backsliding under the increasing moral weight of this sweeping ultimatum, which, quite distressingly, lacks any clear or comprehensive resolution.

Many white New Englanders who buy into the heritability of settler colonial guilt clearly believe that the days of racial reckoning have arrived, and publically perform accordingly. Kathryn Haueisen, a "twelfth generation descendant" of immigrants who arrived on the Mayflower, provides an example in her online "Belated Thank You and Apology" to "Po Pummukoank Anogqs" of the "Royal House of the Pokanoket Nation" (Haueisen 2019). Therein, Haueisen thanks the latter's ancestors for welcoming her "half-starved and desperate" ancestors "four hundred years ago." She confesses that her ancestors neglected "the ways your people have cared for the earth" and "the long and rich history of your people," claiming to be "deeply saddened to think that likely some of my ancestors fought against some of yours."

A reciprocal belief in the heritability of victimhood exists among many Indians. Lorén Spears, Narragansett Indian tribal member and Director of the national award-winning Tomaquag Indian Museum (Grosvenor 2016), describes the intergenerational transmission of historical grievances among Indians in metaphorical terms that she reports hearing from Dr. Elizabeth Hoover, a Brown University professor of American Studies who has since moved on to the University of California at Berkeley:

> Each generation is trying to let one bag off, but it's hard because we're carrying all the pain of all those bags, and when the next generation after that is trying to pull their families back together, they've been so victimized and beaten down that they're carrying the social woes – alcoholism, drug addition, mental illness – just despondency. And you've got to try to start healing from that in order to take a bag off. I think our community has come a long way, but we're still carrying the weight of a lot of those bags on our shoulders. (Spears, quoted in Miller 2015)

Decolonialism would seem to offer Indians an opportunity to shed those metaphorical bags and plot an escape from "the legacies of colonialism." The general public is most likely to encounter the concept of decolonialism in one of the region's many museums that house Indian artifacts. Such is the case in indigenous-owned museums, such as the Tomaquag Indian Museum and the Mashantucket Pequot Museum, as well as non-indigenous-owned museums, such as the Haffenreffer Museum, the Robert S. Peabody Museum of Archaeology, and the institution formerly known as Plymouth Plantation. University students in the humanities and social sciences cannot avoid encountering the decolonial school of thought in their classrooms, and any but the most naïve understand that openly criticizing it, even from a rigorously scholarly position, may be hazardous to their grades and peer relationships. But decolonialism is more than just a quasi-religious awakening sweeping through the region's institutions.

A number of decolonial projects have been launched by Indians themselves, such as the Wôpanâak Language Reclamation Project (WLRP). According to the WLRP website, the project began in 1993 under the direction of Mashpee Wampanoag tribal member Jessie "Little Doe" Baird, who claims to have brought this language back from extinction to return "fluency to the Wampanoag Nation as a principal means of expression." She reports having been inspired by sacred dreams in which she was "given" the message "we are here" by ancestors. In 2010, she was awarded a "$500,000 MacArthur Foundation genius grant to support her continuing linguistic research on behalf of the WLRP and Wampanaog people" (Den Ouden 2012). The WLRP states that "it is the birthright of each Wampanoag child and adult to speak her or his Language given by the Creator" and offers "a no English curriculum for all ages." A school for Wampanoag Nation members ages 3-9 has been established, was awarded a grant of $1.4 million by the U.S. Department of Education in 2018 (Stening 2018), and claims to prepare students "for academic excellence and community leadership by instilling traditional Wampanoag values through Wôpanâak language immersion and culture-based education for decolonization using a Montessori pedagogy" (Mukayshsak Weekuw 2020). In 2020, Baird received the Governor's Award in the Humanities (Spencer 2020a) and was named among *USA Today's* 'Women of the Century' (Carroll 2020) for her work with the WLRP.

A WLRP instructor explains the project's significance in the following terms:

> Being able to bring back the language is … one step towards sort of reclaim-
> ing who … they were millennia ago … it takes one step to start a journey and
> this is, this is part of the journey to, back to a place where, where coloniza-
> tion hasn't happened. I don't know if we can ever go back there, but its's a
> start anyway. (as transcribed from Banda 2020)

A return to indigenous cultural norms from the dawn of colonization may indeed carry certain benefits, though ethnographic evidence
suggests that it would also bring politically elite family lines (Bragdon
1996:178; Ives 2009; Starna 1990:40-42), greater tolerance of domestic
violence (Bragdon 1996:178; Plane 2002), sexual division of labor (Bragdon 1996:107-110, 177-180; Starna 1990:36), and warfare featuring routine collection of human trophies (Bragdon 1996:226; Lipman 2008)
and torture of captives (Hirsch 1988). Young to middle-aged tribal men
are not traditionally called "warriors" for no reason. Though colonialism has visited countless atrocities on the region's Indian people, dis-
mantling a social utopia, at least one that contemporary leftists would
be willing to tolerate, is not among them.

Nonetheless, New England's leftist scholars are often willing to un-
critically endorse just about anything that looks or sounds decolonial.
For example, take Dr. Noam Chomsky, the world-famous linguist from
the Massachusetts Institute of Technology, who applauds the work of
Baird, his former master's student. While delivering the 2011 City of
Sydney Peace Prize Lecture, he opined:

> Recognition of heinous crimes from which we benefit enormously would
> be a good start after centuries of denial, but we can go on from there. One of
> the main tribes where I live was the Wampanoag, who still have a small res-
> ervation not too far away. Their language has long ago disappeared. But in a
> remarkable feat of scholarship and dedication to elementary human rights,
> the language has been reconstructed from missionary texts and comparative
> evidence, and now has its first native speaker in 100 years, the daughter of
> Jennie [sic] Little Doe, who has become a fluent speaker of the language
> herself. She [Jessie 'Little Doe' Baird] is a former graduate student at MIT,
> who worked with my late friend and colleague Kenneth Hale … He was able
> to turn our department at MIT into a center for the study of indigenous lan-
> guages and active defense of indigenous rights in the Americas and beyond.
> Revival of the Wampanoag language has revitalized the tribe. (Sydney Peace
> Foundation 2011)

This lofty, redemptive pronouncement, pressed into a metanarrative of world history as a struggle of innocent indigenous people against predatory European invaders, is safe and easy for Chomsky to deliver. After all, if this language project carries any negative consequences for its young participant-subjects, he would pay absolutely no price.

It is reasonable to speculate that if the Mashpee Wampanoag Tribe creates prosperous industries that enable its members to work with and for themselves, communicating primarily in a language that outsiders cannot understand is a relatively affordable commitment. And more power to them. Bringing a language back from the dead is a triumph of the human spirit virtually unheard of in human history. But the degree to which the WLRP prepares tribal youth to competitively engage today's outside world is a different question. In 2020, the project's first student who qualified to take the Massachusetts State Seal Test for Wampanoag biliteracy took that test and did not pass (Banda 2020). Meanwhile, the WLRP website features photographs of various tribal members holding up signs with messages written exclusively in English, including "My ancestors are pleased with me" and "I speak English because that was my only option." Tribal leaders surely favor such messages of group solidarity, for they divert attention from chronic deficits of "peace, balance, and harmony" in neotribal politics.

Consider that when the Mashpee achieved federal recognition in 2015, Chairman Cromwell declared "this is about controlling our own destiny" (Indianz.com 2015), as if the price of that sovereignty did not include political submission to the plenary power of Congress as a "domestic dependent nation." Soon enough, that reality would corner Cromwell. Since achieving federal recognition, tribal constituents have unsuccessfully attempted to remove him and Vice Chairwoman Baird for alleged "malfeasance" and "wrongful acts" while running a notoriously opaque and extraordinarily well-funded government (Houghton 2019; Stening 2019). As of April 2020, the tribe was over $500 million in debt to the Malaysian casino operator Genting, who had bought them land in Taunton and was bankrolling plans to build a tribal casino there (Conneller 2020). And, according to certain tribal members, roughly $250 million remains unaccounted for. (Note: these estimates vary among media sources.) However, the tribe's federally recognized status not only attracted a windfall of unearned capital from a profit-seeking foreign interest—it also attracted federal oversight. A recent federal grand jury investigation into the tribe's financial and political affairs (Hill 2020a) resulted in a U.S. Attorney indicting Cromwell in accordance with his alleged record of "committing extortion, accepting bribes and otherwise abusing his position" (Fortier 2020) in connection with his "shell entity" (Cote 2020) One Nation Development (Hill 2020c). He has since asked his tribe to pay for his defense (Devin 2020), and Vice Chairwoman Baird has resigned. I wonder what Chomsky would have to say about all of this? Is colonialism to blame?

The Narragansett Food Sovereignty Initiative (NFSI) provides a decidedly different example of a local decolonial project. Though some scholars prefer to sell the concept of food sovereignty as a "radical" decolonial methodology (e.g., Kruk-Buchowska 2018; Matties 2016), the NFSI's application does not appear to indulge in defiant posturing or bitter separatism. According to the NFSI website, the project was launched "to enable the Narragansett people to provide food, health, and wellness through sustainable agriculture, economic development, community involvement, and cultural and educational programs," centering on the concepts of "sovereignty, self-determination, self-sufficiency, sustainability, and food security" (Kirakosian and Tomaquag Museum 2020; Narragansett Food Sovereignty.org 2020). The NFSI holds events that offer practical information on how to farm, while putting people into contact who otherwise might not have many opportunities to cross paths, including those from different tribal communities (Andrade 2018; Ouimette 2019). The NFSI also welcomes non-Indian participation, and networks with local, well-established farmers who seem glad to lend their interest and experience. It is difficult to imagine any forward-facing individual denying the virtue of a project like this—one that brings diverse people together in good faith to figure out how to locally recapture food production and set a cascading series of human benefits into motion.

The next decolonial project that I introduce is the topic of this book. But unlike the WLRP and the NFSI, this project does not appear to have been developed by tribal intelligentsia.

CHAPTER TWO

PLOTTING A COURSE FOR CEREMONIAL STONE LANDSCAPES

CEREMONIAL STONE LANDSCAPE believers share an unorthodox vision of how New England's ubiquitous stone ruins came into being, one that minimizes or rejects the otherwise major role played by historic farmers. They may broadcast their ideological stance by refusing to address ordinary phenomena using ordinary terminology, which is condemned as settler colonial statecraft intended to keep the public from realizing long hidden truths. For instance, they might call stone walls "ceremonial stone rows" to highlight their presumed religious significance. They might call heaps of field clearing stones "spirit stones," or *manitou hassannash*, for the same reason (Figure 1). Regardless of the fact that quartz is among the most common minerals in the earth's crust, they are often excited to discover a chunk or cobble of it in either stone heaps or rows, presuming that someone positioned it there for symbolic purposes. So long as the stone structures in question were not signed and dated by their creators, which they never are, such interpretations are presented as unfalsifiable claims that demand serious attention. And anyone failing to meet this demand is presumed to be complicit with a culturally oppressive settler colonial agenda. If their prevailing attitude were distilled into a manifesto, it might read: *We are awakened to a profound truth and invite you to join us. If you refuse, we may resent you. And if you happen to be white, we will register any disagreeability as certification of your racially oppressive outlook toward Indians.* To examine the origins, political rise, and broader societal implications of this vision, we will take a three-stage approach that follows a variety of threads.

Figure 1: Several Tribal Historic Preservation Officers from southern New England have identified these stone features in Hopkinton, Rhode Island, as *manitou hassannash* (a.k.a. "spirit stones") that articulate to a broader ceremonial stone landscape. I identify the same as examples of agricultural field clearing heaps that can be found throughout the region's reforested hills, usually among the ruins of abandoned historic farmsteads.

In *Part I: The Rise of Ceremonial Stone Landscape Activism*, we learn that the founding fathers of the ceremonial stone landscape paradigm are James W. Mavor, Jr. and Byron E. Dix, a now-deceased partnership of white antiquarians who studied the region's seemingly enigmatic stone ruins. Wielding an alchemy of New Age speculation, counter-cultural sensibility, and an old strain of American Romanticism, these retired professional engineers unveiled a radical new vision of history in their 1989 *opus magnum, Manitou: The Sacred Landscape of New England's Native Civilizations.* They postulated that most dry-laid stonework in today's forests are not agricultural ruins, but ancient Indian ritual landscape architecture that, under covert protection by Indians and white colonial sympathizers, survived the ravages of settler colonial development, and insisted this truth is only evident to those willing to submit to intuition and reject mainstream history and archaeology. Their book drew an immediate cult following from the New England Antiquities Research Association (hereafter NEARA), which had long nursed a resentment toward the mainstream for failing to take more seriously their attributions of the region's stonework to various pre-Columbian European visitors. Mavor and Dix presented a fresh and exciting trajectory for this organization's membership to pursue.

While for years antiquarians answering *Manitou's* call generated a modest, self-referential body of supporting studies, they presented little more to the outside world than a network of middle-class whites over-indulging an Indian cultural fetish. However, one outspoken antiquarian, the late Mark Strohmeyer, broke from the fray by spearheading the first ceremonial stone landscape preservation campaign in 1995. Holding a copy of *Manitou*, he challenged the logic and interpretations of a professional archaeological survey in Carlisle, Massachusetts, but ultimately failed. His lack of professional qualifications in history and/or archaeology, coupled with an absence of Indian endorsement, proved a losing combination. In the aftermath, a handful of more patient and pragmatic antiquarians recognized the political potential of Indian allies, and opened dialogue with federally recognized tribal authorities. A new network of antiquarians, tribal authorities, and a university professor launched a second ceremonial stone landscape preservation campaign in 2005, challenging the same archaeologist working in the same municipality. This time, the professional archaeologist did not have the last word. Following racially-charged media coverage, the municipality acknowledged the otherwise mundane agrarian stonework under debate as Indian ceremonial property and preserved it accordingly. Tribal authorities had successfully exercised a new type of land claim that could be applied region-wide, while antiquarians reveled in a windfall of social authenticity. Before, archaeologists who disregarded their ideas could be accused of closed-mindedness, but now they could be accused of racism.

The nascent Ceremonial Stone Landscape Movement's demand for a tribal figurehead was fulfilled by Doug Harris, Deputy Narragansett Indian Tribal Historic Preservation Officer, who was soon ordained Preservationist for Ceremonial Landscapes by his employer, the Narragansett Indian Tribe. This New England transplant would rise from relative obscurity to become the lead spokesman for an intertribal alliance to protect ceremonial stone landscapes throughout the region, garnering the endorsement of federal agencies, municipal governments, and a range of non-governmental organizations. A charismatic leader representing an ostensibly anti-racist cause, Harris brandished an indigenous moral vanity and explicit distain for "Western" rationalism. Sympathetic eyes saw an unbridled, real-world demonstration of decolonialism, the racialized aesthetic which demanded political subordination of Harris's white settler colonial antiquarian base. Regardless, many antiquarians proceeded to publish a flood of competing, though often incompatible, pet theories, as if to register themselves among the intellectual vanguard of a revolution. Within the broader milieu of an progressively post-truth, anti-establishment, polarized America, ceremonial stone landscape activists declared a standing invitation to New Englanders to "let the landscape speak" and reserve their seat on the "right side of history."

In *Part II: Inconvenient Information*, we take a hard look at what history and archaeology have to say about all of this. At the heart of ceremonial stone landscape claims are the ubiquitous, and typically clustered, stone heaps in the region's wooded hills. Though Harris tends to avoid publically interpreting such in any detail, he routinely anchors their interpretation to the historic Indian "memory pile" tradition of the American Northeast. While this tradition's ideologies remain open to debate, its practices are, arguably, almost as well documented as they are fascinating. A synthetic historical review informs practical working assumptions about how such features were created and where they would most likely be rediscovered. This record predicts that a historic Indian memory pile would exist as a stand-alone phenomenon located beside a well-traveled route that formed through the uncoordinated accumulation of stone "offerings" tossed by travelers. These expectations are not met by the "memory piles" commonly identified by THPOs today, which typically occur in groups, include stones that are too heavy for flesh-and-blood humans to throw, and often exhibit the compact structure of careful placement. Hence, the ceremonial stone landscape paradigm transposes the ideological mystery and power of the Indian memory pile tradition onto something that appears to be historically unrelated and far more abundant.

Ceremonial stone landscape activists generally agree that the notion of historic farmers leaving heaps of stones in their fields is a white supremacist myth, which historians and archaeologists uphold to deny Indians their true religious heritage. Despite its moral gravity, this indictment wilts when it comes into contact with overwhelming contradictory evidence existing outside of its ideological bubble. The vast majority of stone heaps in New England's forests were probably built in the nineteenth century by farmers to clear and impound chronically exposed fieldstones from immediately surrounding, and progressively degrading, farmland. As cheaper farmland became available in the American West, once-ordinary agricultural practices fell silent as local hill farms were abandoned and forgotten. The now-forested farm ruins that remain, including their ubiquitous stone heaps, testify to the mass dispossession of Western Indians in the name of Manifest Destiny, presenting ceremonial stone landscape activists with an irony so profound that it must be denied at all costs.

Part III: Stones of Contention examines issues of contemporary ideology. If one dares cast aside the fashionable lens of political correctness, evidence that ceremonial stone landscape activism derives its political power from the mobilization of "white guilt" becomes glaring. Ceremonial stone landscape preservation campaigns appear to represent collective bargains negotiated across a hard socioracial line. Indian activists gain symbolic recognition, political amplification, and volunteer labor. Their white activist allies are, in turn, released from the otherwise implicit settler colonial stigma of whiteness. The backward, racially paranoid mentality of bargainers on both sides is second-nature in this "land of steady habits," where many descendants of colonial-era populations conceive of themselves as either Indian or white despite centuries of cultural and biological admixture. Ceremonial stone landscape activism re-entrenches this old racial binary while opportunistically subdividing one of its camps, providing a mechanism by which to publically distinguish reformed whites from unreformed whites before the gaze of Indian moral standard-bearers.

Among the most curious aspects of ceremonial stone landscape activism is how professional archaeologists and academics have responded. Most simply avoid the topic as a political third rail. Others, however, declare their position among the angels by applauding ceremonial stone landscape activism's decolonial aesthetic. Their virtue signaling has only exacerbated a growing psychosocial tension in New England archaeology (not to mention North American archaeology in general), where "woke" practitioners were already "interrogating" their field's Euroamerican origins. One state archaeologist's suggestion that the days of "redneck archaeology" are numbered came to epitomize the new vision of professional archaeology as an inherently racist enterprise overdue for major reforms under the direction of morally enlightened intellectuals. And such intellectuals are keenly aware that any criticism of ceremonial stone landscape activism, which has come to be uncritically regarded as an Indian social justice cause, invites the worst consequence they can imagine—racist stigma.

Before the public at large, ceremonial stone landscape activism has gained modest notoriety as an eleventh-hour wild card in municipal disputes. It affords private landowners, who would otherwise be branded as NIMBYs ("not-in-my-backyard"), to reframe their plight to preserve their woodland vistas as anti-racist activism serving Indian beneficiaries. Unfortunately, they are willing to breathe new life into old racial anxieties in return for the political advantages of polarizing discourse and silencing dissent. An effort to thwart a solar farm project in Shutesbury, Massachusetts, provides an extreme example. There, a grassroots alliance of Indian representatives and white activist supporters ostensibly summoned to pursue the preservation of ceremonial stone phenomena not only failed to stop that solar farm, but their words and actions triggered a retrogression of local white and Indian race-relations.

To be clear, this part of this book does not question the otherwise elementary concept that some Indians value stone structures as sacred property. It concerns ideas and behaviors that a movement claiming to celebrate that concept has mobilized within the greater society. And while I do not dispute that some Indians gain information about ceremonial stone landscapes directly from their ancestors through visions, such information is not mine to verify, legitimize, or build upon.

CHAPTER THREE

ON SEEING BEYOND VISIONS

I T MAY BE HELPFUL to understand the key assumptions that guide my writing and analysis, the first of which is my unsophisticated approach toward history. History aims to reconstruct events, trends, and patterns that occurred in a past that are real and irrevocable, regardless of whether that past is four centuries, years, or minutes old. And I see the rhetorical question "Who owns the past?" so frequently used by humanities and social science professors to provoke classroom discussions as needlessly and erroneously planting the idea that a living group of people could "own the past." Surely, any such claim should be taken no more seriously than the cast of *Sesame Street* should they claim to "own the alphabet." Nobody "owns" history either, though individuals may hold copyrights to the versions they produce. History is a fact-based system of knowledge that is of great interest to humanity at large, the lessons and meanings of which are conveyed through interpretive contexts that rank probabilities, even boring or ugly ones, above possibilities.

But the theoretical impossibility of getting history completely right does not justify abandoning all attempts. Nobody is entitled to a history that makes them feel good about themselves or the groups to which they belong. History is too important to sacrifice on the altar of identity because it offers an extensive record of how people succeeded or failed in the past, how some ideas light the way to prosperity and growth, and how others usher in oppression and societal collapse. History matters because the human story is complicated and full of suffering—it always has been—and we could use reliable information to mitigate this condition as best we can, to identify past mistakes and avoid their repetition.

But the prevailing vision of history, as an egalitarian pageant of equally valid, self-authenticating "perspectives" on the past representing the "voices" of particular groups, is dangerous to society at large. It reserves a special place for everyone, which is exciting news for political extremists, con-artists, and megalomaniacs eager to register their self-interested propaganda as legitimate contributions to a "broader perspective" of history. The mainstreaming of postmodern relativist thought and the advent of internet culture have proven a perilous combination, expanding space for any number of disconcerting "historical perspectives" to flourish, including Holocaust denialism among young, far-right activists on an international scale (Busby 2019; Muhall 2018) and neo-Confederate Civil War revisionism among Americans (Hadavas 2020). Information about the past, recent or distant, needs to be handled responsibly because it is in the collective interest.

In writing this book, I have not conducted a single interview, and presume that I missed out on some useful information. But, ultimately, I saw relatively limited value in discovering what people choose to say about a racially charged topic, knowing that it might end up in a book, and was turned off by the prospect of engaging potentially hostile informants. I decided that my time on this topic would be more efficiently invested drawing upon the already ample public record of people's words and deeds. Surely, that I have not consulted contemporary Indians in writing this will raise eyebrows among scholars who intimate that studying Indian pasts without formally affording some group of descendants some measure of control over the process is passé, if not unethical. Though a local collaborative archaeologist's rhetoric of pursuing archaeology "with, for, of, and by Indigenous people" (Silliman 2020) may sound "progressive," I prefer to emphasize that any individual, regardless of their race or ancestry, is capable of independently studying the pasts and presents of groups to which they do not belong and producing useful insights.

I also presume there are no solutions to complex social issues such as racial conflict, which is a major focus area of this book. Any serious student of American history learns that race relations are never "resolved." They are negotiated though tradeoffs among and between a diversity of rational, self-interested actors within ever-shifting fields of opportunities and constraints, from one generation to the next. Those flirting with the idea that our generation might be the one to end racism have a tremendous hubris, an ignorance of the complexities involved, and a tragically flawed imagination of the phenomenon as a metaphysical substance to be "stamped out" rather than an ever-present complex of observable behaviors throughout multicultural societies that inflates or deflates according to circumstances.

Also, I insist that far too many New Englanders, both white and Indian, are clinging to some backward notions about Indians that run counter to social progress. Foremost is the popular tendency to romanticize Indians, which undermines their histories and deprives them of their full humanity in the present. This romanticism, a direct and ongoing legacy of colonialism—a projection of Indians that is only available through the settler colonial lens—lends buoyancy to their presumed innocence, moral integrity, and wisdom. As flatteringly attractive as this projection may appear, it is socially pathological because it "isolates them from rational thought, giving an unrealistic assessment of their abilities and place in the world" (Widdowson and Howard 2008:47). As one archaeologist soberly noted, assuming that "Native peoples are unencumbered by convenience, circumstance, political expediency, or gain" is not realistic (Starna 2017:133). While most Indian identity bearers claiming to seek "peace, balance, and harmony" probably mean it, anyone who doubts that a few actually mean "wealth, territory, and power" suffers from a denial of basic human tendencies.

Fancying Indians as eternal victims of Western society not only denies them equal measures of agency in the past and social responsibility in the present, it also serves as a distraction from (and, by extension, an enabling mechanism for) painful aspects of life in Indian Country. For example, Indians are just as capable of, and often much better positioned for, victimizing fellow Indians than are cultural outsiders. To cite some comparatively benign examples, the temptation to illegally appropriate tribal funds has proven irresistible to a former Sachem (Norwich Bulletin 2016), a former Tribal Director of Housing (Mulvaney 2013), and a former Tribal Chairman (Contreras 2009). I do not air these facts to demonize these individuals. I do so to drive home the point that Indians fully qualify as ordinary people, burdened with all of the familiar shortcomings, temptations, and weaknesses that challenge humanity at large. But their ordinariness goes even further. They drive cars, speak English, own smartphones, go shopping, take out the trash, and pay taxes. And though some change into deer hide and ribbon shirts for certain events, this does not qualify them as any less modern, or any more ancient, than anybody else.

For some readers, a difficult pill to swallow will be my insistence that the centuries-old belief that New England's Indians need intervention from deep-thinking, well-intentioned outsiders in order to thrive is as antithetical to their well-being now as it was when Puritan missionaries first arrived. Today, white New Englanders who see themselves as advocates for local Indians seem as uninterested as ever in considering just how messy and complicated their advocacy might be, or how easily negative effects can spread in the wake of good intentions. The remarkable idea of a privileged socioracial group benevolently lifting a less privileged one should always be met with remarkable skepticism. If this were so, when the Massachusetts Bay Colony put the words "Come Over and Help Us" in an Indian's mouth (Figure 2), perhaps things would be different today.

Figure 2: Original seal of the Massachusetts Bay Colony, showing that some propaganda never goes out of fashion.

In short, I am skeptical of individuals who go out of their way to broadcast their good intentions toward other groups of people at large. Self-concern would seem to be a universal human interest that is chronically under-disclosed though rarely underemployed. In regard to this apparent reality, I am aware of no racial or ethnic exceptions. So to any readers intending to brand this book anti-Indian, by all means enjoy your freedom to do so, but do not neglect to brand it as anti-white in equal measure to reflect my steadfast lack of racial preference.

As you must have already gathered, I am acutely tuned to the frequency of identity politics and am eager to lay bare its chronic ironies, hypocrisies, and absurdities, if only to leaven otherwise disheartening material. And though my prevailing "voice" may sound neo-conservative, know that I am a registered Democrat who has never voted for a Republican and never plans to, a member of the Unitarian Universalist Church, and a daytime fan of National Public Radio who unwinds to the commentaries of Trevor Noah and Stephen Colbert at night. I feel more inclined to criticize the political left than the right because I identify with the former as my tribe of origin, and have never stopped seeing its constituents as kinfolk with whom I can be bluntly honest. To me, the political right appears as a largely unexplored country inhabited by a pantheon of brilliant black scholars whose works do not "matter" to a left-leaning academy that chooses racial hypocrisy over intellectual diversity. Today, I tentatively identify as a radical centrist freshly committed to listening to the ideas of folks staked out on the political extremes without joining their crusades. Valuable ideas are routinely generated by people from across the entire political spectrum, and those ideas should be judged solely according to their own merits. And while certain ideas tend to fall into the orbits of certain identities, they are not bound to one another, nor are individuals bound to either. Internalizing this truth may unlock original, productive, and refreshingly unpredictable discourse that has become alien to the ideologically policed spheres of mainstream media and academia.

Regarding my modestly provocative writing style, I urge one demographic to be especially careful about how they respond—those readers who feel that my arguments are compelling. Resist any impulse toward uncritical embrace, especially if you are the type who is excited by the vision of a person strolling over a hornet's nest wearing nothing but flip-flops. Read this book skeptically, appraise any or all of my sources, and question, challenge, or reject my conclusions as you see fit. You need not be an archaeologist, historian, or one of this book's many featured self-declared stone structure experts to do this. You need only be a free and independent thinker. As someone who has spent a good deal of his adult life seeking and sharing knowledge within classrooms, I have always found the most practical, valuable, and liberating educational experiences without them. And I have tossed the bedazzled straightjacket of cultural relativism into the academic lost-and-found box so that I may more effectively leverage the most "disruptive" force known to our aspiring leftist shepherds—common sense. Common sense is that underappreciated little something that most New Englanders use to get by in their daily lives, that makes it possible for our multicultural society to function as a relatively integrated and navigable whole.

Walking a politically contentious line, I have taken care not to break explicit personal confidences or disclose restricted data, including tribal information that is protected under Section 304 of the National Historic Preservation Act. And though I take the liberty of sharing an assortment of anecdotes and stories drawn from my personal interactions with various people over the years, I have, in accordance with the conventions of personal memoir, stripped them of identities and omit key circumstantial details to ensure adequate protection for the guilty. Regardless of whether or not the COVID-19 pandemic has abated by the time this book is published, I imagine that I will enjoy a special envelope of social distancing in many settings for years to come. I suppose I would rather have my reputation flogged by people who never actually read this book than feel complicit in a silence with far-reaching negative implications for society at large.

And, ultimately, that is why I wrote this book. I felt compelled by a deep-seated fear of loss, the kind many Americans experience whenever they read the news or engage social media. I fear that when enough people rally to the identitarian visions of their choice, and when enough of the remaining population becomes too afraid to openly engage them with honesty and reason, the democracy which otherwise maintains a space for both, will collapse. Lloyd Wilcox, the late Medicine Man of the Narragansett Indian Tribe, once said: "Representative democracy is the finest thing I have ever examined as far as the government's concerned" (Burns et al. 1979). I agree with his statement and will stand behind it to the last.

PART ONE:

THE RISE OF CEREMONIAL STONE LANDSCAPE ACTIVISM

CHAPTER FOUR

BROMANCING THE STONES

I T HAS BECOME FASHIONABLE to disparage Western history and culture for showcasing the accomplishments of so many "dead white men" (e.g., Dafoe 2020; Grady 2019; Pett 2015; Turner 2018). At the risk of disappointing like-minded readers, I must disclose that the founding fathers of ceremonial stone landscapes also fall under this category. They were pale-skinned pilgrims traveling west from the island of Great Britain on what they imagined to be a profound mission. Having committed themselves to exploring the wild hinterlands of a "new England," they carried an unorthodox spirituality aimed at reinvigorating man's relationship to the earth, the heavens, and their timeless, invisible connections. And perhaps their work would even change the hearts and minds of local Indians, whose ancient religious system appeared to have fallen into a state of decay. However, these settler colonial missionaries did not disembark from the Mayflower. They were disco-era Americans returning from a 1978 pilgrimage to Scotland to visit their muse, Dr. Alexander Thom. Anyone who believes they are embarking on a profound mission could use one.

The elder pilgrim was James W. Mavor, Jr. (1923-2006), a naval architect from the Woods Hole Oceanographic Institution who had led the team who designed the world-famous deep-sea submersible, *Alvin*. Having earned his M.A. in naval architecture in 1950 from the Massachusetts Institute of Technology, he "discovered a strong interest in archaeology" after taking a trip to Greece in 1965 (Woods Hole Historical Collection n.d.). He pursued those interests by "investigating Thera (Santorini) in the Aegean Sea as the possible locale for Plato's Atlantis story" (Emery 1969) and published the "exciting if speculative" (Galanopoulos and Galanopoulos 1969) book, *Voyage to Atlantis*, in 1969.

The younger pilgrim was Byron E. Dix (1942-1993), an optical-mechanical engineer who had worked for the Space Research Corporation, designing "a long gun for launching satellites into orbit" (Mavor 1994:43), and for the "Air Force Geophysics Laboratory developing telescopes for a detection and ranging system that uses laser technology," which is today commonly referred to as LiDAR.

Mavor reports that he "retired from engineering two years" after meeting Dix "so that I could help fulltime to continue the work that he had started in the New England countryside" (Mavor 1994:43). He described Dix "as a brother" who "readily became one of the family" and "influenced deeply the lives of many people," including himself. In contemporary parlance, they appear to have shared a "bromance" the likes of which most men never do. After joining Dix, Mavor remembered that:

> All aspects of ancient New England became a consuming passion for both of us. When it became evident that most of what we saw on the landscape had native origins, our primary goal became understanding native America and how the natives interacted with non-natives. We focused on universal behavior to draw cultural comparisons, and decided that astronomy is one of the most powerful tools available for reconstructing the past. (Ibid.:43)

Famed for his archaeoastronomical research into British megalithic sites, Thom was, like his American guests, highly educated though not a credentialed archaeologist. He was a retired engineering professor who became dedicated to recording and explaining patterns in the countryside, such as those found at Stonehenge, focusing on how they might relate to ancient astronomical and ceremonial cycles. Though professional archaeologists found his ideas, most notably his theory that prehistoric Britons measured landscapes in so-called Megalithic Yards (2.72 foot increments) (Thom 1962) fundamentally flawed (e.g., Burl 1979; Kendall 1974), his social legitimacy measured up in the eyes of 1970s counter culture.

In fact, the BBC's *Chronicle* series of documentaries produced an episode in 1970 largely dedicated to comparing Thom's ideas to those of orthodox archaeologists. It was titled "Cracking the Stone Age Code." His search for the lost wisdom of ancient peoples resonated with a middle class that was disillusioned with the notion of so-called Western progress and willing to indulge their New Age curiosity. With a steadfast, aspergery determination, Thom seemed to demonstrate that anyone with a decent handle on astronomy, geometry, and/or geography could rediscover the sacred realities of long-forgotten peoples without formal archaeological training, that it was just a matter of searching for patterns and interconnections. Mavor and Dix followed his lead.

Flaunting their lack of archaeological credentials like counter-cultural credentials, they projected Thom's visionary research approach onto New England, though it was never a good fit. At least the British archaeologists who rejected Thom's conclusions agreed with him on the relative antiquity and inscrutability of British megaliths. New England's archaeologists, however, did not believe that most of the stonework sprawling across the region's rural landscapes was particularly old or mysterious. They presumed most of it was left behind by farmers in the not too distant past. Undaunted, Mavor and Dix:

> ...resolved to follow in Thom's footsteps across the water in North America and he encouraged us. He saw our efforts to bring to light the sacred landscape of New England as a parallel to his long struggle in Great Britain. (Mavor and Dix 1989: vii)

To promote a Thom-esque rediscovery of enchanted landscapes on this side of the Atlantic, Mavor and Dix needed to refute and deny the orthodoxy at all costs.

Mavor and Dix discovered no shortage of mysterious "standing stones," astronomically aligned "stone rows," and calendric "stone circles" throughout New England's forests, just as Thom had in the British countryside. And they published their findings between the covers of a disparate assortment of publications that probably reached limited audiences (Dix and Mavor 1980, 1981, 1982a, 1982b, 1983, 1987; Dix et al. 1980; Mavor 1986; Mavor and Dix 1982). But their *opus magnum*, the 1989 book titled, *Manitou: The Sacred Landscape of New England's Native Civilization*, would reach a much broader audience, appearing in bookstores throughout New England. One reviewer noted that "Native Americans, the environment, archaeoastronomy, and mystical spirituality have become popular fare for general reading audiences since the 1960s" and that "*Manitou* fits within this framework" (McPherson 1994:37). The book presented a bold synthesis of their research across the region since the birth of their partnership a decade before. The distinctive suite of assumptions they articulated therein provides the basis of what would become ceremonial stone landscape theory:

• Most of the dry-laid stonework in New England's contemporary forests is precolonial, astronomically oriented ritual landscape architecture constructed by Indians.
• Under the covert protection of Indians and white sympathizers,
much of this stonework survived colonial-era landscape abuses.
• Today, these truths are only evident to intuitively perceptive individuals who reject mainstream historical and archaeological dogma.

One of *Manitou's* central lessons is that nearly any stone structure in
the woods could be construed as ceremonial in nature; it is just a matter of connecting the dots. For example, potentially "sacred alignments"
could be inferred from just about any arrangement that one could chart
in the immediately visible universe. The direction of a stone wall may
be deemed spiritually significant, as might a line drawn between stone
heaps or from a boulder to a prominent hilltop or celestial (ie., lunar/
solar/stellar) interception of the horizon. Where Mavor and Dix found
artifacts near stone features, such as nineteenth-century bottles or rust-
ed iron implements, they interpreted such as ritual offerings (Mavor
and Dix 1989:150, 292, 300). Where artifacts were lacking, they proposed that this reflected the maintenance of clean ritual areas (Ibid.:12,
15, 120, 228). Throughout the book, their arguments are supported by
ethnohistoric and archaeological anecdotes cherry-picked from cultures from across the Western hemisphere, including, but not limited
to, the Adena, Anasazi, Aztec, Chippewa, Dakota, "Eskimo," Hopi, Hu-
ron, Inca, Maya, Pueblo, Shawnee, Wyandot, and Yurok. They did not
neglect opportunities to cherry-pick from cultures of the Eastern hemisphere as well.

One review of *Manitou* provides a particularly astute breakdown of
its fundamental weaknesses as scholarship:

> The book's general conclusion is that shamanism, vision-seeking, and
> careful solar and stellar observations were among the central motifs in
> this culture's beliefs. How these tenets functioned within the culture
> is generally left to the reader's imagination. Once a site is identified
> by the authors' criteria it automatically becomes "sacred," with one or
> two suggestions as to use but with little proof. Frequent words such
> as "probably," "infer," "appears," "seems," "imagine," and "in our view,"
> are compatible with the authors' beliefs that speculation and intuition,
> based on a sharpened sixth sense, are just as important as documen-
> tation. Although there is interesting guesswork and some apparently
> keen observation, there are flaws in the authors' explanations. The first
> flaw is their wrenching of assumed beliefs out of context and com-

paring them with cultures as diverse as the Chinese, Yurok, Egyptian, Shaker, and Scottish. To do so suggests little variation between cultures, which is not true. A second problem is that much of the evidence presented is circumstantial, skewed, or insufficient to support the conclusions. (McPherson 1994)

I would add that when stripped of its "open-minded" optimism, *Manitou* demonstrates how two well-educated scientists cast off the shackles of disciplined rationality to indulge the pursuit of a consensus-based ideological vision. Of course, I presume that their professional work, which concerned such things as launching satellites and building deep-sea submersibles, was governed by little more than their mastery of exact science. Deviating from the orthodoxy of scientific theory was a luxury that they could never have afforded, unless they believed that failed satellite launches or leaky deep-sea submersibles were within the spectrum of acceptable consequences. But as antiquarians, Mavor and Dix lay claim to a remarkable freedom—freedom to produce ideas and distribute them widely without suffering any personal consequences for being wrong. They had entered into a volunteer trade where no one ever gets fired; where false equivalencies, circular reasoning, and confirmation bias had been standard tools for decades; and where the principle of parsimony is distained with revolutionary flair.

Their book also delivers an indictment against archaeology. Mavor and Dix warn readers away from the knowledge and expertise of archaeologists, who presumably aim to distract the public from realizing profound truths about ancient Native Americans. For example, they criticize archaeologists for classifying "native remains" as belonging to the "Woodland, Archaic or Paleoindian" time periods and for employing artifact typologies because "these are matters that were invented by the white man" to create "artificial boundaries which are distracting in an attempt to comprehend Native American behavior" (Mavor and Dix 1989:4). Hence, archaeologists, whose work reinforces "prejudices of the past," would seem to embody the worst of what "the white man" has to offer. While the authors' critiques of archaeology are generally of the straw man variety, they take special aim at those working for the Massachusetts Historical Commission for having "dismissed" a group of stone mounds in Falmouth "without ever looking at them" (Ibid.:57).

There is little, if any, space for Indians to be thought of as individuals, or even as potentially important contemporaries, in *Manitou*, which populates a wide variety of what I see as historically improbable scenarios with little more than vague caricatures. At every possible opportunity, Indians are qualified simply as environmentalists whose principal concern is to live in some ill-defined "balance and harmony" with nature (Mavor and Dix 1989:2, 3, 12, 117, 118, 124, 127, 140, 165, 172, 326, 344). The importance of maintaining such balance is a pan-Indian sentiment that, for better or for worse, anchors conceptions of what it means to be Indian in the popular imagination. And Mavor and Dix would not seem to have had much use for local contemporary Indians anyway, claiming that most have forgotten traditional ceremonial stone practices, though a "remaining few descendants" (Ibid.:4) may have inherited a "limited understanding" (Ibid.:343).

Instead, they turned to the Yuroks of California to help interpret some of the ceremonial stonework that they attribute to New England's Indians. They qualify indigenous Californians as having been spared the brunt of "cultural decay" suffered by most North American Indians, and so justify "seeking authentic ritual" among them (Mavor and Dix 1989:220). The Yuroks, in particular, are portrayed as a far-flung Algonkian cultural satellite fortuitously distanced from the plague of acculturation and cultural fatality of assimilation, supporting the conclusion that "their ritual probably approaches that of the ancient New England Indians more closely than any other that is known today" (Ibid.:246). Essentially, they employ an organic model of culture, arguing that the true ceremonial heritage of New England's Indians has largely died, but that its core practices survive among this isolated Western group. The myth of the vanishing Indian, which has long undermined the social and political fortunes of the region's tribal people (Geake 2011; Hernandon and Sekatau 1997; Rubertone 2008), finds no shortage of space to stretch its legs in *Manitou.*

While many of Mavor and Dix's ideas come across as generally improbable, some border on offensive. The most flagrant example is their interpretation of a suspected Mohegan "prayer seat" that they discovered beside a powerline transmission corridor running through the tribe's core territory (Mavor and Dix 1989: 264, 271). After explaining how people standing near such transmission lines may sense their electromagnetic fields, Mavor and Dix offered the fantastic speculation that Mohegans secretly built this alleged prayer seat by the power lines so they could electromagnetically supercharge their visions. They reason that "because one of the effects of transmission lines is to cause hallucination and therefore better reception of visions," its "users were and probably continue to be Mohegan Indians" (Ibid.:264). They include a sketch map of this site that is sufficient for anyone with a common topographic map of the area to deduce its exact location (Ibid.:264). I speculate that they felt this was all justifiable in their greater crusade to expose the truth. Looking back on his work with Dix, Mavor claims:

> Most of the work of Byron and myself has been about the spiritual life of native people. The traditional beliefs and wisdom are sacred and respected because they help to maintain the balances in nature that must be if we are to avoid destroying alternatives, making it more difficult to adapt to change. (Mavor 1994:43)

Despite their expressed positive sentiments toward Indian people as a social category, it is clear that flesh-and-blood Indians were not meaningfully consulted in writing *Manitou*. But they were not the choir to which its authors preached. *Manitou* was the antiquarians' New Testament. It was a testament to the heresy of archaeology, the romanticized victimhood of Native Americans, and the potential for white settler colonists to transcend both, armed with little more than faith in their inherent spiritual capacities and a vision of trans-historic redemption.

I find it remarkable that *Manitou* still has a cult following, and that it has come to be regarded as an authoritative source of information among some tribal historic preservationists. Ideas from *Manitou* have even been cited by the Keeper of the National Register of Historic Places (NRHP 2008), not to mention my agency prior to my arrival (Rhode Island Historical Preservation & Heritage Commission 2002). I find it hard to believe that any of the officials involved have taken the time to read this book from cover to cover and critically think through its ideas and their implications. If they had, I imagine they would have disposed of it quite unceremoniously. But I must put this cart back behind the horse.

CHAPTER FIVE

A MODEST CULT FOLLOWING

THE NEW ENGLAND Antiquities Research Association (NEARA), a nonprofit organization founded in 1964 to study and preserve stone structures regionwide, enthusiastically promoted *Manitou* immediately following its 1989 release (e.g., Rothovius 1990; Strong 1990). For many members, it seemed to provide a welcome exit from decades of attributing much of the same stonework to ancient, Old World visitors who presumably transplanted some form of megalithic culture (Gero 1989; Muller 2009:18; Schwartz 2004-5).

That well-worn track had been pioneered by mid-twentieth-century antiquarians like insurance executive William B. Goodwin and professional photographer Malcolm D. Pearson, who published their fantastic 1946 book, *The Ruins of Great Ireland in New England*. Among Goodwin and Pearson's notable finds was a colonial root cellar in Upton, Massachusetts, that they argued was an astronomically-oriented ritual chamber constructed by pre-Columbian Irish Monks (Goodwin 1946) (note: Still referred to as the "Upton Chamber," federally recognized tribal authorities designated it and nearby stone heaps as parts of a broader ceremonial stone landscape that their ancestors traditionally used to time the planting of their crops, an interpretation acknowledged by the Federal Communications Commission in 2011 [Burge 2012; John Milner Associates, Inc. 2012; National Park Service 2017:38-39].) Their work attracted public interest and helped inspire a radical revision of New England history, with antiquarian societies, including NEARA, being founded in the 1960s dedicated to its development and promotion. However, the claims of antiquarians following this thread were routinely discredited by the archaeological community throughout the 1960s, 70s, and 80s (Feder 2010:59; Gero 1989; Neudorfer 1980), to the frustration of many within NEARA. One NEARA member described the "polarization" and "atmosphere of mutual distrust" that had developed between archaeologists and antiquarians as of 1984:

> The general antipathy of mainstream archaeology toward the notion of a transplanted megalithic culture in New England has served to enhance the opinion among megalithic proponents that archaeology is a sacred cow, afraid of change, fearful of any new ideas which the mainstream theorists did not originate themselves. The result of this antipathy has been the growth of resentment and the development of a "persecuted-crusader" complex, i.e., the notion that, mainstream opinion notwithstanding, the amateurs will continue to wave the banner of truth with regards to the "real" pre-history of New England, and someday, the mainstreamers will have to fall in line and admit the visions of a minority were accurate after all. (Devine 1984)

This bitterness was persistent. A professional archaeologist who joined NEARA confirmed that its membership still cultivated an "us versus them" mentality as of 1989, with many continuing to carry "chips on their shoulders with regard to the professional archaeological community" (Potter 1989).

Finally, as one NEARA member acclaimed, the publication of *Manitou* had driven a "thorn in the side of the presently-accepted history of New England" (Lonegren 1993:58). *Manitou's* impact on NEARA was revitalizing in that it valorized antiquarian research, contested the legitimacy of professional archaeology, and offered an exciting revision of history with an open invitation to maverick intellectuals. *Manitou* also landed on bookstore shelves throughout New England, becoming nothing less than a cult classic.

Mavor and Dix's core audience was well-suited to receive their book in any number of regards. *Manitou* immediately rooted within NEARA's predominantly white, middle-class intellectual field, where interests in Indian pasts were already growing on an old compost of American Romanticism infused with the individualistic, exploratory spirit of the New Age. Many of those drawn to NEARA, then and now, are highly educated scientific professionals who thrive in a setting where they may collect data, analyze it for potentially meaningful patterns, and share their findings with colleagues. Their membership was, and still is, well endowed with doctoral degree holders, though trained anthropologists, archaeologists, and historians are ironically scarce. I suppose many get involved because they are looking for something constructive and mentally stimulating to do during their retirement.

My father, a retired aeronautical engineer, would have thrived within their ranks. In fact, he called me several years ago and suggested that I was going in the wrong direction with my take on ceremonial stone landscapes. He insisted I contact his associate who had an abundance of boulders on his property. Apparently, he convinced my father that measurements of their positions demonstrate that someone, presumably ancient Indians, had performed mysterious ceremonies there. My father confidently insisted this was a matter that demanded my attention as an archaeologist. If the phrase "Okay Boomer" had already been coined, I would have gleefully delivered it through the receiver. And if I thought that calling out his lack of competency with history and archaeology would have deflated his confidence on this issue to an appropriate level, I would have. But I know him too well, not to mention the stubbornly single-minded focus that made him such a success in his particular area of competency.

NEARA's relationship to Indian stakeholders had long been ambivalent, and occasionally became uncomfortable. *Manitou's* authors remain silent regarding Indian interests when the circumstances of their research are unfavorable. For instance, they propose that Vermont's Calendar I site "may have been the oldest ritual site that we have seen in New England" (Mavor and Dix 1989:326), and may still be in use. If it was still in use, their extensive field investigations, which involved excavating soil down to the bedrock (Ibid:314), demonstrate a practiced insensitivity toward the place they rhetorically venerate. But NEARA also acknowledged the interests of Indian stakeholders, and attempted to negotiate them in good faith. For example, Abenaki representatives once clarified to NEARA's Vermont Chapter that they wish to be contacted prior to any site investigations, and want locations to remain confidential (Sager 1991:48). One metaphorically described her people as a "small cat" relative to the "Doberman Pinscher" of NEARA. NEARA published this information for their readership to openly consider.

Similar tensions surfaced in 1996 during a NEARA tour of an allegedly sacred Indian landscape in Bebe Woods, a 400-acre reserve in Falmouth, Massachusetts. As Mavor reported:

> There were Native Americans in the groups and their views included the extremes of what I have heard on the subject of religious privacy, from disapproval of the tour because it drew attention to sacred places

to approval because it educated the public. I have no answer to this difficult question, but I have tended, as I have come to respect the sacred places, to keep knowledge of their location to a small circle of people, who I feel are likely to respect them. (Mavor 1998:108)

In regard to that quote, even a word as small and inconspicuous as "the" carries enormous political implications. It sounds reasonable enough for a self-declared expert on "the sacred places" to serve as a self-appointed gatekeeper for related information. But if Mavor had decided to use the term "their sacred places," it would have qualified the phenomena in question as Indian patrimony, and not something for him to be making important decisions about.

Looking beyond the political tensions of their day, Mavor and Dix imagined their book eventually carrying profound benefits for Indian people down the road. As Mavor once explained:

Byron wanted others to follow up on the ideas put forth in MANITOU. He hoped that the results of his research will have a beneficial social effect, that the Indian way will enter the mainstream of American society, that native peoples will be more supported in their efforts to keep their ways intact, that more Americans will consider the native people's history as part of their own. (Mavor 1994:43)

A quarter-century later, their work could be said to have had significant social effects where white-Indian relations are concerned. But I am not convinced that those effects have, in the balance, provided net benefit.

CHAPTER SIX

CARLISLE EPISODE I: A RAINCHECK FOR WHITE VISIONARIES

URING THE 1990S AND early 2000s, NEARA-affiliated antiquarians published several articles following Mavor and Dix's lead (e.g., Ballard 1999; Boudillion 2001; MacSweeney 1999; Muller 1999, 2003; Paul 2001; Waksman 1999). Some seemed to stake out their intellectual claim to certain types of alleged ceremonial features. Edward Ballard established himself as the lead thinker concerning "U-shaped" stone structures, which are, essentially, horseshoe-shaped enclosures built of locally available stones that appear fitting for a person to sit within. He leaned toward Mavor and Dix's interpretation of such as being functionally analogous to the "prayer seats" built by the Yurok of northern California, which seated one person for ceremonial purposes (Ballard 1999). Norman Muller, an art conservator at the Princeton University Art Museum in New Jersey, studied cairns, taking a particular interest in the larger and more handsomely built specimens (Muller 1999; 2003), concurring with Mavor and Dix that they must have been built for ceremonial purposes. But the idiosyncratic interests of such antiquarians did not seem to reach beyond publishing relatively obscure articles, but for one who aspired to activism.

Mark Strohmeyer (1953-1998), a professional grant writer drawn to social justice causes (Long 1998), began lecturing to civic groups about his avocational research into alleged Indian cultural landscapes. He believed that professional archaeologists should seek the instruction of avocational researchers like himself so they could perform their work more effectively (1996). On at least one occasion, he attempted to establish such a relationship.

The town of Carlisle, Massachusetts, intended to develop a property behind the town hall known as the "Conant Parcel" in 1995, and, at the recommendation of the Massachusetts Historical Commission (MHC), contracted the Public Archaeology Laboratory, Inc. (PAL), to identify any historic or archaeological resources thereon for project planning purposes (Leveillee and Harrison 1995; Leveillee 1997, 2001). Alan Leveillee served as the project's principal investigator. After Strohmeyer identified himself to the town as an interested and knowledgeable party, he was referred to Leveillee so they could walk the property together.

Figure 3: 'Winter Solstice Stone Pile' identified by antiquarian Mark Strohmeyer on the Conant Parcel. Used with permission courtesy of PAL, Inc. (Leveillee and Harrison 1995).

Strohmeyer pointed out a variety of phenomena, including stone heaps that he believed were used for astronomical and commemorative purposes. He referred to one built atop the exposed portion of a large, glacially-deposited boulder as a "winter solstice" marker (Figure 3), an interpretation he had already published in an editorial in the local newspaper, the *Carlisle Mosquito*, as part of a series focusing on seemingly enigmatic stonework. He claimed that recently discarded bottles on the property represented "offerings" by contemporary Indians, though he did not claim to know specifically who. He also attempted to point out "a face looking out toward the wetland and the winter solstice" from the crevices of a boulder outcrop, though Leveillee was unable to recognize it. If one thing was clear, it was that Strohmeyer sourced his ideas from

Manitou, which he carried in the field like a bible.

Several days later, Leveillee walked the property with a like-minded informant, Dr. Anita Fast. Like Strohmeyer, she cited *Manitou* as a major influence and had also published contributions in the *Carlisle Mosquito*'s series on enigmatic stonework, particularly in regard to the sacred nature of stone walls. The following passage, from one of those articles, provides a sense of her approach to the interpretation of stonework:

> The earth is a living being, and has energy meridians similar to our human body. (In our bodies, these are the meridians acupuncturists know and use.) Sometimes these energy meridians are referred to as "ley lines." In our white culture, we aren't aware of these energies. In the Native culture the aliveness of the earth, its energy, its changes, its cycles, are integral to the culture. These energy lines are experienced as obviously as we would experience the love exchanged in a hug. The rock walls were built to overtly mark and celebrate these energy meridians. Native people built stone rows to create beauty marking the energy lines. (Fast 1993)

As a psychotherapist and independent holistic researcher who had trained under a "Cherokee medicine woman" in "visioning," she brought a "very particular set of skills" (*sensu* Liam Neeson as Bryan Mills in *Taken* (2008)) that, while mildly intriguing and perhaps even perversely entertaining, were not useful for historical interpretation. She reported having extrasensory insights when meditating near the Conant Parcel's stone heaps, and concluded that Indians must have reserved the area for community ceremonies where children received spiritual instruction. She pointed out what she believed to be ritual landscape architecture, including "solstice stones" and irregularities in stone walls that she referred to as "prayer seats," again, ideas lifted from the pages of *Manitou*.

The next informant arrived by invitation. Onkwe Tasi, an Indian and long-time resident of nearby Dracut, agreed to observe and comment on the features identified by Strohmeyer and Fast. Tasi recognized the stone heaps as the work of historic farmers and noted that they must have required considerable effort to build. But he also explained that his ancestors had no need to construct elaborate calendars or "go to all this trouble and work to mark the rising or setting of the sun." He did not know of any contemporary Indian groups in the area who used such sites for ceremony. However, he acknowledged that a non-mainstream spirituality existed among the public, Indians and non-Indians alike, and respectfully speculated that this was the case here. He clearly knew how to disagree without being disrespectful, which brings the following anecdote to mind.

In the midst of an otherwise casual debate that I had several years ago with a ceremonial stone landscape activist (who is also a white doctor of anthropology), I made reference to Tasi's statements on that matter. Said activist, who had been growing progressively irritated with my lack of agreeability, blurted out that Tasi's opinions counted for nothing because he was "just a parade-float Indian!" I had never heard the term. It sounded like a bad penny picked up in "Indian Country," that indigenous counter-dimension from which people like this activist so loftily pretend to speak. Perhaps a "parade-float Indian" is the Indian equivalent of what many blacks call an "Uncle Tom." If so, that penny had clearly not enriched the content of its new bearer's character. But I digress.

Leveillee conducted a final walkover of the Conant Parcel by himself the next month to refine his maps and further examine the landscape. Intriguingly, he found that four clusters of quohog shells, none of which were previously present, had been left in various locations, including on top of the "solstice stone." Quohog shells are ideologically powerful symbols in the eyes of many of New England's contemporary Indians, in part because they furnish the raw material for the purple-colored variety of wampum, the small tubular beads that their ancestors famously produced back in the days of the fur trade. So these shell "offerings" certainly gave the appearance that contemporary Indians were using the Conant Parcel for some ceremonial purpose. Interestingly, quohog shells have been noted as materializing on or around stone features on other proposed developments in southern New England after those features had been declared ancient Indian ceremonial constructions (e.g., Walwer and Walwer 2005).

PAL concluded that the stonework in question was generated by farmers and, ultimately, the town never recognized the Conant Parcel property as ceremonial. Strohmeyer contacted PAL after reading their report to express his regret that its authors had, as Leveillee put it, "failed to become enlightened" (Leveillee 2001). Like Mavor and Dix, Strohmeyer assumed that intuitively perceptive individuals could identify and interpret Indian ceremonial landscapes without Indian involvement. What he did not understand was that he lacked the political traction needed to compel an institution such as a town to recognize a property as an Indian ceremonial space. His lack of credentials in the fields of anthropology or history presented a fundamental limitation. To be taken seriously by the world at large, he would either need to go back to school, which would have contradicted his anti-establishment persona, or outsource his political legitimacy to any Indian cultural authorities willing to underwrite his claims. Having died in 1998, Strohmeyer would never see how remarkably effective the latter approach would prove among his colleagues. Regardless, I think we would be justified in recognizing him as an early activist for the preservation of what would eventually be called ceremonial stone landscapes, regardless of the fact that many Indians would have identified him as white.

It is worth noting that there were controversies over the origins of woodland stone heap sites in southern New England during the 1980s and 1990s, where Indian cultural authorities were consulted. Several, such as Chief Spotted Eagle of the Nipmuck Indian Tribe (Acciardo 1983), Three Bears of the Wampanoag Indian Tribe (Acciardo 1983), and Ray Lussier (aka. Chief Looking Glass) and Dan King (aka. Wounded Pony) of the Abenaki Nation (Leveillee 1998), insisted that the stone heaps in question marked human burials. Examples were disassembled by archaeologists, but no human remains or grave goods were located. Thus far, I have found no clear or compelling evidence of the ceremonial stone landscape paradigm being promoted by Indian cultural authorities prior to the new millennium, and, to be more precise, prior to 2003.

CHAPTER SEVEN

CONVERTING "THE INDIANS" BACK

N EW ENGLAND'S SETTLER colonists have intervened to alter the cultural systems of Indians repeatedly over the past few centuries. It happened in the mid-1600s when fourteen Indian "praying towns" were established across southern New England under the authority and design of Puritan clergy and politicians. Their goal was not only to convert resident Indians to Christianity, but to compel them to relinquish their traditional cultural norms and practices in exchange for European customs and lifestyles. It happened again in the mid-1700s with the 1754 founding of Moor's Indian Charity School in Lebanon, Connecticut, where Indian students were groomed to become Christian missionaries to fellow Indians. The effects of this intervention were profound, and included a mass westward migration of the region's christianized Indians. And it happened again with the 1879 establishment of the Carlisle Indian Industrial School in Carlisle, Pennsylvania, which operated for nearly three decades with its stated goal to "kill the Indian" to "save the man." The school drew in students from across the country, and some from New England's surviving tribal communities.

As I see it, another settler colonial intervention has been underway for the past eighteen years, though this one appears to have originated at the grassroots level rather than from established seats of power. This time, settler colonists have not been trying to convince Indians to embrace any form of Christianity. Rather, they have been trying to convince Indians to embrace an ill-defined form of spirituality that they imagine must have existed prior to colonization, to go back to something that they figure Indians lost at the hands of their British colonial predecessors. Long-dead Christian missionaries and Indian medicine men alike must be spinning in their graves, though for different reasons. The political alignment of some of New England's Indian cultural authorities with local antiquarians is an 18-year-old phenomenon that deserves to be taken seriously. And while this alignment pursues and promotes an ideological agenda, personal and political motivations have also been at work since the beginning. This chapter explores that beginning, when antiquarians and tribal authorities banded together for the first time to confront a perceived common rival— professional archaeology.

First, it is important to understand that archaeologists have never been popular with local Indian cultural authorities, especially Tribal Historic Preservation Officers (THPOs), for many reasons. Developers have long paid professional archaeologists to identify and interpret Indian cultural resources to comply with historic preservation laws. This is not always the case for THPOs, who still receive voluntary information requests from such archaeologists billing their developer-clients for time it took to send those requests. Whenever federal agencies passively delegate their tribal consultation responsibilities to project proponents, contract archaeologists, often the only parties directly communicating with THPOs, seem to personify the failed ideals of the government-to-government relationships supposedly endowed by federal recognition (Ranslow 2014). And this does not necessarily reflect bad intentions within the web of individuals involved. The framework for federally-mandated project-related consultations, as anchored to Section 106 of the National Historic Preservation Act, is not always easy to negotiate.

And at a deeper level, THPOs reviewing professional archaeological reports find their ancestral cultures described in alienating language and must be willing to stomach the occasional discussion of "mortuary data" from Indian burials excavated before the passage of the 1990 Native American Graves Protection and Repatriation Act. As plainly stated by a Navajo archaeologist, "in the minds of many Indians, archaeologists are stigmatized as grave robbers" (Wellner 2005:37). And archaeology's calling card—the masonry trowel—does not necessarily inspire joy among people who see it routinely used to systematically dissect their ancestral places. In such contexts, it is not at all difficult to see archaeology as an instrument of settler colonial oppression. But THPOs are not the only stakeholders with reason to view professional archaeology cynically.

Professional archaeologists represent a different brand of villain to another group. For years, antiquarians could not independently usher *Manitou's* vision into the public eye as legitimate, nor could they convincingly rebuff the archaeological community's skepticism. Some reached out to Indians for help, and to tremendous effect, as antiquarian Dr. Peter Waksman reports:

> My friend from Carlisle, Jic Davis started calling the Native Americans. He called the Narragansets [sic]. He called them once a month for two years. And they always said, "No. We can't talk to you. We've busy. Sorry. Out of the office. Not here. Try again. Some other time." After two years, he finally got someone to pick up the phone, and he'd been calling them for two years. He said, "You've got to come look at this stuff I have in Carlisle. I think it's Native American stuff. You got to come out here and check it out." Jic's very sociable. He got the Indians out of their shell, and they came up. Medicine men, tribal elders, ethnographers, whole troop. (Concord Oral History Program 2010)

Let us be clear: according to Waksman's account, Davis reached out to the Indians first, and only received a response after considerable effort.

Curiously, Dr. Curtiss Hoffman, who was, at the time, a professor of anthropology and associate of Waksman, portrays the Indians as the initiators in his 2019 book, *Stone Prayers*. He reports that the Narragansett Indian Tribe became inspired to take the "lead in promoting these structures as 'stone prayers' of their people and other tribal groups," during a meeting of their tribal council. They agreed that so many sacred sites were "disappearing under the threat of suburban development" that they needed to reach out and find allies "with whom they could partner" to protect them (Hoffman 2019:44). Next, he reports that tribal medicine woman "Ella Sekatow, and her son-in-law, Doug Harris, set up a meeting with local antiquarians (Timothy Fohl, Jic Davis, and Peter Waksman) early in 2003 in the town of Carlisle" and that he was also invited because he was known to be "sympathetic to their claims." Then, he, the antiquarians, and the tribal representatives present at that meeting "agreed to form a working group and do what we could to encourage local towns to engage in preservation efforts."

Who is giving the more accurate version of this beginning, Waksman or Hoffman? I do not have enough information to provide a definitive answer. But I will note that Waksman's prose tends to be politically unfiltered, characterized by extreme candor, and makes no attempt to valorize Indians. On the other hand, I wonder if Hoffman's Indian subjects are endowed with so much wisdom and foresight that they are prequalified to be cast as the initiators regardless of actual historical circumstances?

Like earlier colonial-era missionaries, these folk appear to have been aiming to change the hearts and minds of a handful of Indian cultural authorities recognized as "the voices" of indigenous people. Anyone familiar with America's colonial history understands that Indian subjects should always engage such folk skeptically because unstated self-interests may be at work. Of course, it is possible that Davis' interest in contacting these Indians was noble. However, Waksman claims that it was motivated by his hope that they "could help him protect his land from real estate lawyers" (Waksman 2010). Davis, a forester and landscape designer, lived in Carlisle, Massachusetts, where his property abutted an extensive tract of woodland known as the Benfield Estate. According to Waksman, Davis "didn't want a whole housing development" next door and "was trying to figure out some way to interfere" with lawyers who planned to divide the Benfield Estate and "sell it off to the highest bidders." Waksman credits himself for giving Davis the idea of using "Indian archaeology" to stop development. Hoffman includes no such details in his recount of events (Hoffman 2019:44-45).

Tribal representatives and their new associates conferred in person on several occasions, walking through the woods to examine stone structures that the latter claimed were of Indian origin. Waksman's accounts suggest that they did not see eye to eye at first, and that his camp had to court the Indians until they came around. For example, Waksman recounts one tribal member showing "puzzlement when I first showed her a rock pile—wondering if it wasn't from field clearing and dismissing similar structures from her back yard" (2018a). He also recalls *Manitou* being "repeatedly mentioned by the Indians" on these walks, and claims they noted it as an "important and sensitive" book while agreeing that "it is difficult to read" (Waksman 2009). Perhaps lured by the prospect of recovering sacred aspects of their past culture, and possibly enthused by the possibility of challenging professional archaeology, these "native voices" would eventually join with those of Hoffman and his antiquarian colleagues.

As Waksman reports, Harris reportedly took the antiquarians very seriously:

> I took Doug Harris on many walks, maybe five walks, maybe three walks, in the woods. And I showed the stuff to him. I said, "See? This is what it looks like. This is where it's found." It's found where water comes out of the ground, is where rock piles are, where water comes

out of the ground, or, places that face west, one thing like that. And I showed him, and I showed him, and I showed him. And then he started revealing that they knew this stuff. How much he knew beforehand, let's say it doesn't matter. I really do believe that the Indians built this. I don't believe that today's Indians remember much about it. (Waksman 2010)

Claiming Cheraw and Cherokee ancestry, Harris had already moved to New England, married into a Narragansett family, and had started working for Narragansett Indian Tribal Historic Preservation Office (NITHPO) (Poli 2017). But it was through his association with local antiquarians that he found a sense of purpose that would come to define his career as a tribal historic preservationist.

Harris took measures to politically endorse and culturally authenticate what he appeared to have been learning about from Waksman and company in the forests of Massachusetts. In 2003, Harris introduced a resolution to the intertribal congress known as the United South and Eastern Tribes, Inc., titled "Sacred Landscape within the Commonwealth of Massachusetts" (USET 2003). The resolution passed, acknowledging that there "exists a sacred landscape which is of particular cultural value to certain USET Tribal members" which includes land within the municipalities of Acton, Boxborough, Carlisle, Concord, Lincoln, Littleton, Stowe, and Westford. Waksman claims to have personally supplied Harris with this list (Concord Oral History Program 2010). The resolution explains that "for thousands of years before the immigration of the Europeans," tribal medicine people "used this sacred landscape to sustain the people's reliance on Mother Earth and the spirit energies of balance and harmony," and proposes that member tribes partner with the named municipalities to provide for their permanent protection. The word "stone" does not appear in the title or language of this resolution, and would not find its place between the words "ceremonial" and "landscape" for several years.

CHAPTER EIGHT

CARLISLE EPISODE II:
WE HAVE "THE INDIANS"

A s EXPLAINED IN Chapter 7, the 1996 campaign to register a stone feature complex on the Conant Parcel as an Indian ceremonial site had failed because it lacked Indian endorsement. This chapter reports on a similar campaign that took place in 2005 under remarkably similar circumstances. It occurred in the same municipality, concerned the same sorts of stone features, involved the same archaeological firm, and included antiquarians who were versed in the book *Manitou*. It was almost like a controlled sociological experiment. But one key variable was different during this trial. Native American cultural authorities were involved.

The town of Carlisle was planning to authorize the construction of affordable housing and a playing field on a subject property called Benfield Parcel "A." This was the project that Davis had apparently been planning to oppose for at least two years, and PAL was surveying the property at the recommendation of the Massachusetts Historical Commission for project planning purposes.

Waksman describes how he facilitated getting "the Indians" onto Benfield Parcel "A:"

> We arranged for it to look like Mr. Benfield invited the Indians to come. Actually, Mr. Benfield might've been more or less awake when he signed the thing that said to, "Please, Indians, come." He didn't actually write the thing that said, "Please, Indians, come." I had something to do with that. But anyway, a letter was signed by Mr. Benfield inviting the Indians to come, so the lawyers couldn't say, "No the Indians aren't

allowed to walk here." They had a signature. So, they came and then walked, and they saw. And they said, "This is ours. You cannot just bulldoze this." And this began a little bit of a ripple in the planning of the conser- Carlisle Conservation Fund, or Foundation. (Concord Oral History Program 2010)

An unprecedented alliance revealed itself to support an Indian ceremonial interpretation of the property, one that included antiquarians, tribal authorities, and a credentialed archaeologist. They conducted their own survey of the property and submitted their findings to the town in a report (Fohl, et al. 2005). Its first author was Dr. Timothy Fohl, a "neighbor of the Benfield property" (Heaney 2005) and published NEARA member, with a career specialization in the science and technology of light sources and lighting systems. The THPOs identified him as an "avocational survey field specialist." Its second co-author was NITHPO's Doug Harris. Next was Dr. Curtiss Hoffman, Chairman of the Department of Anthropology at Bridgewater State College, whose research interests include New England archaeology, world mythology, and culture and consciousness. The last co-author, with whom we are also already familiar, was Dr. Peter Waksman, a software engineer specializing in geometry and language who was also a published NEARA member. The THPOs identified him as an "avocational survey field specialist" as well.

Figure 4: One of many stone features on the Benfield Parcel "A" property, which antiquarians and tribal authorities determined to be sacred. Used with permission courtesy of PAL, Inc. (Leveillee and Waller 2005).

Their report claimed that the most enduring evidence of Indian spiritual life in New England consists of clusters of stone structures (Figure 4) and that they had found over 60 on the subject property, including rows of rocks pointing to solstice sunrises or sunsets, stone arrangements thought to resemble human and animal figures, and a large boulder that appeared to have been "carved out" (Heaney 2005).

Harris and Cheryl Andrews-Maltais, THPO representatives from the Narragansett Indian Tribe and the Wampanoag Tribe of Gay Head (Aquinnah), respectively, leveraged the powers of their offices to defend this "sacred ceremonial complex." They wrote a joint letter to the Board of Selectmen asking the town not to allow excavation within its boundaries. Their claims captured the public's interest after appearing in the *Boston Globe*. Its title: "Indian Tribes Say Carlisle Site Bears the Signs of Sacred Past, Building on Hold Pending Survey" (Heaney 2005). The story included the following transcription from their joint letter:

> We are constrained by Tribal tradition from offering public detailing of the practices at such sites. But in general terms, this complex was used by our region's medicine people and tribal women for ceremonies relating to the maintenance of balance and harmony with the spirit realm, with our Creator, with the spirit of our Mother the Earth and the healing energies of her springs and fresh flowing waters. (Heaney 2005)

Harris also went on record with a warning that the Tribes "don't want to become legally combative on this with people we prefer to be working with. That does not rule out engaging in legal battle if we have to" (Heaney 2005).

Andrews-Maltais sent a letter to the U. S. Army Corps of Engineers in what appears to have been an unsuccessful attempt to get the project brought under federal oversight, which would have provided significant political advantages where tribal interests are concerned. Therein, she clarifies her office's position toward the involvement of professional archaeologists.

> …[T]he site is of great significance and importance to our, and other Tribal Nations. Any invasive archaeological surveys and/or ground disturbance in the areas we have identified as part of the Sacred Ceremonial Site will forever destroy the integrity of the site. These proposed invasive assaults will have a devastatingly profound effect on the site, effectively eliminating our ability to protect what is so important

to us. (Andrews-Maltais 2005a)

Andrews-Maltais and Harris sent a highly-charged joint letter to the Massachusetts State Archaeologist, insisting:

> For more than 350 years, Colonial and Post-Colonial slaughter and persecution of the medicine people and related practitioners of this ancient tradition has created a chilling effect on the open practice and communication about this tradition. (Andrews-Maltais 2005b)

These approaches appear to have effectively pushed concerns over historical interpretation aside, putting racial identity politics on the front burner.

The report that PAL submitted to the town of Carlisle diagnosed the presence of a generally unremarkable historic agrarian landscape on the Benfield Parcel "A" property (Leveillee and Waller 2005), which was in step with their assessment of the nearby Conant Parcel property a decade before. But this time, the archaeologists did not have the last word.

As I see it, the question of whether significant archaeological site areas exist on the property had been fully eclipsed by a more politically consequential question. What town officials are going to publically disagree with Indian representatives bearing accusations of racism and religious oppression? Not the town officials of Carlisle. They acknowledged the property as an Indian ceremonial space and committed to a redesign of the proposed housing project to avoid impacting any of the stone features. It was an historic first. Municipal and federal officials would make similar decisions under similar circumstances as the years progressed. This decision by the town of Carlisle was, essentially, the down payment on a political upgrade for stone structure research—from an antiquarian hobby to a tribally-endorsed mission. As Waksman exclaims: "So this property, given to the town of Carlisle by Mr. Benfield, became the first acknowledged Native American ceremonial site in the northeastern US" (Waksman 2011). He also adds, "out of this time frame came the 'Indian Rock Defense'...as a new way to fight against land development" (Waksman 2018a).

The political and ideological implications of this turn were profound. Tribal authorities had successfully tested a new type of cultural claim that could be applied to almost any New England property bearing stones. And they could make this claim without any deference or reference to the knowledge or opinions of archaeologists. During the Benfield Parcel "A" preservation campaign, Harris rightfully asserted that "properties of traditional religious and cultural importance to an Indian tribe" are identified by "Indian tribes, not archaeologists" (Heaney 2005). He had made a valid and important point. But what followed could be described as a decolonial divorce settlement within the sphere of cultural resource management. The Indians take moral custody of the beautifully weathered, lichen-festooned stone heaps and give them the attention they have long deserved. The professional archaeologists go back to their labs with their handfuls of ancient stone tool-making debris and historic trash.

This political precedent had also unlocked a new synergy that allowed antiquarians to bear, by proxy, the moral authority of Indians as an aggrieved socioracial class, endowing their research products with the social authenticity of activism. Before, anyone who disregarded their ideas could be accused of closed-mindedness, but now they could be accused of racism. Like sacred cows, their ideas became free to roam into new precincts, such as environmentalism, social justice, tribal historic preservation, and eventually, mainstream academia. Harris found himself holding a considerable, though quite slippery, sociopolitical power to harness, presumably on behalf of all Indians under the auspices of decolonialization.

CHAPTER NINE

A WONDERFUL WEAPON

W HILE THE TERM CEREMONIAL stone landscape is not ancient, it appears to be of Indian origin. It publicly debuted in a resolution adopted by the United South and Eastern Tribes, Inc., in 2007. Introduced by Harris, it states that "sacred ceremonial stone landscapes and their stone structures" such as "massive or small structures, stacked, stone rows or effigies" had long been used "to sustain the people's reliance on Mother Earth and the spirit energies of balance and harmony" until colonial oppression (USET 2007). It contends that archaeologists and State Historic Preservation Offices (SHPOs) often mistake these structures "as the efforts of farmers clearing stones for agricultural or wall building purposes" and "categorically thereafter, dismiss these structures as non-Indian and insignificant, permitting them to be the subjects of sacrilege of archaeological dissection and later destruction during development projects." This resolution provides the most authoritative public definition of ceremonial stone landscape available to date, though it seems more concerned with indicting the archaeological establishment as an instrument of settler colonial oppression than providing substantive information on the nature of the stone structures in question.

It was around the time of this USET resolution that Harris was endowed by his office with the unique title *Preservationist for Ceremonial Landscapes*. A charismatic orator, he became the Ceremonial Stone Landscape Movement's de-facto leader and is largely responsible for elevating its cause to political consequence. This is attested to by an impressive and expanding list of institutional supporters, including the U.S. Forest Service, the U.S. National Park Service, the National Trust for Historic Preservation, and various land trusts and environmental advocacy non-profits.

Under Harris' lead, a coalition of THPOs from the Mashantucket Pequot Tribe, the Mohegan Tribe, the Narragansett Indian Tribe, and the Wampanoag Tribe of Gay Head have established themselves as the sole authenticators of any and all ceremonial stone landscapes in New England. Though this "Sacred Landscapes Coalition" (*sensu* Hoffman 2019:40) may seem to present a consensus Indian voice for the region's indigenous people, this is not the case. Leaders and spokespeople from most of the region's other tribal entities have yet to voice a public opinion as to whether or not they endorse the ceremonial stone landscape paradigm. And THPOs from two other federally recognized tribes with relevant histories in the region, specifically the Stockbridge-Munsee Band of Mohican Indians and the Mashpee Wampanoag, have openly disagreed with it (Hoffman 2019:234-235). As Bonney Hartley, THPO for the Stockbridge-Munsee Band of Mohican Indians succinctly explained regarding the interpretation of woodland stone heaps as Indian ceremonial constructions: "There's not a consensus on this one" (Bellow 2017). For this, Harris criticized her in the media for "taking a non-spiritual position."

From the moral high ground of an indigenous warrior rebelling against the settler colonial state, Harris rallies others to join his cause. Take, for example, this quote that can be found on the National Park Service's website: "I would ask that those of you who have ceremonial stones of this sort in your region, persevere. Use the National Historic Preservation Act. It is a great tool and in some instances, a wonderful weapon" (Harris 2014).

A key principle explained by Harris is that moving any stones on a ceremonial stone landscape is sacrilegious.

> Stones, it was believed as the oral history tell us, could resonate with the voice. So if you prayed into a stone and you placed it on the earth mother's body, you would be communicating to her and that communication or that prayer would continue to resonate. One of the things that we are very much against is movement of these stone groupings because if you move them then the prayers are broken and the powerful balance and harmony that the medicine people have sent down to us as the reason they were doing this would be broken. Then the balance, the precarious balance that we are in with our earth mother would be in worse shape, we believe. (Harris 2014)

It naturally follows that once a THPO has identified a particular property as a ceremonial stone landscape, or suggested that it has the potential to contain one, disturbing any stone thereon might be seen as deeply offensive and should therefore be carefully avoided. Accordingly, the only politically safe position that property owners wishing to develop stone-bearing lands could assume is one of complete deference to THPOs, who seem to be endowed with a preemptive moral claim to the very integrity of such properties.

Harris' strategy of appealing directly to municipalities to protect ceremonial stone landscapes has proven remarkably successful. The 2016 Comprehensive Plan of Hopkinton, Rhode Island, includes the following language:

> There are places in Hopkinton which may be of ceremonial importance to the Narragansett Indian Tribe. The Town of Hopkinton will make efforts to work with the Narragansett Indian Tribal Historic Preservation Office (NITHPO), the New England Antiquities Research Association (NEARA) and the Rhode Island Historical Preservation and Heritage Commission (RIHPHC) to identify and protect important ceremonial sites in Town. The Hopkinton Land Trust has acquired a 14 acre property to protect the ceremonial landscape where over 700 stone structures thought to be indigenous have been documented. The Historic District Commission, Conservation Commission and Hopkinton Historical Association are all involved in this preservation and research. (Hopkinton 2016:26)

The 2016 edition of the Community Comprehensive Plan of Smithfield, Rhode Island, takes a similar position, explaining that "many cultural and ceremonial practices, including ceremonial use of stones, stone structures, and stone landscapes were suppressed," and that many, which are "easily mistaken" for "the results of early agricultural activities," are "now located on privately owned land" and are "threatened by land alteration and development activities" (Smithfield 2016:217). In 2008, the Conservation Commission of Carlisle, Massachusetts, listed various municipal properties as containing Indian "stone piles," (pg. 46) "ceremonial sites," (pg. 46) and "ceremonial structures" (pg. 46) (Carlisle Conservation Commission 2008). The town of Wayland, Massachusetts, has also expressed interest in the ceremonial stone landscape concept (Harris 2012) and appears to have commissioned a report by Ceremonial Landscapes Research, LLC, for municipal land management purposes (Ceremonial Landscapes Research, LLC, 2015).

In 2017, the Historical Commission of the Town of Wendell, Massachusetts, signed a memorandum of understanding with the THPOs of the Mashantucket Pequot Tribe, the Mohegan Tribe, the Narragansett Indian Tribe, and the Wampanoag Tribe of Gay Head (Aquinnah) "to identify and protect ceremonial stone landscapes within the town's jurisdiction" (Wendell Historical Commission 2018:9). The Town of Upton, Massachusetts, purchased what is now called the Upton Heritage Park, which features a stone chamber (probably a colonial root cellar) that certain members of the Upton Historical Commission believe is a ceremonial stone landscape (Spencer 2012). And though it does not appear to be a municipally-controlled organization, the Hopkinton Area Land Trust, which serves Hopkinton, Massachusetts, has also adopted a position of advocacy for the recognition and preservation of ceremonial stone landscapes (Hopkinton Area Land Trust, Inc., 2018). Clearly, ceremonial stone landscape recognition and preservation has moved into New England's Overton window.

THPOs routinely engage development projects concerning the presence or potential presence of ceremonial stones. For instance, a ceremonial stone landscape identified by NITHPO in Hopkinton, Rhode Island, that was slated for private housing was purchased by the town's land trust for conservation in 2014 (Drummond 2015) and designated the *Manitou Hassannash Preserve* in 2017 (Drummond 2017). NITHPO won support of its own tribe's leadership in 2015 to relocate the new Narragansett Indian Health Center to preserve a ceremonial stone landscape, and to teach tribal youth "geometry and astronomy on their own property" (Harris 2014). And several energy-related projects subject to federal oversight have been redesigned to avoid impacting stone structures that southern New England THPOs have identified as ceremonial (Harris and Robinson 2015). Some preservation campaigns have fallen short, such as an attempt to prevent a gas pipeline construction from disturbing stone structures in Massachusetts' Otis State Forest (Bellow 2017). Regardless, ceremonial stone landscape activism has become a political force to be reckoned with.

CHAPTER TEN

INDIGENIZING THE MOVEMENT

After Harris became the de facto leader of the Ceremonial Stone Landscape Movement, the enthusiasm and outspoken nature of the antiquarians who had laid the groundwork may have presented as much of an asset to be mobilized as a problem to be corralled. Waksman recalls the situation around 2003:

> I would call Jic up and say: "lets go out" and occasionally he would take walks with me and add the insight of his observant (I claim un-filtered) perceptions. Those insight came from inside his head and (still later) when he would ask Doug Harris about something, Doug would get annoyed that Jic was projecting so much into the subject and asking questions Doug could not answer. (Waksman 2018a)

And not long after, Harris heard that his antiquarian associates were being credited for their pioneering role in the nascent Ceremonial Stone Landscape Movement by the chairman of the United South and Eastern Tribes, Inc.:

> When Doug first started to get the idea, he was excited and went to the USET congress (an official meeting of united, south, and eastern, tribes) and they issued a "resolution" that names the 8 towns (the ones I had identified) and that was the start of an official story about rock piles. I listened with great intent when, at a subsequent NEARA meeting, they had the chairman of USET speak these words: "We did not know about these things...you showed us the way." That nails it for me. Before these events, ceremonial stone landscape was NOT part of Indian thinking in the eastern U.S. I should mention in passing that

the USET chairman's voice was transmitted to the audience during a
NEARA "expert panel discussion" about rock piles that was organized
by Doug Harris and included Tim Fohl, Ted Ballard, and tribal officers from Mashpee and Aquinna. I was not asked to be on that panel.
(Waksman 2018a)

Sharing the ideological and political helm of this movement does not
appear to have been among Harris' long-term goals.

Rather, he insists that any ceremonial stone landscape study must
use techniques developed by Indian tribes (Serreze 2016b) as rightful
cultural resource gatekeepers (Harris 2014). Initially, THPOs appear
to have had no other choice but to tap the talents of antiquarians who
could draw data from project areas and perhaps even help develop interpretations. Harris explains this as the will of the "Creator and the
ancestors" who "began to deliver the people with all of the pieces of
the puzzle" (Harris and Jones 2018:149). As of 2013, Technology Integration Group, Inc., of Carlisle, Massachusetts, conducted ceremonial
stone landscape mapping for regional THPOs (Harris and Robinson
2015). Though TIG, a "light and optics technologies" firm, never advertised a connection to the cultural resource management sector, its
now-retired president, Dr. Timothy Fohl, was the lead author of the
tribally-endorsed Benfield Parcel "A" property report (Fohl et al. 2005),
a published antiquarian (Fohl 2003; 2010), and an emerging non-Indian
authority on Indian ceremonial landscapes (Eldred 2009; Heaney 2005;
Lepinoka and Carlotto 2015:38; Martha Lyon Landscape Architecture,
LLC, et al. 2016:3).

TIG's curious side gig as a ceremonial stone landscape service pro-
vider was soon superseded by Ceremonial Landscapes Research, LLC
(CLR), of Massachusetts, which was incorporated in 2014 specifically
to work "with federally recognized Tribes in the Tribal process of mapping, describing, analyzing, and preserving ceremonial landscapes as
identified by the Tribe(s), in accordance with the National Register of
Historic Places standards" (CLR 2017). Its staff originally included a
GIS expert, astronomer and historical researcher, photographer, and
Registered Professional Archaeologist who were presumably "culturally sensitized" by "Southern New England Tribes" (USET 2014). Aside
from the Registered Professional Archaeologist, Dr. Alexandra Martin,
the other staff members appear to fall under the antiquarian umbrella.
CLR's reports are confidentially submitted to federal agencies presiding
over the review of undertakings that have the potential to impact Native

American traditional cultural properties, which have come to include ceremonial stone landscapes. State historic preservation offices may be excluded from seeing these reports, in accordance with the special government-to-government relationship that federally recognized tribes and federal agencies share.

In 2015, CLR's methods were reportedly taught to twelve tribal specialists through a course sponsored by the Narragansett Indian Tribe, the Mohegan Tribe, the Mashantucket Pequot Tribe, the Wampanoag Tribe of Gay Head, and the National Trust for Historic Preservation. The graduates, including representatives from the sponsoring tribes, in addition to the Mohawk, Shinnecock, and Passamaquoddy tribes, received Ceremonial Stone Landscape Field Specialist certification (Rapkin 2016). Perhaps it signaled a further transfer of intellectual authority from the antiquarian base into the tribal wheelhouse. If so, that transfer was not sufficient to eliminate a continuing demand among THPOs for CLR's services.

Harris would seem to cast Indians as the ceremonial stone landscape paradigm's ideological architects. Take, for example, his opening statement at a lecture he gave in 2017 at the Institute for Native American Studies in Washington, Connecticut, where many antiquarians were in attendance:

> Let's get one thing straight; you're not in Scotland anymore. They are not cairns…That's a European word. They are not rock piles or stone piles, not anything else. They are Manitou Hussanash, Sacred Stones, Spirit Stones." (transcribed on Rockpiles.com)

It logically follows that naming a stone feature in English may constitute a microaggression toward Indians. Caught in the tractor beam of these identity politics, professional archaeologists Charity and Matthew Weiss have pledged to henceforth avoid using terms like "cairn" or "chamber" in their research, according to their "disrespectful, racist, or imperialistic undertones" (Weiss and Weiss 2017:errata). And while Harris acknowledges Mavor and Dix as intellectual trailblazers, it is unclear as to how extensively he credits them with developing the ideological framework that he appears to espouse.

Instead, Harris points to the late Medicine Man of the Narragansett Indian Tribe, Lloyd Wilcox, as the movement's ideological patron. This could be seen as a remarkably ironic choice, though to understand why requires considerable background. A fitting place to start is by recalling one of the last major public ceremonies in which Wilcox participated.

It was held on May 19, 2004, at Unity Park, in the village of Turners Falls in Montague, Massachusetts, a village named in honor of Captain William Turner, who, on May 19, 1676, led the killing of roughly 200 to 360 Indians on the opposite side of the river during King Philip's War. Euro-American historians have long referred to this event as "The Battle of Turners Falls," while some Indians prefer to call it the "Peskeompscut Massacre." Today, there is an initiative aimed at renaming this village "Great Falls" (Urban 2020.) During this ceremony, a reconciliation document was signed by several Montague Select Board Members, in addition to Wilcox and Chief Sachem Matthew "Seventh Hawk" Thomas on the behalf of the Narragansett Indian Tribe. The goal of this ceremony has been described by a local journalist as giving "closure to native groups regarding the name of the village" (Curtis 2014) and by Harris, who was also present at the ceremony, as a means by which to "bury the hatchet" (Harris 2016).

The thing about burying the hatchet is, someone usually remembers where it was buried. Historian Christine DeLucia explained:

> The town's commitment to a more respectful chapter in its relations with Native people and polities faced a test only a few years after this reconciliation and would return to contest the nearby Turners Falls Municipal Airport expansion project a couple of years later when he [Doug Harris] led the intertribal coalition to preserve the Turners Falls Sacred Ceremonial Hill site. In 2007 plans developed for a runway extension at the Turners Falls Municipal Airport. Located slightly southeast of the falls, it serves regional air traffic. (DeLucia 2018:279)

This affair has had a lasting negative impact on the local municipality, which was cash-strapped to begin with and was looking to expand economic opportunities. At a 2012 Montague Board of Selectmen's Meeting, Mark Fairbrother reminded his town:

> As we sit here in 2012, the project is still far from complete, the taxi way hasn't been touched, some of the navigational aids haven't been installed yet. It was supposed to be a 4200 foot taxiway and runway, its 3200 feet. I was on the commission at the time so I had a front row seat. While there were other guilty parties as well, where we are today has been driven by the actions of certain tribal leaders pressing their points of questionable veracity on the Town and leaving us in a very bad position, we have lost the funding for infrastructure im-

provements for hangers that we could have already been getting rental fees for. In the mean time we had this project fall apart with no end in sight, the tribal leaders involved have been paid not quite $100,000 for their activities at the airport…despite what you may have heard, I do not hate Native Americans. I have great respect for Native Americans. There are however 3 or 4 specific tribal leaders who were the ones promulgating all this, they are the ones I'm not happy with. If it had been someone else other than Native Americans, and gotten us to the same point, I wouldn't be their friends either. (Town of Montague 2012)

Wilcox withdrew from the public eye just as Harris took the Ceremonial Stone Landscape Movement's helm, and passed away in 2019. But throughout Wilcox's final and publically quiet decade, Harris seems to have cast him in the role of a decolonial visionary who would have been pleased by the power he and allied THPOs were exercising over large, federally regulated undertakings such as the Turners Falls Municipal Airport expansion project, armed with ceremonial stone landscape ideology and the "wonderful weapon" known as the National Historic Preservation Act. I can neither confirm nor deny that the victories allied THPOs have secured include payments, termed within the cultural resource management industry as "mitigations," for project-related damages to ceremonial stone landscapes. These are intended to serve as compensation for the loss of significant cultural property that would otherwise play a vital role in maintaining the continuing cultural identity of tribal constituencies.

In the eyes of many stakeholders, well-funded, federally regulated projects with broad public interest that need to follow a tight schedule present money trees worth shaking. Indian stakeholders who may take this approach are in good company. Fundamentally, this is not a racial issue at all, but an otherwise predictable expression of rational economic decision-making. A range of other organizations and interest groups, such as local historical societies and tourism foundations, may grab branches as well. But where federally recognized tribes are concerned, some of these grabs reach halfway across the country, as when THPOs from western tribes who monitor Section 106 consultation listings request to be included in New England projects. They then advise project proponents to solicit comment letters from them determining whether or not their tribes have potentially significant cultural resources within the subject properties that may merit protection. Their comment letters inevitably conclude that their tribes have no such resources, but are accompanied by invoices running into the hundreds of dollars.

As the late economist Milton Friedman often said, "There's no such thing as a free lunch." The real-world costs of these transactions, both well-justified and poorly-justified, local and distant, Indian and non-Indian, are not borne by wealthy CEOs who feel compelled to forgo their annual holiday bonus so they can give it "back to the community," though that would appeal to a popular vision of social justice. These costs are generally passed on to an under-informed public indirectly in such forms as utility bill inflation, which, of course, disproportionately impacts the poor, and delays in such things as service upgrades and maintenance. Understanding that wealth always comes from somewhere, it is worth considering that people who have no choice but to go to work five days a week, productively interact with people from other cultural backgrounds, and pay their utility bills every month include most of the Indian adults inhabiting New England.

Proponents of large-scale energy projects have doubtlessly become wary of the potential steep costs of delays that THPOs may attempt to impose at relatively small costs to themselves through federal consultation process detours or crowdfunded litigation (e.g., Climate Action Now 2017a, 2017b). Hence, it is logical to presume that under such conditions, satisfying THPO demands quickly and quietly may present the most logical choice. Hypothetically speaking, such negotiations would be carried out under the oversight of Uncle Sam, in the form of whatever federal agency happens to be on the hook in a regulatory capacity. The system for such negotiations was created through federal legislation, and THPOs who choose to avail themselves of its opportunities should be expected to do so in a way that is economically rational. And the point that most Indians are rational economic decision-makers would not have missed Lloyd Wilcox, who made his living as a master stonemason.

It is not clear whether or not Harris knows that Wilcox (1933-2019) espoused conservative libertarian principles, at least in 1979 when he was interviewed for an oral history project when he was in his forties (Burns et al. 1979). During those interviews, he extolled the benefits of hard work on personal character, condemned the media's selective appetite for victimhood stories, nodded to the universal wisdom of "The Ant and the Grasshopper" fable, and accused government social welfare programs of disintegrating Indian nuclear families by undermining the traditional gender roles on which they are structured, thereby "building the poverty cycle." He seemed to reserve a modest contempt for fellow tribespeople who choose to avail themselves of government assistance, arguing that self-sufficiency would increase "if you get him [Uncle Sam] out of the way," so that "these people have nobody to rely on but themselves." Having insisted that "Uncle Sam" is best kept out of people's "pockets," it is difficult to imagine a ca. 1979 Wilcox being impressed with the practiced trajectory of ceremonial stone landscape activism under Harris, whose political rise appears to have been built on getting Uncle Sam *in the way* where deep pockets exist.

Nonetheless, Harris routinely explains in his public presentations:

> We had remembered what the elder medicine man of the tribe had told us. He said, do not rely on tribal oral history or tribal lore to win the day on these issues. They – archaeologists and other naysayers – will deny the significance. What you must do is let the landscape speak for itself. And let the tribal oral history and lore stand as its witness. I thought I knew exactly what he was talking about when I left his office, and I realized later on I did not have a clue what in fact he really meant. But as we went through this process, what we learned was that the landscape in fact would begin to speak for itself. (Harris 2014)

With these poetically enigmatic words, Wilcox would seem to have pulled Harris out of his otherwise ordinary life and set him on an adventure of spiritual discovery, as Thom did for Mavor and Dix, and as Obi-Wan Kenobi did for Luke Skywalker. One need not be a Jungian psychologist to understand that archetypal tropes such as the "old wise man" make for compelling storytelling. "Let the landscape speak" has become the Ceremonial Stone Landscape Movement's public relations slogan, though its precise meaning is anybody's guess. It brings to mind Noam Chomsky's observation that "the whole point of good propaganda" is to "create a slogan that nobody's going to be against, and everybody's going to be for. Nobody knows what it means, because it doesn't mean anything" (Chomsky 2002).

But to be clear on a related point, I do not question that Wilcox recommended "letting the landscape speak," and that there is tribal wisdom for some to be had in that statement. I merely add that sufficient evidence exists to postulate that a younger Wilcox may have been more interested in letting conservative libertarian economists such as Drs. Milton Friedman or Thomas Sowell speak, and that ceremonial stone landscape activism appears to draw upon an isolated shred of the wisdom that he has offered the world at large.

CHAPTER ELEVEN

ANTIQUARIANSGONEWILD.COM

As Indian authorities moved to the front lines of ceremonial stone landscape activism, antiquarians promoted their idiosyncratic theories with renewed fervor, as if scrambling to be recognized as unique figures among the vanguard of a social revolution. For instance, Waksman hypothesized that many now disheveled-looking stone piles in the forest were once quadrilateral pyramids containing chambers (2012). Edward Ballard continued positing the interpretation of semi-circular stone arrangements as "prayer seats" from which astronomical phenomena would be viewed (2006), while James and Mary Gage have continued to consider the spiritually symbolic potential of empty spaces between or underneath stones (2011, 2015a, 2015b, 2017). And Timothy MacSweeney argues that many, if not most, stone walls were originally constructed as models of antlered serpents that doubled as fire-breaks to facilitate controlled burnings of the woods (2010). He maintains a website where he regularly posts photos of the ends of stone walls that he believes resemble serpent heads, onto which he often superimposes eyes and antlers. In this manner, all of these antiquarians appear to have carved out very distinctive places for themselves on "the right side of history."

A unified theory seems unlikely to precipitate from this intellectual pageantry, unless endless repetition of the general notion that "most or all mysterious stonework is probably Native American" qualifies as such. And the ceremonial stone landscape vision has not come into any greater focus since its pursuit merged onto the misinformation highway known as the World Wide Web. As NEARA's Norman Muller explains, online publishing has made it possible to "sneak under the radar screen" (NEARA 2004:26) and promote "a blossoming of information on previously ignored lithic sites that archaeologists are slowly coming around to considering as important" (NEARA 2014:38). As of June 2017, relevant open-access websites include:

- Ceremonial Stoneworks of the Northeast
- Celebrating the Ceremonial Stone Landscapes of Eastern North America
- Indian Ceremonial Rockpiles of Eastern Massachusetts
- Native American Stone Constructions
- Rock Piles
- Rock Piles – Stone Walls
- Sacred Ceremonial Stone Landscapes
- Stone Structures of Northeastern US
- Two Headwaters Stone Piles
- Waking Up on Turtle Island: Native American Cultural Landscape

Without direct consequences for being right or wrong, their webmasters present a flood of seemingly authoritative, though often incompatible, information for public consumption.

And the public is consuming it, as boasted by Waksman on the eleventh anniversary of his Rock Piles blog website:

> Google gets its own ideas baked into its own definition of "relevance" and 11 years of Rock Piles blogging has convinced Google THIS is the source for information about such things. No conventional wisdom academic view will ever catch up. So as far as the internet is concerned rock piles are antiquities left by Native Americans for ceremonial purposes....it says so on the Google! (Waksman 2017b)

He attributes the success of his blog to the fact that it answered "search questions about rock piles, at a rate of perhaps 100 new people a day, for long enough that academic rejection of Native American stonework never took place" (2018a). Misplaced sense of accomplishment aside, it is difficult to imagine a more reckless approach toward public knowledge-building. In October of 2018, Waksman's blog ranked 26 on Feedspot's "Top 40 New England Blogs and Websites to Follow in 2019."

As I see it, the post-millennial explosion of self-declared New England stone structure experts provides yet another expression of the nationwide trend described by Tom Nichols in his 2017 book, *The Death of Expertise: The Campaign Against Established Knowledge and Why It Matters.* Therein, he argues that Americans have entered an age when rejecting publically recognized expertise, particularly within the domains of public policy and social science, has become a popular virtue. Accordingly, ceremonial stone landscape activists would appear to present a remarkably virtuous crowd, at least in their own estimation. Take this quote from "Norman," who wokescolds the U.S. at large for failing to have become similarly enlightened:

> Unlike most advanced western countries, the U.S. has a population that has little knowledge about the unusual stone features that are sometimes encountered in the woods, fields, and hills. And because of the historical disconnect with our Native American past, we treat these features as something of little importance historically or culturally, and consequently they are often treated as not worthy of preservation. (comment, following Waksman 2020a)

Despite their sense of moral superiority where Native American cultural heritage issues are concerned, ambitions to produce research breakthroughs have, for some, sidelined good judgement. The most notorious example is marked by the 2014 arrest of Frederick F. Meli, known to his NEARA colleagues as "Dr. Meli" (Waksman 2008), by the Rhode Island State Police Financial Crimes Unit under charges of perjury, forgery, and obtaining money under false pretenses (Providence Journal 2014). Reportedly, this former University of Rhode Island instructor had used a forged doctoral degree in anthropology to secure a contract from the North Smithfield Town Council to study stone structures (Narragansett Improvement Co. v. Wheeler, 21 A.3d 430, 433-34 [R.I. 2011]; Henry 2008; Szep 2007). He was pursuing the idea that the town's abundant stone heaps mark highly ritualized Indian burial complexes, ultimately, at the expense of his legitimacy as a contributor to any future discourse.

Some antiquarians seem ambivalent about the rise of Indian authority in ceremonial stone landscape activism. James Porter insists that the success of the movement will not be delivered by tribes because they have "been working on that for centuries with little success" (comment posted by James Porter, following Waksman 2017a). Waksman does not look upon this turn through rose-colored glasses either, remarking that Harris does "not spend time with people just for the fun of it" and that his "visiting me, while being introduced to the rock piles, was something he benefited from" (see comment following Waksman 2009).

In fact, in an October 2018 Rock Piles blog post that he titled "Indigenous Landscape—Creating a New Mythology," Waksman admits feeling "slightly hurt" by Harris, who he claims is deliberately omitting the "paternity of ideas" underlying ceremonial stone landscapes that he and others developed (Waksman 2018a). He adds in a later post: "I get a little miffed about the spread of fake history" (Waksman 2018b), revealing an ironic circularity, that of a radical revisionist of ancient Indian history experiencing an allergic reaction to the perceived filtering of his own recent history by a representative of the people whose ancient history he set out to revise in the first place. This situation also presents a rare, if not unique, political unicorn—a white settler colonist suggesting that a local Indian has appropriated his ideas and then erased him from history. Perhaps Waksman feels that he is "still here" in much the same sense as the proverbial invisible Indian. But, realistically, Waksman cannot lodge any recognition-related grievances within ceremonial stone landscape activism's ideological bubble, where sympathies are deeply racialized and only flow down, away from the privileged crest of Mount White where, like it or not, he remains permanently seated.

Waksman, a seminal promoter of the ceremonial stone landscape paradigm, is beginning to critically reflect on the trajectory of the movement that has carried it forward, and perhaps even the intellectual legitimacy of the movement's figurehead. In an October 2020 blog entry, he asks some stark questions:

> If Doug Harris already knew about rock piles, then why would he take multiple walks with me? If he already knew about rock piles then why did the USET resolution appear (Resolution 2003:022), identifying eight towns, only after I gave Doug the names of those towns? Had the main purpose of the USET resolution been the political aspect of working with New England towns, then Doug, who is an extremely busy person, would have gone to the towns first and not bothered taking walks with me. (Waksman 2020b)

Responding to Waksman's post, "Norman" identifies himself among the handful of antiquarians who "showed Doug Harris and other Native Americans stonework that their ancestors had constructed, but which they were completely unaware of. At the same time, they were embarrassed to admit they didn't know anything about it. Just my opinion."

Regardless of whether or not such antiquarians like it, THPOs politically transformed one of the fundamental principles of ceremonial stone landscape theory as established by Mavor and Dix. The allied THPOs would not recognize the potential of just anybody to intuitively perceive ancient ritual landscape architecture. Rather, they insisted that only Indians carry that ability, though they might afford limited credence to a small echelon of "culturally sensitized" non-Indians willing to submit their thoughts and interpretations for tribal approval. These THPOs installed themselves at the top of the scene's moral and intellectual legitimacy hierarchy in no uncertain terms, as Harris clarified in a presentation to the Massachusetts Forest Rescue titled "The Meaning, Importance and Cultural Significance of Preserving Native American Ceremonial Stone Landscapes and Burials in the Forests of Massachusetts." In that forum, Harris declared that only federally recognized tribes can "certify" the sacred status of an Indian site. A NEARA member who attended this presentation piously trumpeted Harris' message to the rest of his organization: "For no Native American Cultural Stone Landscape (CSL) can be officially identified by a non-Indian, as it should be" (Kreisberg 2017).

So it is overly simplistic to imagine ceremonial stone landscape activists as a kindred alliance of THPOs and antiquarians opposing a unified archaeological front. Ceremonial stone landscape activism is, in large part, a grassroots movement whose ever-shifting ground holds plenty of space for ideologues to compete for attention, status, and power. Nonetheless, a categorical association of archaeology with settler colonialism and racism hangs in the memosphere, as does a vision of Indian victims joined by morally outraged defenders. From this core position, ceremonial stone landscape activism finds sufficient clarity and gravity to press its ultimate question—which side are you on?

That is, of course, a culture war ultimatum intended to trigger a feelings-based response among the under-informed. But the thing about such ultimatums is that they tend to collapse when fact-based contexts are brought to bear. So let us take a serious look at what history and archaeology have to say about two entirely unrelated New England stone traditions that ceremonial stone landscape activists conflate to support their vision of the past.

PART TWO:

INCONVENIENT INFORMATION

CHAPTER TWELVE

WAYSIDE MEMORIES

HARRIS DISCLOSES LITTLE about the nature or use of *manitou hassannash* (phenomena I typically refer to as "stone heaps") publicly, presumably in the interest of keeping culturally sensitive information from falling into unsympathetic hands. Among the few insights he has shared is that many mark a site of historical trauma, such as where an animal killed someone (Bellows 2017; Wisniewski 2018). He has explained that a medicine man would mitigate such trauma by speaking a prayer into a stone and placing it on the site. Other tribesmen would follow suit and "what we end up with are 'memorial piles'" that maintain "balance and harmony" in that location, so long as the stones remain undisturbed. If Harris is correct, the implications are tremendous. A large proportion of New England's wooded hilltops would, essentially, represent extensive memorial sites where large numbers of Indians died traumatically. It would seem logical to presume that Indian folklore would warn tribal members not to travel through the uplands, due to the extreme danger of such geographies. It would also imply that the historic farmers who collectively deforested and intensively farmed these geographies for decades on end, causing extreme environmental degradation along the way, somehow remained committed to preserving hundreds of thousands of these *manitou hassannash* in place.

But the problem is, straightforward readings of historic records do not support this vision. In fact, a close examination of them suggests that Harris is, unwittingly or not, promoting a false equivalency of epic proportions. Though historic records describing the phenomenon known as Indian "memory piles" bear little, if any, relation to the otherwise ubiquitous stone heaps found in New England's forested uplands, they provide a window into a downright fascinating dimension of Indian spiritual history and heritage that is certainly worth appreciating. The goal of this chapter is to establish beyond any shadow of a doubt that Indians have indeed piled stones for ritual purposes throughout this region for centuries on end.

Since early colonial days and perhaps before, Indian travelers have offered a rock, stick, or other object to wayside locations for purposes that could easily be qualified as sacred. While local beliefs and protocols certainly varied, historical accounts point to a common goal of securing good fortune. Authors have variously referred to the objects of this practice as memory piles, sacrifice rocks, stone heaps, and taverns (Handsman 2008; Jett 1994; Lavin 2013:290; Rubertone 2001). For the convenience of discussion, I refer to this cultural phenomenon simply as the memory pile tradition. While history stands guilty of disregarding a wide range of Indian cultural practices, it took a remarkably sustained interest in this one, as attested to by written accounts from colonial days up to the recent past. Familiarity with this record would seem to be a prerequisite for anyone wishing to develop a well-informed opinion on the historicity of ceremonial stone landscape claims.

The earliest written account of an Indian wayside memorial concerns holes more than stone piles. In 1624, Plymouth Colony's Edward Winslow reports that Wampanoags would dig a round hole, roughly one foot deep, along a pathway to commemorate a remarkable act (Winslow 1910:352-253). It would capture the attention of travelers who would ask others what it commemorates. Such "memory holes" were cleared of overgrowth and re-dug as needed to ensure the persistence of associated memories and mitigate the tedium of travel. Anchoring the memory hole concept in deep time, a Wampanoag creation story reports the hero figure Maushop having a pleasant visit with folks on Cape Cod's north side (Crosby 1993:36). In commemoration, he dug an enormous hole, piling the earth in a mound to the south (Reynard 1924:26). The hole filled with rainwater, becoming Scargo Lake in Dennis, while the mound, presumably Scargo Hill, which rises from the lake's south shore, grew over with pine trees.

For over two centuries, travelers in eastern Massachusetts have remarked on "sacrifice rocks" along the ancient trail from Plymouth to Sandwich, historically called Old Sandwich Road. The custom of casting a stone or stick onto wayside rocks there was first reported by Ezra Stiles, eighteenth-century Congregationalist minister and scholar. He explains that wood offerings, used in lieu of locally scarce stones, burned off periodically whenever Indians fired the woods to promote deer habitat (Dexter 1916:161-162). Reluctant to discuss their custom, Indians even took a bypass trail to avoid one such rock when travelling in English company. He claims that some made offerings because their elders had done so, while others believed that a failure to do so brings bad luck, particularly in deer hunting. In 1796, Rev. Gideon Hawley, missionary to the Mashpee, remarked that in "every part of the country, and among every tribe of Indians" there are heaps of stones or sticks, specifically noting "sacrifice rock, as it is termed, between Plymouth and Sandwich, to which stones and sticks are always cast by the Indians who pass it" (Hawley 1835:59; Ruttenber 1872:373-374). He interprets such as sacrifices to, or acknowledgement of, a spiritual presence. In 1807, author Edward Kendall estimated two "sacrifice rocks," possibly those described by Stiles, at ten to twelve feet long, one being six feet tall, and the other ten (1809:49-50). They were mantled with oak and pine branches, both fresh and decaying. He also tells of an "aged missionary of Marshpee" who saw two women drag a pine tree and hoist it atop "sacrifice rock." The women were initially "disconcerted" by the approach of the missionary, who interpreted their act as honoring Divine Providence. Rev. Timothy Dwight notes that sticks were still being placed atop "sacrifice rock" in 1823 (1823:3:109).

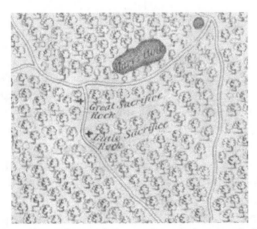

Figure 5. Detail from "Map of Plymouth settled in 1620" showing the "Great" and "Little" sacrifice rocks along Old Sandwich Road in Plymouth, MA (Bourne 1830).

Two "sacrifice rocks" along Old Sandwich Road, near its intersection with Ship Pond Road, are regularly included on nineteenth-century maps of Plymouth (Figure 5). In the late twentieth-century, historical archaeologist Constance Crosby describes two sacrifice rocks along this road (1993). One, not publicly marked, is mantled with a thick mat of rotted pine needles and oak leaves that support pine saplings. She believes it was used at least into the 1880s. The other is located on property donated to the Plymouth Antiquarian Society in 1928. The Society marked it with cement posts in 1940, installed a commemorative marker around 1960, and replaced the latter with a metal plaque in 1991 (Plymouth Antiquarian Society 2012). Crosby recalls late-twentieth-century motorists stopping and instructing their children to throw a pebble onto it for good luck (1993:40). Offerings are still being added today, consisting mostly of small sticks, pebbles, and coins.

Anthropologist Frank Speck also took interest in the memory pile tradition, beginning with his 1907 visit to the Mashpees (Prince 1907:495). Tribal informants reported that, according to their former beliefs, spirits of the dead often appeared on paths and required an offering to clear the way. Consequently, Mashpee ancestors built "great square flat-topped" spirit lodges as places to offer gifts, often food or whiskey, and hold religious meetings. Speck claims that Mashpees still superstitiously offered a stick or branch to the decaying remains of what they believed to be these lodges. Speck described and photographed three such "brush heaps" during later visits. One, at a junction in South Mashpee's pine barrens, was 8-10 feet across, shoulder high, composed of pine branches and twigs, and contained an empty whiskey bottle (1945). Before photographing it, Speck and his brother each "tossed an offering of a dead pine branch upon the heap." An informant specified these as "payment" to the victim of some tragedy that happened there, ensuring the safety of travelers passing on dark nights. At another junction in 1922, Speck photographed a brush heap that Butler notes in 1946 as "now overgrown with scrub" (1946). "Conservative" tribal members maintained it and "even held a powwow at the site to emphasize its sentiments," probably during the 1930s (Speck 1945:22). Mashpees called these "lucky stick piles" and "taverns" by the 1930s (Hutchins 1979:139; Simmons 1986:255; Tantaquidgeon 1935:49). One informant, remembering her childhood in the 1920s and 30s South Mashpee, explained that a traveler would take a stick or small tree, spit on it, and throw it on the mound to ward off evil spirits (Bingham 1970:20). In 1935, Gladys Tantaquigeon, the Mohegan medicine woman and anthropologist who partnered with Speck, reported that highway construction had destroyed several local "taverns," though three others remained

(1935:49). She qualifies two as "old," noting that the third was recently established on the tribe's summer meeting grounds. Locals generally denied knowing anything about them, with a couple of exceptions. One informant still made offerings based on superstition or tradition, while another respected the taverns marking places where people had been murdered in days long past. Tantaquidgeon also reports a claim by Eben Queppish, who led the tribal revitalization efforts of the 1920s, that the largest tavern ever made was built on the remains of a lodge or wigwam.

The Mayhew Memorial of Martha's Vineyard marks a centuries-old memory pile site still venerated by locals. In 2008, the National Society of the Daughters of the American Revolution rededicated the Mayhew Memorial, which marks "the place by the wayside" where, according to tradition, missionary Thomas Mayhew Jr. performed his last service for Wampanoag converts in 1657 before perishing at sea. Tradition holds that Hiaccomes, a local convert, placed a quartz pebble at Mayhew's feet, which the Aquinnahs added to through the centuries (Banks 1911:1:230). In 1901, the tribe and the Daughters of the American Revolution installed a boulder and plaque next to the pile, which diminished through souvenir collecting (Norton 1923). Speck described it as a "small pile of round cobblestones" marked by an enclosure (1945:22). The Mayhew Memorial was rededicated in 2008 following a two-year, $13,000 restoration of the miniature park surrounding it. Attendees left small beach pebbles there (Cabot 2008).

Another notable memory pile, the "Stockbridge Stone Heap," lies near the state's western end, in Great Barrington, by Monument Mountain's base. It was described by three eighteenth-century missionaries: Ezra Stiles, John Sergeant, and Gideon Hawley. Observing it in 1734 while traveling with an Indian interpreter, Sergeant estimates its volume at "ten cart loads," explaining that it grew from individual stones cast by Indian travelers, though the custom had largely fallen out of practice (Sergeant, quoted in Brown 1958:47). He notes that it was reputedly built over a sachem, who died after Mahicans arrived in the region. Also, an Indian informant claimed it marked a territorial boundary respected by the neighboring Mohawk, and that the Mahican are entitled to hunt on any land within a day's journey. Stiles had seen the Stockbridge Stone Heap and sketched it (Figure 6) in 1762 as 18 feet long and six feet high with a concave center (Dexter 1916:161). Hawley saw it also, writing in 1796 that the "the largest heap I have ever observed is that large collection of small stones on the mountain between Stockbridge and Great Barrington" (Hawley 1835, quoted in Ruttenber 1872:373-374). He notes its position along a trail near a stream where his party refreshed their horses. Their Indian guide found a stone nearby and "cast" it into the heap, but was reluctant to discuss why, only sharing that his father had taught him to do so.

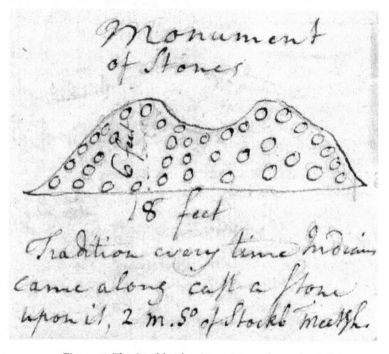

Figure 6: The Stockbridge Stone Heap, drawn by Stiles.
(Yale Digital Collections)

Yet another missionary, Rev. Timothy Dwight, describes the Stock-bridge Stone Heap in 1823 as an obtuse cone with a six- to eight-foot di-ameter base (1823:2:362, and 3:408). He claims it formed by "slow accu-mulation of rocks thrown upon it one at a time by passing Indians" and marks a prominent Indian's tomb, adding that local Indians have, for many years, felt "released" from the obligation to make offerings. Once, when passing the monument, he lamented that it was "broken up," pre-sumably by relic-hunters or would-be grave robbers, providing one of several historic accounts of vandalism. Joseph K. Pelton, who lived by Monument Mountain's base in the early nineteenth century (Hosmer 1885:34-35, 45), met two Stockbridge Indian descendants who came from "the west" seeking this memory pile (Taylor 1882:46). They did not know its precise location, relying on Pelton as an escort, but seemed familiar with its ritual protocol. Pelton reports "after standing for some time thoughtfully and in silence about the pile, each cast a stone upon it and turned away."

Tradition holds that a stone heap once standing on Sachem's Plain in Norwich, Connecticut, marked the spot where Uncas, a Mohegan sachem, executed Miantonomo, a Narragansett sachem, in 1643. Anthropologist Eva Butler is confident that colonial-era Indians maintained a stone pile there, though Miantonomo was likely executed elsewhere (Butler 1946:6-7). Historian Frances M. Caulkins suggests that local colonists associated Miantonomo with this feature, which may have signified something entirely different among Indians (1866:34-39). According to his reading of a manuscript by Rev. Richard Hyde of Norwich, historian William Williams claims that the "large heap of stones" at Sachem's Plain was originally erected over Miantonomo's body, but later culled by locals for building material (1833:135). In 1841, a group of Norwich citizens marked its original location with a monument (Caulkins 1866), which was relocated in 1904 to Sachem's Park where it remains.

Several other memory piles have been reported in Connecticut. Speck observed "a modest mound construction" on a ledge overlooking the road from Norwich to Hartford believed to have marked the northern boundary of Uncas' seventeenth-century domain (1945). Speculating that it was once taller but had settled through two centuries of disuse, the spaces between rocks contained dirt and leaves that he attributed to natural deposition. He also describes a memory pile on the Schaghticoke Reservation in Kent as several feet tall onto which travelers "cast" stones. By one informant's account, some Indian visitors poured whiskey there for the "ghost of a murdered comrade whose shade abode there." Dwight reports another memory pile on the summit of western Connecticut's Falls Mountain in 1823 as a "circular enclosure" that was unlike the "obtuse cone" of the Stockbridge Stone Heap (1823:3:403). Noting that Indians had long ceased casting stones onto it, he claims it was erected over a Schaghticoke leader who was executed for a heinous crime. Young medical students reportedly destroyed it in a futile attempt to "dig up the bones of the deceased chief." A later nineteenth-century historian, Samuel Orcutt, provides a romantically embellished discussion, identifying the deceased sachem as Waramaug and encouraging all travelers to add stones (1822:111). Butler contends that Orcutt's discussion is largely fabricated because the mound was already destroyed, and an earlier history claims that Waramaug lay buried in a cemetery elsewhere (Butler 1836:475). In a 1788 letter to Stiles, Dr. Noah Webster recalled from his youth a wayside stone pile on the road from Hartford and Farmington that locals thought marked an Indian burial (1790:207). He describes it as a 25 foot round pile formed from stones added by Indian travelers. Curiously, Webster also reports a custom, which he qualifies as a vulgar form of ridicule, whereby travelers passing this pile attempt to trick any uninitiated companion into removing their hat—in a manner evocative of honoring the dead—by telling them that an insect was on it.

At least two memory piles are reported from Woodbury that presumably no longer exist. One was believed to mark the grave of Pomperaug, a Potatuck Sagamore who died shortly before English settlement. Historian William Cothren locates it beside a large rock on the west side of Main Street, describing it as a "large heap" of small stones, some of which were not sourced locally, that had been cast by passing Indians (1854). He provided an illustration (Figure 7). The 1938 publication, *Connecticut: A Guide to Its Roads, Lore, and People*, claims that Pomperaug is buried beneath the large rock, but makes no mention of an accompanying stone heap (Federal Writers Project for the State of Connecticut 1938). Cothren reports another stone mound near Nonnewaug Falls thought to mark the grave of Nonnewaug, another local sachem. He recalls a "hillock, or mound, raised over the grave" when he visited it in the early nineteenth century, but adds that the landowner had since "plowed it down" (1854:2:884-885). Recalling it as about ten feet long, six feet wide, and four feet high, he supposes that it was formed "in the same way, as in the case of Pomperaug's grave."

Figure 7: "Pomperaug's grave" (Cothren 1854:2:88).

Though we have focused on New England, it is important to note that the use of memory piles is in evidence along much of the East

Coast. This tradition extends west and south of New England (Jett 1994) and is relatively well-documented in New York State (Speck 1945). For example, Edward M. Ruttenber, a nineteenth-century journalist and historian, reports Indians in the lower Hudson Valley casting stones on roadside piles, which he presumed signaled to other travelers that a visit occurred. Carlos Westez, an Indian and ethnographer who worked with Speck, reported in 1944 that he and a bicycling companion "resumed an old Montauk custom of piling stones at Poggatticut's resting place" in eastern Long Island "every time we pass the spot." Tradition holds that the 1651 funeral procession for this Manhasset Sachem briefly rested at this location before continuing to his grave. Speck also reports a tradition of maintaining "memorial brush heaps" in Sussex County, Delaware, noting one that local Euro-Americans continued using for over a century.

The memory pile tradition is neither extinct nor exclusively Indian. It clearly struck a chord with colonial and early Euro-American observers. Otherwise, they would not have written about it. But why? First, consider that Indians did not introduce Puritans to the idea of piling stones commemoratively. Revisiting Kendall's account of Mashpees' "aged missionary," it is revealing that the missionary decided not to criticize the women who paid homage to the "sacrifice rock." Instead of interpreting their act as heathen, he viewed it as an acknowledgement of Providence. While presentism may tempt us to imagine that his reaction reflected a multicultural worldview, it more likely betrayed a sense of the familiar, as the Christian Old Testament references monumental stone piles. In the Book of Genesis, Jacob and Laban consecrate their covenant before God by building Galeed, a stone "witness pile." The Book of Joshua describes Gilgal as a pile of twelve stones carried from the Jordan River, memorializing the first camp of the Israelites after completing the Exodus. An association of New World memory piles with Old World theology is plainly evidenced by the nineteenth-century historian who describes Miantonomo's Monument as a "Gilgal or heap of memorial stones reared in the wilderness" (Caulkins 1866:34-39). And Dwight qualifies the use of the stone heaps at Stockbridge and New Milford as "nearer to the custom of the Israelites" (1823 Vol.3:387).

But the receptivity of Euro-Americans to the Indian memory pile tradition may reflect more than just ideological familiarity. Butler points out that "people who were not Indians but who were interested in perpetuating the old customs of the Indians, have periodically attempted to revive it." Speck proposes that generations of Euro-Americans continued to pay tribute to Indian brush piles in Sussex County, Delaware, for protection against a vaguely understood spiritual threat, a practice "transmitted to the colonists and their posterity as an American folk tradition" (1945:23). Crosby suggests that Stiles' and Kendalls' accounts of the "sacrifice rocks" on the road from Plymouth to Sandwich unintentionally promoted "an incorporation of these particular memorials into the Euro-American cultural and historical landscape" (1993:39-40). Before photographing the "tavern" at the junction of Mashpee and Waquoit Road, Speck and his brother each added a dead pine branch to the heap—a performance that contributed to its physical character. Additionally, Crosby recalls children throwing pennies onto Plymouth's "Sacrifice Rock" for good luck, which is a practice that may represent an ideological crossover of the northern European wishing well tradition, which is similarly aimed at securing good fortune and still prevalent among contemporary New Englanders. These accounts indicate that while Indians generally created memory piles, non-Indians often took up their use. We may speculate that memory piles provided Euromericans with an outlet for their own superstitious tendencies, or, at some level, satisfied their desire to engage Indian heritage. As historical archaeologist Lynette Russell has observed, "people want to belong, they want to know a geography and unproblematically fit into a landscape" (2012:415). Accordingly, the accessibility and democratic spirit of memory piles should appeal to anyone wishing to feel personally invested in the place, regardless of their group identities.

These last thoughts on memory piles are for anyone genuinely concerned with their rediscovery and preservation. While the local practices and meanings comprising the memory pile tradition varied over space and time, and the historic record concerning them is idiosyncratic, three general expectations are plainly evident. First, we expect a memory pile to occur as a stand-alone phenomenon immediately beside a well-travelled route. Second, we expect stone offerings, where present, to be small enough to toss. Third, we expect a memory pile to lack any organized structure, understanding them to be products of incidental and uncoordinated contributions of travelers over a period of years, decades, or perhaps even centuries. Therefore, we expect them to bear little, if any, resemblance to the stone heaps generated by farmers, which, as we shall learn in the next chapter, typically occur in groups, are usually beyond the range of a trailside toss, and almost always include stones that are too heavy for flesh-and-blood humans to have thrown, resulting in a structurally sound position. Put simply, these two puzzle pieces do not fit together.

But powerful ideological visions are at work in today's New England, visions that are not interested in being reconciled with the genuinely fascinating historical evidence that we have just reviewed or the evidence presented in the following chapter.

CHAPTER THIRTEEN

FORGOTTEN FARMS

"WHEN YOU HAVE A FARM, you have to move stones." This is what the owner of a small farm in Foster, Rhode Island, said regarding fieldstones he had heaped onto boulders in one of his pastures (Figure 8A). I had seen his handiwork from the road and brought my camera and some questions that must have sounded trivial. But he was not trivial to me. He was the only living farmer I knew who generated multiple, discrete stone heaps in functioning field and pasture lots. Fortunately, he was glad to show me a range of curiosities, including a quartz outcrop upon which he heaped fieldstones (Figure 8B) that he periodically hauled away to fill holes and ruts. He also pointed to the base of a tree that he had encircled with fieldstones, which he had no plans to relocate (Figure 8C). But I was most intrigued when he led me to a woodlot to inspect several low-lying stone heaps centered on bedrock outcrops (Figure 8D). Beneath veils of shadow and leaf litter, they looked ancient and mysterious. He said they were there when he bought the farm, having won it at auction after retiring from his non-agrarian career, and wondered who made them. In reply, I presumed they were left by previous farmers who also found stone-moving unavoidable, though I am not sure he was convinced. Regardless, he planned to leave them for future generations to admire, which left me wondering what those admirers might think if his farm reverted from its present state of development to forest. Would they understand that most of the stone heaps were unceremoniously created by an early twenty-first-century farmer with a flair for improvisation? If not, my incidental notes and photographs would stand as the best insurance against their unnecessary mystification.

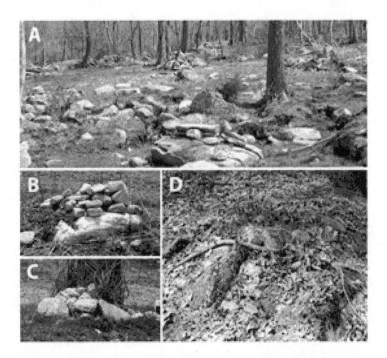

Figure 8: Stone heaps photographed by the author on farm in Foster, Rhode Island, May 2015: A) Modern stone heaps on boulders in a pasture. B) Modern stone heap on a shallow quartz outcrop in the middle of a planting field. C) Modern stone heap around the base of a tree by the edge of the same planting field. D) One of several, leaf-obscured historic stone heaps sited on shallow outcrops in a woodlot.

My contention that nineteenth-century hill farmers built groups of stone heaps across the region has been repeatedly condemned as mere "mythology" by ceremonial stone landscape proponents. Regardless, independent existing evidence indicates otherwise. This chapter presents the results of a historic journal/newspaper search that I conducted, which recovered numerous incidental accounts of nineteenth-century farmers constructing stone heaps, some of which were clearly built by hand in active fields and pastures. These findings call into question ceremonial stone landscape proponents James and Mary Gage, whose historic journal/newspaper search into historic agrarian field-clearing practices apparently failed to turn up similar accounts (2014), which seemed to confirm their previous assertion that only Indians "intentionally built *compact* and *carefully* constructed" (2011:159) stone heaps, and that "a group of cairns indicates the presence of a Native American ceremonial site" (Ibid.:193).

By examining these historical accounts, I also offer modest sociocultural insights into a marginally documented but geographically
widespread rural phenomenon that is no longer indexed in our collective memory. First, a semantic note is warranted. Elsewhere, I have
termed individual stone heaps "cairns" and groups "cairnfields" (Ives
2015a). But seeing as these British borrowings appear in none of the
accounts featured herein, I have decided to use the historically germane
term "stone heap." And for the purposes of this chapter, eastern New
York State is considered an "honorary" part of New England, which is
consistent with the approaches of stone wall historians (Allport 1994;
Thorson 2002, 2005).

To appreciate when and why stone heaping appears to have become
widely practiced in New England's hills, a broad-brush overview of their
agricultural history is useful. Bear in mind that, by necessity, this historical context addresses the region's interior lands in generalized terms,
in accordance with the notion that "across central New England there
has been great similarity in the regional pattern of land use in terms
of the extent and timing of deforestation, major agricultural uses, and
the history of farm abandonment and reforestation" (Foster 1992:768).
Of course, broad-brush overviews are poor substitutes for more accurate microhistories, and this particular one may hold little relevance to
coastal and riverine sub-regions that were extensively farmed prior to
the American Revolution.

Colonists began establishing farmsteads in the region's interior hills
following King Philip's War (1675-8), which left their original, indigenous landlords politically subjugated. Endowed with considerable timber reserves for building construction, fencing, and fuel, colonial hill
farms operated for decades with little reason to consider sustainability.
They usually encompassed less than one hundred acres, were economically self-sufficient, and produced few market products.

However, a generation of young farmers brought up during the
post-Revolutionary War baby boom was determined to meet, if not
exceed, their parents' success. In the opening years of the nineteenth
century, they largely finished transforming southern New England's interior into a rolling tapestry of farms that were generally modest in size,
partly according to the tendency to divide landholdings among multiple
descendants. Among them were many of the entrepreneurs who drove
local industrial development. The small mills they built along tributaries
gave rise to villages and hamlets, which, in turn, opened new markets

for local agricultural produce and a keener orientation to macroeconomic trends. Unlike previous generations, this one would run headlong into sustainability issues, as wood, land, and fertile soil grew scarce.

Farming the progressively deforested hillsides invited soil degradation, particularly from 1810-1840 when wool production became a principal venture (Allport 1994; Bidwell 1921:689; Wessels 1997). During this period, sheep flocks grew rapidly, (Baker and Paterson 1988:98; Bidwell and Falconer 1941:406-407) as did the number of small wool processing mills (Sturges 2014:487), contributing to a so-called "sheep fever" or "wool craze" driven by commercial demands and market speculation (Bullion 1988: 88). This trend was most pronounced during the 1830s, a decade dubbed the "Golden Era of sheep raising" (Day 1954:187). In 1853, a seasoned farmer recalled the economic rationale of those days, when one would profit better from converting "his old fields into sheep-pastures" than raising crops, which had higher labor costs (Brown 1853:443). But the environmental costs of wool's easy, short-term profits were undeniable. As terrestrial ecologist Tom Wessels notes, "a large percentage of the exposed bedrock found in the region today owes its presence to past overgrazing by sheep (1997)." Uplands were left stonier every time their silty runoff choked streams and rivers. If environmental historian Brian Donahue is correct, many of the region's farmers "were skinning the land, and they knew it" (2007:19).

Yet even during this "Golden Era," the decline of hill farm culture loomed on the horizon. By the 1830s, westward migration had become a topic of widespread concern, as reflected in the advice of a "Green Mountaineer" urging fellow Vermonters not to sell off their land "to your rich neighbors for sheep pastures" (Fessenden 1835:128). But soon enough, many the region's progressively run-down hill farms would hardly be worth selling. After peaking in the early 1840s, the region's sheep population declined as many farmers turned to dairying to satisfy expanding urban markets (Wilson 1990:23-33).

As the mid-century passed, ruralists continued pursuing economic opportunities in cities, manufacturing towns, and the West, leaving, in the words of one agricultural historian, "less thrifty and less enterprising" family members behind (Turner 1919:222-241). Consequently, the "long-established habits and traditions" of the self-sufficient hill farm were quietly falling out of practice (Bidwell 1921). Bear in mind that while New England's net agricultural productivity, if indexed to output per farm acre, did not plummet until after 1900 (Bell 1989:456); lowlands had been increasingly shouldering the balance for decades prior.

The "old pastures," criticized as "painful evidences of the wretched system of husbandry that has prevailed among us for the last half century," were noted as littering the countryside by 1860 (*Country Gentleman* 1860). The region's market-oriented farmers, especially those working marginal lands, could not compete with the bounty arriving by rail from the west. And though the Civil War temporarily revitalized local wool production, it chiefly benefited that dwindling echelon of sheep farmers in northern New England, who bought out smaller farms to provision their large flocks (Cole 1926; Wilson 1935).

Following the war, state governments began grappling with a challenge that would carry on for generations—figuring out what to do with abandoned farmland (*Hartford Courant* 1898; *Maine Farmer* 1891; *Michigan Farmer* 1898; Vaughn 1929; Wilson 1892:10). Of course, reforestation met pockets of resistance, such as where farm houses were repurposed as weekend estates (*Boston Sunday Globe* 1898; *Critic* 1893), where locals continued haying viable hillside fields regardless of who owned them, and where loggers worked. Nonetheless, as the twentieth century progressed, state and non-governmental institutions amassed abandoned farmland for conservation under which their secondary forests became sociopolitically ordained as "natural" spaces.

Upon encountering old farmstead ruins in the wooded hills, remember that "by far the greater part of the westward migrants" in early-to-mid-nineteenth century America "were the sons and daughters of New England" (Thistlethwaite 1967:100). The prairies and woodlands that they developed into farms along western frontiers were, of course, originally inhabited by any number of Indian tribal groups. But the young nation's Indian removal policies ensured the availability of fresh land for yeoman farmers from the east who "exported" their land clearing tradition (Pfaff 2000). Accordingly, it would be shortsighted to regard our stone heaps, walls, and cellar holes merely as relics of an agricultural heyday. They are also silent testimonials to the mass displacement of western Indians in the name of Manifest Destiny. Against this historical backdrop, let us consider the historic record of stone heaping among New England farmers.

An early account of stone heaps sited on farmland is provided by Johnston Verplanck, a New York City resident who journaled throughout his month-long tour of upstate New York in 1822, a journey he took to avoid the height of a yellow fever epidemic. With satirical flair, Verplanck composed entertaining descriptions of countryside settings. For instance, when near Milford, he facetiously drew a cultural link between ancient Egyptians and local farmers:

> People in this part of the Country, must be of course, of Egyptian ex-
> traction, and by the way, stones are actually piled up in the fields in
> a pyramidical manner, which either proves the hypothesis, or clearly
> shows, that the Egyptians took the hint in the construction of their
> pyramids from our ancestors. (Verplanck 1968 [1822]:39-40)

He went on to marvel at the surplus of stone in this "Queer country,"
where "in many places looks as if it had rained stones instead of water."
Apparently, impounding fieldstones within "pyramids" was one way local farmers managed their surplus.

In 1910, a Maine resident recalled heaping stones when he was a
young farmer. In regard to the latest winter weather, he wrote, "This,
to some extent, duplicates the month of January 1876, when the snow
went off and the writer picked up a field of stone heaps, since turned into
pasture; but the stones are there yet to remind us of the fact" (*Oxford
Democrat* 1910). That farmers often left stone heaps in place, rather than
carting or sledding them away, is evident in several of the accounts that
follow.

The most detailed historical account of agricultural stone heaping
known to the author appears in an 1895 issue of the *Providence Journal*
in an article about rural curiosities in Connecticut's northeasternmost
town of Thompson:

> On the Josiah Dyke place, in this region, are a number of curious heaps
> of stones, piled up without mortar into pyramids so well and so solidly
> built that although built 60 years ago they are still in as good condition
> as ever, except where mischievous boys have torn them down. They
> were placed there over half a century ago by an uncle of the owners of
> the property. He was demented and spent his whole time in the fields,
> which are full of stones of all sizes, picking up the stones and placing
> them with great care in heaps which tapered slightly and reached a
> height of six feet or more. The work was so well done that it became
> a wonder of the countryside, and people came from far and near to
> look at the stone heaps. Now they remain in the fields, visible from the
> road, although their builder has long since passed away, and few of the
> farmers in the locality know their history. (*Providence Journal* 1895)

A mere five sentences long, this passage is wonderfully dense with
information. First, it dates the construction of these particular stone
heaps to the 1830s, at the height of the "sheep craze." The stone heaps

were assembled from "stones of all sizes," suggesting that any fieldstone would have been suitable to include. Their maximum height generally corresponds to the practical limits of a typical adult's reach when standing. And having been built with "great care" in "tapered" forms, the stones they contained were clearly intended to stay in place. Perhaps the most interesting implications are social. First, the fact that their builder is qualified as "demented" probably means that he suffered from progressive cognitive impairment, the price many pay for longevity. In regard to this account, stone wall historian Robert Thorson qualifies the stone heaps as "a testament to dementia," acclaiming the therapeutic "value of stonework in happily passing the time as a form of engagement with the world, even when one's mind is slip sliding away" (2018). Thorson also notes that the "micro-history of this demented builder faded away in only six decades."

This account leaves us wondering why certain farmers would take such care in constructing stone heaps, rather than simply tossing them in sprawling piles. There may be several practical benefits, none of which conflict. As proposed by science and natural history author Susan Allport, farmers in New York and New England built stone heaps almost as well as their walls "so they wouldn't occupy more land than necessary or tumble down" (1994:76). Her explanation is in step with an early twentieth century American agricultural handbook stating that fieldstones should be "compactly piled" to inhibit weed growth while occupying as little land as possible (Hays 1912:39). And previously, I proposed that the principal benefit of carefully stacking fieldstones from degrading pastures on the already unproductive surfaces of boulders was to increase the surface area available for vegetation (Ives 2015a). A Vermont farmer said as much in 1882 when he stated, "We pile all stones in the pasture, causing two spears of grass to grow where only one grew before" (Anderson 1882). Interestingly, in his 1824 landscape painting of the seaport village of Blue Hill, Maine, Reverend Jonathan Fisher chose to include in the foreground a pasture where fieldstones appear heaped on a bedrock outcrop, out of the way of a nearby horse. Of course, cattle are less likely to break legs, and horses less likely to throw shoes, on terrain that is not littered with stones.

But pastures were not the only spaces where farmers heaped stones. For example, an 1848 account on improvements to a Massachusettes farm notes "an old orchard which had been in grass a long time, the soil thin, and the field covered with stone heaps" (*Vermont Phoenix* 1848). And hayfields are implicated in an 1844 newspaper story about

Silas Wright, the U.S. Senator from New York who would soon serve his state as governor. When Martin Van Buren visited Senator Wright at his small farm near Ogdensburg, New York, he found the future governor "in a linsey Woolsey dress, piling stones into heaps to save the scythe of the mowers" (*New York Herald* 1844). And stone heaping probably occurred in vegetable fields as well, as suggested by two of the subsequently discussed accounts (*Boston Journal* 1903; *Providence Journal* 1888).

It should come as little surprise that stone heaping was also often relegated to children. Such work would not demand much, if any, supervision, nor would it require draught animals or heavy equipment. For example, a report published in 1820 mentions a group of Vermont children who "seven years ago last spring…were at work together, heaping stones in a field" (*Freeman's Journal* 1820). Among them was a boy, specified to be "about ten years old." And among the many "Hints to Farmers" published in an 1834 edition of the *Genessee Farmer*, a New York publication, was advice on how to keep children busy. It specified, "Let them pick up stones about your farm, and pile them in heaps, to make a wall, repair the roads, or at least be out of the way of your scythe, hoe, or ploughshare" (Tucker 1834). The notion of children heaping stones was sufficiently relatable to serve as a literary trope, as evidenced in the short story titled "The Orphan and the Fairy: A Story For Children," which appeared in an 1856 issue of a Vermont newspaper. It opens with the protagonist, "little Melody," being sent off "early one Monday morning in Spring" to "a distant field to pile stones" (*Green-Mountain Freeman* 1856). The expectation that children would perform such work may have been strongly reinforced in some families. An extreme example is described by a New York farmer and politician in his 1836 newspaper article titled, "Industry. An Address to the Young."

> A certain father who was deeply convinced of the importance of forming his sons to habits of industry, used to set them to pulling down heaps of stone, and then putting them back again. He has been known to employ them many a day alternate removing and replacing of stones. (Buel 1836)

Whether or not these exercises instilled the desired "habits of industry" was not reported, though the author warned that they risked "disgusting the young."

And stone heaping, presumably a monotonous and demanding exercise, was not easily forgotten by the experienced. This is evident in an

1886 political commentary on President Grover Cleveland's nomination of N.D. Bates for United States Marshal for Connecticut. Praised for his "shrewd Yankee head," Mr. Bates was touted as long-accustomed to hard work, having "had to hoe corn and wear his fingers to the bone picking up stones in the pasture lots when he was a boy in the hills of Preston City" (*New York Sun* 1886:3), Connecticut. And childhood memories of stone heaping are colorfully related in an 1873 account from a Vermont newspaper:

> How well I remember, writes an ex-farmer, those warm, relaxing spring days on the old farm, when I was just large enough 'to pick up stones.' What tedious, dull, back-aching, hand-rasping, boy-disheartening days those were! But I do not remember what force it gave us boys when we were told in the morning, 'Boys, pick up a dozen good, large heaps of stone and then go a fishing for the rest of the day!' (*Putnam County Courier* 1873)

Throughout the nineteenth century, consolidation, mechanization, and specialization came to signify progress across all industries, including agriculture. Accordingly, traditional labor practices of small family farms would become gradually stigmatized as inefficient, outmoded, and perhaps even shameful. As one agricultural historian observed, "the ideal of the yeoman" in the popular imagination gave way to "the emerging image of the rube" (Bell 1989:464). As one might expect, farmers who left stone heaps strewn about their fields in plain view triggered certain progressive-minded critics. The editor of the *Farmer's Monthly Visitor* exhibited such a slant in 1839 when he insisted that "not a solitary stone pile is found encumbering the fields" of a certain "praiseworthy" farm in Canterbury, New Hampshire (*The Farmer's Monthly Visitor* 1839). With an overtly negative spin, a commentator in an 1837 issue of *The Union and Easton Journal* suggested that the appearance of "stone heaps" in "mowing fields" is a signature of farmers who disregard common standards of routine farm maintenance. And an 1872 *Vermont Farmer* article titled "Removing Stones from Tillage Land" bluntly insisted that "progressive farmers" do not leave "small heaps scattered over" their fields. If stone heaping carried any practical value on working farms—which, presumably, it did; otherwise we are left to conclude that their owners were idiots—progressive critics appear to have filtered such information out of their public discourse.

Some critics simply argued that stone heaping was inefficient, such as an 1855 commentator in the Vermont-based *Burlington Free Press*, who insisted that stone picked from fields should be thrown directly "into a cart" because "the labor of constructing stone heaps, is labor thrown away." Farming advice published in another Vermont periodical, the *Orleans County Monitor*, in 1874, specifies that mowing around stone heaps that "lay in the field year after year" is "poor economy." The Maine Board of Agriculture similarly once commented that "it is surprising that some farmers will clear their fields of stone and put them into heaps, or piles, which are constantly an interference in cultivation" (1860:197).

Other critics seemed to condemn the personal character of farmers who generated stone heaps. For example, an 1842 commentary in an agricultural journal argues that any farmers "who mean to act up to the intelligence of the age" are obligated to remove all such obstructions from their fields (Adams 1842). A patronizing article titled "A Few Hints for the Farmer," as featured in an 1849 edition of a Vermont newspaper, insists that "stones should never be accumulated in heaps in the fields" because it is "a slovenly practice" (White 1849). This sentiment is echoed in an 1865 edition of another Vermont newspaper by a commentator who did not "like to see the rocks picked up and left in heaps" (*Vermont Transcript* 1865). He condemned such practice as "a shiftless and thriftless way" that "spoils a good deal of good land, and makes bad work in the mowing."

By the close of the nineteenth century, hill farmers were seen by many as backward-facing reminders of an agricultural heyday that had clearly passed. This sentiment flavors a 1903 article published by a correspondent for the *Boston Journal*. Regarding the discovery of gold deposits in Bridgewater, Vermont, he wrote:

> Some of the people of this section are going wild over the reported discovery of gold here. Farmers who have piled up stones for years and years from their potato fields are now standing over some of these same stone piles with clubs whenever anyone appears who looks like a geologist. (*Boston Journal* 1903)

The image of club-wielding farmers defending their stone heaps from an invasion of gold prospectors is amusing, but probably not realistic and certainly not flattering. From such an angle, stone heaps would seem to stand in passive defiance against some progressive gaze.

However, others developed an affinity for the very same objects, affording them a certain dignity. By the late nineteenth century, the so-

cietal turbulence of the industrial age had pressurized a nostalgic un-
dercurrent through popular culture, therein which stone heaps became
material reminders of a simpler time, be it real or imagined, when families worked together day in and day out.

Figure 9: A) Undated historic photograph of Woodvale Farm, now
part of the University of Rhode Island's Alton Jones Campus, in West
Greenwich, Rhode Island. The pasture shown here contained stone
heaps, three of which are magnified for detail (source: University of
Rhode Island). Though these stone heaps were removed decades ago,
the pasture is still grazed by cattle and appears much the same today. B)
Detail from a ca.1870 stereo view of a farmstead in Lincoln, Vermont,
showing stone heaps similarly scattered throughout what appears to
be a pasture (Source: University of Vermont, Consulting Archaeology
Program).

In the late nineteenth and early twentieth centuries, stone heaps
were still familiar elements of New England scenery (Figure 9) and still
widely recognized as the handiwork of rural farmers, though often from
prior generations. For instance, a New Hampshire property owner wrote
in *The Rural New Yorker* that his estate includes "a woodlot of about a

hundred acres" with a "well-built cellar hole, while around through the woods are the eternal little stone piles that meant hard work and clear mowing" (1918). He recognized these stone features collectively as the remains of an abandoned farmstead and valued them as objects for introspection. Claiming that "no one around here knows how old it is," he reported that "when I feel blue on a Sunday, I go up there and sit down and smoke my pipe and wonder if the 35-cent dollar drove them out." A Vermont property owner similarly reported owning a reserve of pine timber in what once constituted an "old field" (Pattee 1886). He noted the visibility of "rock heaps among the pines" and an "old cellar hole… over which a numerous family of boys and girls were born."

Similar accounts exist from southern New England. For example, one appears in a report published by a botanical club in an 1884 edition of the *Providence Journal*. In regard to the area of North Smithfield, Rhode Island, known as "The Blunders," they wrote, "an interesting thing about the pine woods is that a little more than thirty years ago the ground was a level, cultivated field," which is betrayed by "occasional stone heaps as thrown together in days long gone by." If their context is accurate, those stone heaps occupied a local landscape that was open and farmed during the mid-nineteenth century. Today, the forest floor at The Blunders is still dotted with stone heaps, perhaps the same as those noted in 1884.

In 1888, the editor of the same newspaper published a letter submitted by a Rhode Islander who contended that the state's extensive, abandoned farmlands should be brought back into production. He characterized much of these lands as covered with "stone piles" that "stand moss-grown and covered with briars, among oak trees that have the growth of a life-time, when men on the verge of 80 years hoed corn and potatoes in their boyhood" (*Providence Journal* 1888). If his context is accurate, that boyhood work took place during the second to third decades of the 1800s.

The value of stone heaps as familiar rural imagery is evident in a short story written for the *New York Weekly* and reprinted in the *Waterbury Evening Democrat*, a Connecticut newspaper, in 1891. With the title "To the City. And the Sad Home-Coming of a Wayward Boy," most readers were probably not surprised to find that it was a parable on the moral and spiritual decay of young adults who forsake the wholesome life of a hometown farmer to pursue greater fortunes in the city. When the story's headstrong "New England boy" left "his good home" for the city, the narrator laments, "Farewell to the broad rough uplands, with familiar stone heaps dotted over" (Harker 1891). The boy tragically returned the following year in a casket, after "the city ground him up and spit him out."

We may never know what percentage of New England's fieldstones were quite literally ground up and spit out for roadbuilding projects in the late nineteenth and early twentieth centuries. As reported by an upstate New York writer in 1902, farmers were "demanding pay" for the "stone heaps that dot their fields" in response to the "scarcity of free stone near where the crushed stone is being used" (*Ogdensburg Advance and St. Lawrence Weekly Democrat* 1902). Some predicted that this infrastructure boom would effectively eliminate stone heaps from the countryside. At the turn of the twentieth century, a Vermonter predicted that "A generation hence there will doubtless be but comparatively few stone walls or piles of stones scattered about the fields to be seen. They will either be in drains or used for permanent roadmaking" (*Barre Evening Telegram* 1900). This is precisely what a writer had encouraged farmers to do in an 1892 issue of a newspaper based in Brewster, New York, a town not far from the Connecticut border:

> There are in all directions in this town piles of stones on various farms, which the owners, at their own expense, would gladly draw to the road, providing the stone, when crushed, was used upon the roads in their vicinity. It is remarkable that the farmers do not move in this matter. (*Brewster Standard* 1892)

Fortunately, for those who admire historic stonework today, early road-building projects did not provide land owners with enough incentive to categorically eliminate stone heap sites. Modern observers have reported them from every New England state and New York State.

Future research may recover additional accounts of nineteenth-century farmers heaping stones, offering a clearer view into the topic. But meanwhile, if we agree that the accounts reviewed here causally relate to the relatively abundant stone heap sites in New England's rugged forests, we have not resolved a great mystery. Rather, we have been introduced to a once ordinary strain of knowledge that dropped from collective memory. Yet, there is multivocality worth remembering here from a cultural-historical perspective, understanding that agrarian stone heaps have held different meanings for different people over time. They embodied the pragmatism of hill farmers who endeavored to keep their most stone-riddled fields productive, affording both young and old family members opportunities to prove their worth. They were framed as objects of disdain by at least a few progressive farmers who defined their ideological vision against that of outmoded "others." And they became objects of quiet reflection for certain industrial-age folk who pined for a simpler and more satisfying way of life. But with the continuing re-forestation of the region's hills, a certain social amnesia appears to have followed.

In the twentieth century, it appears that many people reinterpreted New England's ubiquitous stone heap sites to be Indian burial grounds. State archaeologists from Connecticut, New York, Maine, and Rhode Island have all spoken with constituents who claimed that local stone heap sites are Indian cemeteries (Nicholas Bellantoni, personal communication 2013; Christina Reith, personal communication, 2013; Arthur Spiess, personal communication 2013), and some property owners in Connecticut and Rhode Island specify that they learned so from a parent and/or grandparent. For example, a Rhode Islander raised on a farm in Cranston during the 1920s and 1930s provides one account (Leveillee 1998:17). His childhood memories include finding stone heaps scattered throughout the local woods, which "old timers" occasionally referred to as an "Indian burial ground." An archaeological investigation of the site in the late 1990s concluded that those stone heaps were products of ag-ricultural field clearing.

Similarly, an Italian-American Rhode Islander once explained to me her family's long-standing belief that a group of stone heaps on their wooded hillside property constitutes an Indian burial ground. Her childhood memories of the 1950s include hiking through the woods with her grandfather, who cautioned her to behave respectfully when-ever they walked past the deceased, who supposedly rested beneath the stone piles. A federally funded professional archaeological investigation of the site a few years ago found that many of its stone heaps contained not bodies but mid-to-late-nineteenth-century farm refuse. I have not cited the report because tribal authorities concluded that its data are extremely sensitive.

Bear in mind that large numbers of European immigrants arrived in southern New England in the early twentieth century, and many of them turned to farming to make their livings. Lands that were most affordable and available to immigrants were typically the stoniest—the final hin-terlands cleared during the agricultural climax of the early-to-mid-nine-teenth-century and subsequently abandoned. Derelict farms were often auctioned by the state or sold by the last surviving family member, who transferred the land strictly as a commodity. Under such circumstances, new owners clearing decades of forest regrowth discovered stone heaps built by people they would never meet. And even if an intimate knowledge of these lands could have been passed on, the ethnic majority viewed recent immigrants as aliens. Social partitioning within an ethnically diversifying population could only have hastened the forgetting of once-common stone heaping practices. Nonetheless, people seek to understand the places they inhabit, finding comfort in the familiar. Accordingly, many new farm owners, especially immigrants, were probably left to imagine meaning into and from their new surroundings.

Also, consider that popular history had declared local Indians extinct by the early twentieth century, and took the liberty of rewriting their pasts with romantic flair and, often, generous speculation (O'Brien 2006). Meanwhile, many local Indians were pursuing a cultural revitalization that not only sought to revive indigenous practices and traditions, but also sought to regain the recognition of a public that was remarkably ignorant of their existence (McMullen 1994). Under these circumstances, viewing stone feature complexes in forested areas as the secret haunts of Indians may have satisfied the interests of Indians and non-Indians alike.

But the Indian burial ground hypothesis failed to pan out in so many instances that it seems to have largely burned itself out of popularity. And looking back, this makes a lot of sense. There is a reason that the nineteenth century's numerous skeleton-seeking medical students and antiquities collectors did not waste much time digging in, around, or beneath hillside clusters of stone heaps. There were simply no bodies or grave goods to be found in such places. Recognizing the turbulence and mutability of collective memory across industrialized Western nations (e.g., Anderson 2006; Halbwachs 1992; Hobsbawm and Ranger 1992; Ricoeur 2006), I find it remarkable that some anthropologically trained archaeologists carefully sidestep the possibility that New Englanders are, once again, reinterpreting nineteenth-century agrarian stone heap sites through a romantic lens.

Over the past several years, there have been numerous archaeological studies of specific stone heap sites from across the region, and they have persistently pointed to nineteenth-century agrarian origins. This is in step with the historical information just reviewed. We will take account of this evidence in the next chapter.

CHAPTER FOURTEEN

ARCHAEOLOGICAL EVIDENCE

MY CONTENTION THAT most stone heaps in New England's forested hills were generated by nineteenth-century farmers is not based solely on historical records. It is also informed by basic observations I made in Rhode Island over the past several years, and a handful of key archaeological studies from across greater New England. To begin with the former, if you ever visit Rhode Island and wish to search for local stone heap sites, you can find them easily by accounting for three factors.

First, Rhode Island stone heap sites are typically on soils that geologists refer to as melt-out till, which was locally deposited about 16,000 years ago when debris-rich glacial ice stagnated and melted in place, leaving an unsorted layer of sediment that includes boulders, cobbles, gravel, sand. These soils, which are often found thinly covering the crests and sides of New England hills, are poorly suited to plowing or mowing because they are frequently interrupted by boulders and bedrock outcrops. The positions of melt-out till deposits have been mapped by the United States Department of Agriculture and can be reviewed on their Web Soil Survey portal.

Second, Rhode Island stone heap sites typically occur within or near historic stone-wall farmstead complexes that were abandoned in the nineteenth century. The 2011 statewide hillshade LiDAR (Light Detection and Ranging) mapping accessible through the Rhode Island Geographic Information System's online portal is handy for identifying them. This technology provides a topographical model of the ground surface minus the tree canopy, which allows users to discern abandoned cellar holes and their surrounding stone wall networks (ie., the fossil hearts and skeletons of historic farmsteads) with relative ease. Comparing those locations to a diachronic series of historic maps can provide a sense of whether any given farmstead was abandoned before the twentieth century. For example, if the location of a cellar hole matches the location of a house that was mapped in 1840 and 1860, but that house was not depicted on an 1890 map, that cellar hole marks the location of a house that was probably abandoned in the second half of the nineteenth century.

Figure 10: Examples of "stone corrals" from various Rhode Island sites that exhibit a common construction approach. The specimen from Exeter is a rare example that was never finished, exhibiting the typical outer wall of two-handers but lacking the fill of one-handers. The North Smithfield example is in the previously discussed area known as "The Blunders."

Third, Rhode Island stone heap sites almost always occur beneath forest canopies, which is a consequence of farm abandonment. So long as those forest canopies persist, a relatively intact record of historic land use is usually present underneath. But if the area was clear-cut and bulldozed for a solar farm or housing complex, any stone heaps that may have existed are probably gone. In sum, if you overlap these three factors - melt-out till + abandoned nineteenth-century farm complex + secondary forest canopy - and search target locations accordingly, you will have no trouble finding stone heap sites. And I feel compelled to add that the "settler colonial state" is not a major threat to such sites. On the contrary, most stone heap sites reported to the Rhode Island Historical Preservation and Heritage Commission by antiquarians are located on forested tracts that are already under long-term conservation, with the chief conservator being Rhode Island's Department of Environmental Management.

Figure 11: A single wall built with "two-handers" (background) expands into a double wall filled with "one-handers" (foreground). From a functional perspective, I see the double wall as the stone corral's linear cousin. Amos Greene Farm, Charlestown, Rhode Island. Photo credit: Chris McCabe.

Should you observe several Rhode Island stone heap sites, you would gain insights concerning the form and distribution of stone heaps both within and between sites. For instance, stone heaps throughout an individual site usually exhibit a range of structural variability. Some may be low and sprawling, composed of variably sized fieldstones that appear to have been dumped together. Others may be modest, consisting of a few fieldstones perched together on a boulder. You would also come to recognize a modal form of stone heap, which I will loosely refer to as a "stone corral" that can be found from one site to the next (Figure 10), and I believe understanding their form is key to understanding the nature and purpose of agrarian stone heaping in general. The stone corral features a carefully constructed outer wall of large "two-handers" that impounds a disorganized fill of small "one-handers." One-hander versus two-hander is an old Yankee taxonomy denoting how many hands are required to carry a given fieldstone. Clearly, a two-stage process of construction was involved. I presume that almost anyone tasked with going into a rocky field to heap stones of variable sizes would have, through trial, error, and logic, independently discovered the advantages of this approach, which concentrates surplus fieldstone into stable impound-ment structures within footprints that were often agriculturally useless. Their method of construction appears to be much the same as that used to build a "double stone wall," whereby two stone walls, composed chief-ly of "two-handers," are built in parallel to each other to provide a linear landfill to accommodate a multitude of one-handers. The stone corral is, essentially, a rounded and self-contained version of the classic double wall, but unlike the double wall, it could not provide the added benefits of marking linear property boundaries, dividing fields, or controlling the movement of livestock. Stone corrals appear to have functioned strictly for impounding stone with a minimum expenditure of energy. (Figure 11.)

I am not the first to describe this type of stone heap as a "corral." In fact, I adopted the term from NEARA member Daniel Leary, who coined it in his insightful 1988 article titled "Field Cairns: A Study of 18th and 19th Century Field Clearing Techniques — a Homogenous Study and Analysis." He observed that the corral was a modal form at New England stone heap sites, and reported examples that appear to have been built as attachments to pre-existing stone walls, apparently to receive one-handers that continued to surface on surrounding farm-land.

So, contrary to the general impression that I have given thus far, my opinion of NEARA is not entirely negative. This organization has pro-duced archaeologically useful studies, such as that published by member Suzanne Carlson in 2004. It was an archaeological investigation of what I would characterize as a hilltop stone heap site in Bingham, Maine, that NEARA undertook in partnership with a professional archaeologist. Carlson qualifies that archaeologist as "open minded," which is a com-pliment that NEARA members seem to reserve for outsiders who come across as intellectually non-judgmental. This site in question was found to contain eight stone features that were spread out at relatively equal distances. The team deconstructed a specimen and noted:

> Excavation of Cairn #7 revealed a construction pattern which involved rolling, leveraging, or using a sled to drag large rounded cobbles (ap-parently from the foot of the knoll, or perhaps the river) into a closely fitted doughnut shaped ring nearly three meters across the exterior and a little more than one meter in the interior. Smaller cobbles were then

piled into the hollow center and upward until all the larger basal stones had been covered and the center more or less rounded over. Surface inspection of the other cairns suggests indications that the same process had been used in their construction. (Carlson 2004:38-39)

Let us not overlook that parenthetical statement, which expresses a line of wishful thinking that is still in use by ceremonial stone landscape proponents today. It goes like this. Reasonable question: What farmer would have carried these stones uphill to pile them? Reasonable answer: Probably none. Flawed implication: Then a farmer probably did not build them. The flaw in that implication is that it presumes that the stones composing a hilltop stone heap were not sourced from the very same hilltop. To her credit, Carlson considers the possibility that those "large rounded cobbles" were there to begin with. But she also affords equal consideration to the possibility that the features in question served as ritual seats for Indians on vision quests. If this were the case, I believe the first thing those Indians would have envisioned was a more comfortable place to sit.

Perhaps dwelling on the possibility that stones within heaps were painstakingly lugged uphill for spiritually profound purposes provides an entertaining distraction from dwelling on natural principles that otherwise explain why stone became so abundant on formerly farmed lands. I pose these principles as questions with responses. Question 1: Does erosion cause exposed soils to thin most quickly on hills, valleys, or plains? Answer: On hills. Question 2: When stony soils erode, are larger stones exposed in place? Answer: Yes. Question 3: Does frost heave (the incremental elevation of near-surface stones where denuded, saturated soils experience freeze-thaw cycles) exacerbate the surfacing of fieldstones? Answer: Yes, to the dismay of generations of New England farmers (Allport 1990:59; Thorson 2004). If one is willing to acknowledge these natural principles, and that they often operate in concert, one may easily envision how overworked hill farms became stonier, and why farmers decided to consolidate some of their unwanted fieldstone surplus into heaps (Figure 12).

Now, let us turn from my processual modeling to insights gained from a handful of key professional and academic archaeological surveys. A 2004 professional archaeological survey of a proposed housing complex on Buell Hill near Killingworth Center in Connecticut concluded that its abundant stone heaps were generated by farmers (Walwer and Walwer 2005). The hill's namesake reflects the fact that this reforested hill was historically farmed, as betrayed by an extensive network of stone walls by the Buell family, as far back as the eighteenth century. The Buells were known for raising cattle, and the property was found to contain "a parallel set of walls appearing to represent a cattle fun towards livestock pens also constructed of stone walls" (Walwer 2015:117). The survey also identified 381 stone heaps from across the property, the "great majority" of which were "clearly placed on underlying boulders." However, some of the heaps were noted to be "quite impressive, consisting of very wide, double-coursed forms that allowed for precision and symmetry in construction."

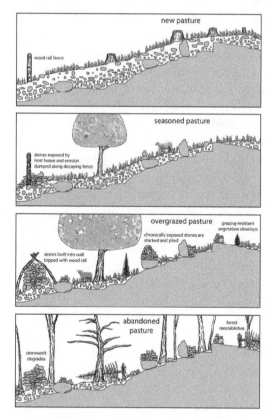

Figure 12: Hypothetical illustration of a hill pasture experiencing soil deflation and chronic exposure of fieldstones, and how a farmer would be able to clear and consolidate those fieldstones without moving them far. From Ives2015a. Used with permission by *Archaeology of Eastern North America*.

The Buell Hill survey somehow attracted the attention of the small, nascent alliance of antiquarians, tribal authorities, and Dr. Curtiss Hoffman, who had become involved with the Benfield Parcel "A" property in Carlisle, Massachusetts. Dr. Greg Walwer, the Buell Hill survey's principal investigator, hosted a site walkover attended by archaeologists Dr. Nicholas Bellantoni (Connecticut State Archaeologist) and Dr. Kevin McBride (Professor of Anthropology, University of Connecticut), and members of the aforementioned alliance, including Doug Harris (Deputy NITHPO), Dr. Timothy Fohl (NEARA member, and Benfield Parcel "A" abutter), and Hoffman. Walwer reported:

> While hesitant to declare anything about the features, there was a broad consensus that the stone piles, including those of impressive construction, were most likely historic Euro-American in origin. And while one of the tribal members pointed to various orientations and forms of some of the features as clearly deriving from a Native American context, the other tribal member called out that the features were Colonial in origin, and that they should leave the premises. So in trying to keep an open mind, all I could think was, what on earth are we supposed to do now? (Walwer 2015:118)

Walwer ultimately concluded that the stone heaps were of agrarian origin. Hoffman independently generated his own report to contest Walwer's, arguing that the stone heaps were constructed by Native Americans for non-agrarian purposes (Hoffman 2005, 2015).

Walwer directed a similar survey of a 100-acre property in the Fort Hill section of Groton, Connecticut, in 2007. It contained the remains of multiple small historic farmsteads, which he identified chiefly according to the presence of cellar holes and related domestic trash deposits. These farmsteads, collectively designated the Morgan I Site, were variably occupied from the late eighteenth to early twentieth centuries. He also identified, mapped, and photo documented 76 stone heaps from across this relict agrarian landscape, noting that the "great majority" were visibly "constructed on large boulders variably exposed at the surface" (Walwer 2015:114). During his survey, Walwer was "advised that some opponents to the project declared the stone features of the property to be related to prehistoric or pre-Contact Native American ceremonialism" (Ibid.:113), and was probably aware of the recent success of activists at Benfield Parcel "A." As he put it, "In a paranoid attempt to make sure that the stone piles did not possibly represent sensitive Native American feature contexts such as burials" (Ibid.:114), he archaeologically dissected one specimen. It turned out to be built on a portion of a boulder that was exposed at ground level, so it was unlikely to present a burial. Another stone heap was observed to contain a nineteenth or early-twentieth-century barrel hoop, while another contained a brick. Such discoveries, in combination with archaeological testing results and background research, afforded Walwer little choice but to archaeologically conclude that he had encountered the handiwork of farmers from just beyond the edge of social memory.

Even archaeological studies of stonework on local Indian reservations have yielded disappointing results for ceremonial stone landscape activists. Dr. Brian Jones, the late Connecticut State Archaeologist and former employee of the Mashantucket Pequot Museum and Research Center, published a study of historic stonework from across 140 wooded acres containing the remains of "Indiantown," a collection of farmsteads occupied by Pequot tribal members and Anglo-American lessees from roughly 1780-1820 (Jones 2015). Most of the stonework he recorded appeared to be associated with historic agricultural use, taking the form of cellar holes, stone walls, and stone heaps. Walled lots entirely cleared of stone tended to be found close to farmstead ruins, while outlying walled lots frequently contained numerous stone heaps. He concluded that this trend reflected abandonment "by its faming families while it was still in a state of 'improvement'" (Ibid.:58). He also noted how the many "carefully constructed" stone heaps "permitted a greater volume of stone to be stored" in one location, and that they tend to occur "on large boulders or ledge outcrops that could not be moved" (Ibid.:61).

Sarah Hasho, a UMass Boston graduate student in historical archaeology working under collaborative archaeologist Dr. Stephen Silliman, directed a survey of historic stonework across the currently forested Eastern Pequot Reservation from 2009-2010, the findings of which she synthesized in her master's thesis (Hasho 2012). The stone heaps she recorded were not aesthetically inspiring, consisting chiefly of crudely heaped, unsorted fieldstones. What was interesting was their relatively young age. Her survey, which integrated archaeological testing with GIS mapping, documented a network of cellar holes in the center of the reservation dating to the eighteenth and early nineteenth centuries, pointing to a phase in reservation history when family homesteads were centrally located. The stone wall networks and stone heaps extending more broadly across the reservation, on the other hand, had little if no meaningful spatial relationship to this older occupational signature, and were built over that signature's archaeological deposits. Hasho postulated:

> ...[H]ouses often preceded the creation of extensive stone pile and field wall systems, suggesting that the intensification of agriculture on the reservation may have post-dated the late 18th century for certain households, or more likely, took place after the middle 19th century when several houses in the center of the reservation were no longer occupied. Ultimately, this thesis demonstrates that the changes in the usage, organization, and construction of the landscape and architectural features of the Eastern Pequot reservation are the result of the active decision-making processes of Pequot people and must be accorded archaeological and historical attention. (Hasho 2012:v)

Her study suggests that even an Indian community which occupied their land base for centuries may, just like surrounding settler colonial populations, forget their own relatively recent historic agricultural practices and rediscover them through archaeological inquiry. Though some antiquarians (e.g., Gage 2014, 2015a; Gage and Gage 2017; Lepinoka and Carlotto 2015; McLoughlin 2017) and archaeologists (e.g., Cipolla 2018; Harris and Robinson 2015; Hoffman 2015, 2019) who have since published perspectives on the ceremonial stone landscape paradigm do not acknowledge the existence of Hasho's topically relevant thesis, it indeed exists and remains freely available on the Eastern Pequot Tribal Nation's website.

Unfortunately, I am not at liberty to share details from the most compelling and methodologically rigorous archaeological survey of a stone heap site that I have read. It was conducted several years ago by professional archaeologists in a New England state working on behalf of a federal client on federally owned property. The survey concluded that the stone heaps were constructed by nineteenth-century farmers on the surfaces of boulders and outcrops using the same "corral" structure commonly observed at New England stone heap sites. It also confirmed that the land on which they were documented had indeed been farmed, and rather intensively. However, some of the region's tribal authorities declared the site to be ceremonial in nature. According to a source who shall remain anonymous, the "Native community" expressed concerns that publication of the report, which was originally intended for publication, could result in a broad brush of all such sites throughout the region as being agrarian in nature. The report continues to be withheld from the public by presiding officials in accordance with what I have no doubt is a well-intentioned cultural sensitivity. But ultimately, as I see it, this provides another example of how data that are potentially threatening to the ceremonial stone landscape vision are quietly cleared, like unwanted stones, from the intellectual field.

In closing this chapter, I wish to be clear that emphasizing the probability that most stone heaps in the New England landscape are of agrarian origin does not discount the fact that Indians across the region have manipulated stone for millennia, and not only within the context of the memory pile tradition. As archaeologists know, ancient habitation sites sometimes contain massive roasting pits, the interiors of which are filled with stones. And Indians have not neglected to build formal structures in stone either. An archaeological investigation of an ancient rock-shelter in Middleboro, Massachusetts, determined that its main living space was originally enclosed by a "curved wall of dry-laid stacked angular stones" (Blancke and Speiss 2006). Contextual evidence indicates that this wall, which had been preserved beneath younger sediments, was constructed roughly four thousand years ago. Indians have also, for millennia, built fish weirs across streams and rivers throughout the region where bottoms were shallow and stone abundant (e.g., Goodby et. al). Perhaps the most dramatic example of Indian stonemasonry is at the Queen's Fort Site in Exeter, Rhode Island (National Register of Historic Places 1980). Here, sitting on a hill of glacially deposited boulders, is a stone construction resembling a fort with defensive bastions. According to local tradition, it was built by Stonewall John, reputedly the first Narragansett trained in English stonemasonry, at the direction of Saunksqua (which roughly translates as "Queen") Quaiapen for the protection of the Narragansett people during King Philip's War (1675-8). Furthermore, it is well known that there are Indian families throughout the region who have worked as stonemasons for generations, building farm walls, estate walls, decorative pilasters, foundations, stairways, and chimneys (Levitt and Dekel 2008). There is no shortage of Indian stonework to be found in this part of the world. And I think it is reasonable to presume that Indians have built stonework for ceremonial and/or spiritual purposes that archaeologists cannot readily identify. But, as I see it, none of these facts or ideas conflict with, or constitute any sort of argument against, the likelihood that stone heaping was rampant on nineteenth-century hill farms, and that evidence of that behavior is widely manifested beneath modern forest canopies.

PART THREE:

STONES OF CONTENTION

CHAPTER FIFTEEN

ROOTS AND BRANCHES OF RACIAL PARANOIA

T HE NATURE OF CEREMONIAL stone landscape activism may seem largely mysterious to anyone who fails to perceive the racial paranoias that it channels, both in regard to the Indian people whose interests it claims to champion and the white identity bearers to whom it appeals. This chapter provides an overview of the history and texture of Indian racial paranoia in New England. And it begins in a place of ignorance that I occupied during the years immediately surrounding the turn of the millennium.

As a young contract archaeologist in my twenties, I sometimes felt dismayed when consulting with flesh-and-blood Indians, because they did not always meet the starry-eyed expectations that I had gained during my undergraduate university education. Indians were supposed to be progressive, open-minded folk who fought to overcome racism and oppression. According to my predominantly leftist instructors, they were nothing less than unsung heroes of the American story who were poised to lead the rest of us to a better tomorrow. Of course, some fit that profile. But my professional experience gradually painted a far messier, and otherwise predictably human, picture that I struggled to reconcile for years.

One of the most eye-opening experiences occurred when I was working on an otherwise routine assignment—monitoring a construction project where ancient, unmarked Indian burials might be encountered. I was proud to consider myself an "applied anthropologist" working in partnership with a young, equally under-experienced tribal representative. But I was rendered speechless in our first hour of working together, as conversation took a shocking turn. He invited me to bond over a presumed mutual dislike of "n---ers," who he explained were bringing down the quality of life in his neighborhood. He assumed that because I was white, I would be a bigot, and I assumed that because he was an Indian, he would not. In the long, painfully awkward silence of my response—an incredulous stare—I believe we both realized the errors of our assumptions. I remained utterly perplexed by this interaction for quite some time.

After years of diving deeply into the region's history and interacting with contemporary Indians, I became gradually more aware of a troubling reality. New England's Indian people have lived with racial paranoia for centuries, and many are still plagued by it today. The reason the aforementioned tribal representative started dropping n-bombs was, I believe, to demonstrate to me that he did not identify as black in the most socially efficient and authentically performative manner possible. And to be honest, if I had met him in a different time and place, and he did not communicate to me that he self-identified as Indian through words, attire, or adornment, I might have casually presumed that he self-identified as black. As tasteless as it was, his bigotry served a practical purpose—social registration. And then there was my response, an "incredulous stare." I could not come up with a verbal reply to fit the circumstances. I would like to have told him that using the n-word in that way is an excellent way to disgust people, including me. But it was like a certain epistemological handicap was standing in the way. In my mind, I registered as "white" and he a "person of color." Therefore, I lacked the moral authority to criticize him on any race-related issues. Ignorance and racial paranoia prevailed in that moment, aided and abetted by both of us.

Race can be a hair-trigger topic in indigenous circles. Their society has been internally knotted by white, red, and black racial tensions for centuries. Of course, colonial culture has a long record of weaponizing the notion of racial purity to divide and disenfranchise the region's tribes. But part of what made that long-term project so remarkably effective is that so many Indians were willing to turn that same weapon on their own kinfolk to compete for whatever tribal power and resources remained. Consequently, the racial heritage of one tribal member may be very different from that of another. One individual may come from a family that has a reputation for stigmatizing others as black. Another may come from a family that has long been denied influence in tribal affairs. Another may have identified since childhood as black, until a federally recognized tribe notified him that he possessed tribal ancestry and invited him to enroll. Yet another may come from a family line that passed as white for generations before allowing their Indian identity to publicly reattach. Of course, there are some Indians who seem to have moved beyond this drama and are not inclined to engage in racial discourse. More power to them in an age when the simple act of declining to get on the racial rhetoric train presents a modest form of public heroism.

Though New England's media has placed an exceedingly high bounty on the topic of race in the twenty-first century, it has, to my knowledge, not succeeded in reporting any instances of a white individual arbitrarily singling out an Indian individual to harass in a public setting. Spontaneous acts of racism targeting anonymous Indian identity bearers do not appear to be a major phenomenon in this part of the world today, probably, in part, because local Indian faces have become so diverse in character over the centuries that it would be challenging for most non-Indians to confidently single any out, especially in a multicultural crowd, without obvious, fashion-based clues.

A genetic case study of 28 members of the Seaconke Wampanoag Tribe of Massachusetts published in 2010 (Zhadanov et al. 2010) sheds some light on this issue. It reports identifying maternal (i.e., mitochondrial) DNA haplotypes belonging to "African and West Eurasian" lineages, with "African haplogroups encompassing the majority." No evidence of maternal Indian lineages was found. Rather, the "main female ancestor of the tribe, a Wampanoag woman," was determined to have possessed a mitochondrial DNA type that is generally diagnostic of African ancestry. Paternal (i.e., Y-chromosome) DNA analysis similarly pointed to "predominantly African and West Eurasian lineages," though it also revealed a haplogroup "widespread among Amerindian populations" that the authors propose reflects "intermarriage with an individual having Cherokee ancestry several generations ago," as tribal history suggested. They also identified a paternal DNA haplotype "commonly observed" in "populations from Papua New Guinea and Melanesia" that they attribute to a "primary male ancestor of the tribe." Comparing this discovery to the tribe's genealogical records, the authors propose that the male ancestor introducing this gene "was an eighteenth-century sailor from Australia who settled in the New England area, and married a Wampanoag woman." In sum, the authors concluded that "the high frequency of nonnative haplotypes in this population, along with the paucity of Native American haplotypes, reveals the substantial changes in the genetic composition" of the tribe.

Any anthropologist who is well versed in New England's Indian history assumes that most of the local Indian representatives that they work with possess a fraction of Indian ancestry reaching back to the precolonial era. Interestingly, the DNA Discussion Project's sample of 217 self-identified European Americans in and around Philadelphia determined that 22 percent possessed African DNA (Lawton et al. 2018). In making these statements, I do not suggest that that any contemporary New England Indians are racially illegitimate, or that a population of illegitimate whites has been discovered in Philadelphia. I am illustrating the fact that sociocultural dimensions of racial identities in America often carry far more weight and momentum than biological ones. Nonetheless, an underlying fixation with notions of biological ancestry and racial purity still exist in New England's Indian Country, a fixation that can be deeply consequential.

To appreciate how this situation came to be, we must understand a history that "revolves around tales of mixed unions" (Carocci 2009) within the context of an overarching determination to survive deeply oppressive conditions of the region's colonial order. We only need to go back about three hundred years to accomplish this. By the year 1700, the region's indigenous population had been reduced through a century of epidemic diseases on the order of 90 percent (O'Brien 2001), and subjected through military conquest. Under the "cumulative impact of the colonial experience, a great many New England Indians found themselves landless, a diasporic population vulnerable to the institutions of English colonialism" (O'Brien 2001). Tribal landholdings were reduced to scattered reservations as the colonial agrarian economy expanded across the region's interior. Though Indian people were not enslaved in large numbers during the 1700s, their economic opportunities and personal freedoms were deeply circumscribed. Adults were routinely manipulated into a state of perpetual, judicially-enforced debt to colonists, and their children were frequently indentured into colonial families (Newell 2003: 108; Silverman 2001).

Oral history reaching back into the colonial era remembers that "Narragansett women always outnumbered men" (Hernandon and Sekatau 1997:440), which is consistent with the region-wide trend. Throughout the eighteenth century, southern New England's Indian men tended to find work away from reservations and remained absent for long stretches. The emerging whaling industry created opportunities for many, some of whom used their earnings to independently purchase land bases in their ancestral territories where "several extended family networks or communities of color emerged" (Mancini 2008:40). Hard work and sacrifices aside, the scarcity of such men on New England Indian reservations had become a well-known phenomenon by the turn of the nineteenth century (Mancini 2008:29). It is because "women performed virtually all of the agricultural labor in their societies" by tradition (O'Brien 2011) that men preferred to support their families through occupations that involved significant personal risk, such as military service or maritime work, which accommodated traditional male gender roles. This proved to be a persistent cultural predilection.

Records indicate that through the nineteenth century, most Indian men were employed in the whaling industry, where racial discrimination wilted under an economic meritocracy that rewarded hard work and personal ambition (Shoemaker 2015). In fact, Indian whalemen of those days often rose higher in shipboard hierarchies than the majority of their white colleagues and were generally compensated at levels that were equal to, and sometimes slightly higher than, others of the same rank. Though whaling was a remarkably dangerous profession, these stouthearted world travelers understood all too well that a permanent return to New England's landlocked sphere could threaten their professional fortunes and perhaps even their dignities. Some of their male relatives living on the mainland found themselves without land or credit, and were routinely greeted by racial discrimination as they moved from town to town in search of employment (Rubertone 2020). But Indians were not the only oppressed racial group in colonial New England.

As Morgan James Peters, a self-identified "black Wampanoag" who directs the African and African-American Studies Program at the University of Massachusetts, Dartmouth, has pointed out, African ancestry among today's southern New England tribes is largely an outcome of colonial-era demographic trends that intertwined the destinies of many blacks and Indians (*Bay State Banner* 2014). One historian has argued that "from 1725 to 1807, what has been called the 'American slave trade' might better be termed the 'The Rhode Island slave trade'" (Coughtry 1981). Though most of the African men who were brought to places like Rhode Island were soon sold and transported elsewhere, this was not always the case. Some were forced to work on large, local farms alongside Indians, who also worked on such farms under debt bondage or as indentured servants (Melish 2016:29). And other blacks who purchased their freedom or were manumitted made their living as free laborers, farmers, and craftspeople.

Blacks presented an alternate pool for Indian women seeking partners. Originating from a part of the world where men traditionally engage in farming, many may have been more likely to remain local to help raise their families within the socioracial confines of the mainland economy. Consequently, intermarriage had become a notable trend among some Indian tribes by 1750 (Mandell 1998:471), and following the Revolutionary War, white observers remarked on what they believed to be the increasing scarcity of "pure blooded" Indians and the corresponding rise of "negroes, mulattoes, and poor whites" among them (Mandell 1998:471). What had developed was an economy of marriage "born out of necessity" (Zhadanov et al. 2010:2). Ironically, one of its first order effects was to trigger racial policing within its very own communities, before the close of the eighteenth century. Another effect, which would not be fully realized until the mid-to-late nineteenth century, was the dominant society's campaign to call the legitimacy of most indigenous communities into question according to accusations of their progressively "mixed" blood.

The division of indigenous society along racial lines became evident during the Brothertown Movement. Under the leadership of Reverend Sampson Occum, a Mohegan preacher who rose to prominence in the aftermath of the Great Awakening of the 1730s and 40s, this movement aimed to resettle Christianized members of various southern New England tribes to Oneida territory in upstate New York. There, they would establish a settlement modeled after a "Connecticut town," where they could pursue Christian religion and agricultural development free from the constraints and corruptions of English colonial society. Following the Revolutionary War, they began their migration to what is still called Brothertown, New York. As one ethnohistorian observed: "[T]he Brothertowns shared the same prejudices of mainstream eighteenth century American society; equal privileges of citizenship were denied to either women or Algonquians of Indian-black descent" (Menta 1994:361). Among its early ordinances was a ban on marriage with "persons of negro blood" (Mandell 1998:477).

An unofficial legacy of their exodus was a popular belief that New England's "pure-blooded" Indians had left the region long ago, leaving behind a higher proportion of "black Indians." Perhaps more significantly, their exodus subtracted intellectual capital from southern New England's Indian population during a critical period. Being a literate subset of that population, the Brothertowns acquired inside understandings of settler colonial politics and attitudes that might have been useful for empowering tribal interests within their ancestral territories. But this was not the path they chose. And their path did not end in up-state New York, where they faced "troubles with their white neighbors" (Menta 1994:364) in the early nineteenth century. Under pressure from the United States government, the Brothertowns relocated to Wisconsin in the 1830s, where they accepted United States citizenship and private land allotments to avoid being displaced again. Many of their descendants, principally among today's Brothertown Indian Nation, still live there.

The nineteenth century witnessed a number of state-sponsored "investigations of the number and circumstances" of Indian people generally aimed at dissolving tribal landholdings and politically disenfranchising their communities (Mancini 2008:42). For instance, in 1856, the state of Connecticut planned to auction off 800 acres of Western (Mashantucket) Pequot reservation land following a determination that its tribal owners lack "clear blood." An 1832 report on the Narragansett Tribe concluded that its members were "negro paupers" and that its council was "not of the genuine Narragansett blood" (Mandell 1998:483). In an 1862 report, the Massachusetts Commissioner of Indian Affairs concluded that tribal communities in his state were of mixed blood and should trade in their tribal membership for state citizenship (Thee 2006). Consequently, many Indian men developed a "very bitter feeling" toward blacks who married into their communities largely out of concern for family resources and autonomy (McMullen 1994:130; Mandell 1998:476). Among the Narragansetts, controversies over race, land, and power led to factionalism and political fragmentation (Mandell 1998:483-484), while the "increased socioeconomic mobility of mixed-race descendants" favored "their assimilation into the dominant society" (Mandell 1998:485).

Concerns over the purity of Indian ancestry went hand-in-hand with the development of a region-wide "last Indian" mythology. Scores of nineteenth-century municipal histories written in honor of their town's bicentennial begin with the poetically tragic demise of the last full-blooded Indian (Mandell 1998:474). These books are still sitting on library shelves across New England. A prominent ethnohistorian has observed:

> These histories, which would become a nineteenth century cottage industry in New England that moved well beyond justifying Euro-Amer-

ican conquest, pressed another insidious claim; that New England Indians were on the verge of extinction, if they had not already passed
from the scene. (O'Brien 2006)

Meanwhile, flesh-and-blood Indians were being classified out of existence by record-keepers who simply registered them as "colored,"
"negro," or "black," a process that has been described as "documentary genocide" (Hernandon and Sekatau 1997: 437, 446). In the balance,
"race and culture became rigid and artificial categories that could not
contain the histories or identities of real New England Indians" (O'Brien
2006).

The late Dr. Ella Sekatau, ethnohistorian and Medicine Woman of
the Narragansett Indian Tribe (and recipient of an honorary Ph.D. from
the University of Rhode Island), explains the depth of tri-racial resentment that developed under these conditions:

> Some grew to hate white people for grouping Indians and Africans
> together without regard for their heritage, and some grew to hate the
> latter as well, for being the group that the Narragansett were conflated
> with. That hatred surfaced at 'crying rocks' and unmarked graves,
> where some native mothers abandoned babies fathered by non-Indi-
> ans. (Hernandon and Sekatau 1997:447).

Figure 13: Detail from Rev. Ezra Stiles' 1761 "Map of Charlestown and
South Kingstown" showing "Bastard Rocks," which he seems to have
included as a culturally and geographically significant point of reference. These may or may not be the "crying rocks" referenced by Hernandon and Sekatau (Yale Digital Collections).

According to local tradition, Crying Rocks is a locality on the Narragansett Indian Reservation where "unwed mothers abandoned their illegitimate or deformed children" (Simmons 1986:127), which, apparently, took on an even darker interracial significance under colonialism (Figure 13).

White racial prejudice and bigotry continued through the twentieth century, though many of the Indians suffering its insults and injuries were not necessarily targeted because they were indigenous. Often they were targeted because they did not look white. For example, some elder Narragansetts who remember finding seasonal work on Rhode Island's South County potato farms, most of which have been converted into twenty-first century turf farms, remember being generically referred to as "potato n---ers" (Richie 2004). But racial aggression directed specifically against members of known Indian groups also occurred. Perhaps the most shocking example was in 1976, when nine members of the Mashpee Wampanoag Tribe of Massachusetts were arrested by local police wearing riot gear (Peters 2016). Their crime—"disturbing the peace" by drumming too loudly. And, as a youngster growing up in the midst of publicly elevated racial tensions surrounding the Mashpee land claims suit of 1976-1983 (United States Department of the Interior 2006:67), Mashpee tribal member Morgan James Peters remembers hearing racial slurs including "white n---er" and "n---er Indian." These are not words from a distant past. These are words burned into living memory.

And racism, of course, continues today. As reported in the *Providence Journal's* award-winning "Race in Rhode Island" series, Narragansett Tribal Member Lorén Spears explains how her family members have been, and still occasionally are, racially harassed by local police:

> We're tailed because we are brown in an area of Rhode Island that is very white. I know there are good police officers, but the fact is that our family members get harassed. My mother was stopped not too long ago. Somebody didn't believe it was her car because she drives a Volvo. (Miller 2015)

Petty bigotry toward Indians as a socioracial category is, of course, still not extinct. It recently surfaced in Warwick, Rhode Island, where a federally-mandated municipal sewer construction project has, for years, been grappling with the question of how to move forward without impacting unmarked Indian burials located throughout the area. In August of 2019, a Warwick Sewer Authority board member reportedly stated: "Forget all the stuff with the Indians and do it the conventional way" and "Pocahontas and Tonto have had their day. It's over" (Howell 2019). There is no reason to assume that such petty bigotry is rare, even if it rarely comes into public view. As John McWhorter, linguistics professor at Columbia University, recently pointed out, the assumption that "all people have a racist bias is reasonable—science has demonstrated it" (McWhorter 2020a), while Shelby Steele lends some additional perspective when he insists that "racism is endemic to the human condition, just as stupidity is."

In view of this long, racially fraught history, it should come as little surprise that the idea of "blood" underwriting Indian legitimacy is also still very much alive in contemporary New England. The Mashantucket Pequot Tribe of Connecticut, having mixed Indian, white, and black ancestry among its members, came under considerable racial scrutiny following the financial success of their Foxwoods Casino. Accusations of diluted bloodlines were leveled by critics, including future President Donald J. Trump, who infamously commented that their tribal members "don't look Indian to me" (Lightman 1993), without elaborating on what he expected an Indian to look like.

A 2007 feature in the *New York Times* discussed this situation: "Several years ago, to prove their ancestry, the tribe started testing its members' DNA. Several people learned that they were not Pequot at all. Others learned that their children were not their own, tribal members said" (Kershaw 2007). One of the tribe's top administrators added that "It was a disaster," comparing it to *The Jerry Springer Show*. Reportedly, the tribe has since stopped this program, except in regard to one particular demographic. As of 2018 the tribe required genetic testing for all newborns, a practice that remains controversial among some of its members (Kaplan 2018). The tribe suffered another minor public image setback in 2018, when the media reported that the Mashantucket Pequot Chief of Staff, who oversaw police and fire services, had served four years in San Quentin back in the 1980s. When living in California at the age of seventeen, he reportedly stabbed and paralyzed another teenager. Prosecutors say that on the night of the attack, he told others riding in the car that he intended "to kill a white boy."

Twin sisters recently learned via Facebook that they had been removed from the rolls of the Mashpee Indian Tribe immediately after applying to the tribe's COVID-19 relief program (Hill 2020b). Like the Narragansett Indian Tribe (Henry 2007), the Mashpee exhibited a disenrollment spike at about the same time the media started reporting that they were planning to get a casino (Vosk and Brennan 2008). Perhaps the availability of COVID-19 relief funds incentivized additional scrutiny of membership among the Mashpee. Reportedly acting on a paternity allegation, the Tribal Enrollment Committee is requiring that the sisters submit to a DNA paternity test, the results of which would be compared to those of a similar DNA test administered to their alleged biological father (providing he is willing), as a precondition to considering their re-enrollment. Their mother, who is of Cape Verdean descent and claims not to know this alleged father, maintains that her daughters were disenrolled simply because "they are dark." She notes that they have both been enrolled since birth and have been active in tribal affairs, serving as tribal dance instructors and becoming "champion dancers of the Eastern Blanket and the Fancy Shawl" categories. None of her three sons have been disenrolled. The sisters are suing the Enrollment Committee in tribal court. This affair would seem to represent a bizarre blemish on the tribe's otherwise outstanding response to the COVID-19 pandemic (Spencer 2020b). Another recent report suggests that intentions of removing "dark-skinned" tribal members may be a repeating phenomenon among the Mashpee (ReelWamps.com 2020).

Figuring out who to marry seems to be a racially fraught issue among some tribal people. The previously mentioned Adrienne J. Keene, who teaches at Brown University, provides a thought-provoking commentary on the tension some Indians experience when trying to negotiate the ideals of love versus racial identitarianism in their search for a partner:

> Colonialism leaves a helluva legacy, doesn't it? That to me is the saddest and most frustrating part of all this. Notions of 'blood fractions' are a complete colonial construction, designed to 'breed out' Indians, and now they've been internalized and are being used by our own communities to further restrict not only the futures of our tribes, but our right to love. So is reclaiming your right to love whomever you want an act of decolonization? Or is it weakening modern tribal sovereignty? I'm still not sure. (Keene 2013)

A National Public Radio producer and member of the Mashpee Wampanoag Tribe provides a brave commentary on how and why she wants to find an Indian to father her children:

> For me, the hierarchy has always been clear—if not Mashpee Wampanoag then Aquinnah or Herring Pond. If not Wampanoag then Nar-

ragansett. Then Pequot. And if you find yourself too far from home to lock down an Eastern Woodlands man to father your children, he damn well better be Indigenous to somewhere on this continent. Find yourself a Native man. Good blood for your babies. I know how messed up it sounds. But it's about survival. Here's the thing about blood quantum: it's not real...but it's got all these smart people—traditionalists, university students, Indigenous language revitalists—running around doing mental math, convinced it's our best shot at keeping our cultures alive. I won't pretend that I'm above it. The prospect of having kids even more mixed than I am makes me anxious. If, in a century, the Wampanoag tribe no longer exists—if we lose our land, our traditions, our language—will it be my fault? If my babies end up looking like him, if they feel more white than Wampanoag, have I wasted my ancestors' sacrifices? (Maher 2018)

Believing that the future of her tribe may depend on her willingness to submit to a reproductive agenda aimed at racial conservation reveals an intergenerational burden that most New Englanders do not carry at this day in age. Her account humanizes this challenge, providing rare insight into its psychology while acknowledging the sorts of people who are promoting it—apparently, people she believes are "smart," the "traditionalists, university students" and "Indigenous language revivalists." John Peters, the Massachusetts Executive Director of Indian Affairs and member of the Mashpee Wampanoag Tribe, points out that this mentality is, in part, a consequence of the Indian Reorganization Act of 1934, whereby the federal government anchored tribal political legitimacy to blood quantum (Clark 2020). But he also points out that "you can't keep marrying your cousins."

Since race appears to be the unifying thread of all contemporary public discourse, I may as well work toward the end of this chapter with some related commentary. So, what would happen if I stated that I wanted my children to "look like me?" Just imagine the scandal. Leftist scholars, the self-styled champions of the non-judgmental approach of cultural relativism, would be eager to decry that statement as an unambiguous expression of white supremacy. When Indians want their children to "look like them," the very same scholars would applaud them as bearers of a rare, hyper-legitimate strain of humanity whose members are born special and are perhaps even morally obligated to ensure that their children are born with that same gift, generation after generation, amen. As a defrocked leftist, I understand this mindset all too well—a mindset where every tribe seems to present an endangered group crying out for shelter from the never-ending storm of settler colonialism, and where the human capital of individual Indians is easily overlooked.

As a twenty first century parent, I wonder what percentage of Indian youth are being taught to see the conservation of bloodlines as a high calling, local outsiders as invaders, local landscapes as their stolen birthright, and racism as a primary barrier to their success in life? Would such beliefs inspire them to passionately pursue their talents, to recognize the full horizon of opportunities before them, and to demand nothing less from themselves than excellence? Or might this vision conspire against others from the deepest recesses of their own hearts, whispering a ready alibi against the unmitigated pursuit of their full potential? These are politically incorrect questions, the kinds of questions that someone who looks like me presumably lacks the moral authority to ask. But to not ask them here would feel like a betrayal.

Recently, Princess Natasha Gambrell of the Eastern Pequot Tribal Nation communicated to the media that "On October 12, 2005 – Columbus Day, the United States government took away our federal recognition [and] in doing so, they kind of left us desolate on this reservation" (Jackson 2020). It is a powerful statement. She did not share that her tribe's reservation, on which nobody is required to spend their life, is located in the wealthiest country in the world, in its fifth wealthiest state, within comfortable commuting distance of two of that state's largest employers who happen to be Indians who prefer to employ fellow Indians. But, then again, if her tribe retained their federal recognition and built their own casino, happy endings for individual members still might not be guaranteed, particularly among a first generation born into wealth.

Consider the case of Gambrell's next-door neighbors, the Mashantucket Pequot Tribe. They retained their federal recognition and eventually opened a casino (est. 1992) built with funding from Genting. Following their overnight success as a casino giant, the tribe was applauded nationwide as an example of an indigenous group overcoming the long and dark oblivion of settler colonial oppression. Unfortunately, the Mashantucket Pequots lacked special immunity to a certain second-order effect of rapid economic success, the age-old curse of the *nouveau riche*. The Haywards explained in 2007 that too many tribal youths given money from an early age have become idle and drawn to drugs, admitting that certain members of their own family were refusing to work or attend school (Kershaw 2007). Michael J. Thomas, the Tribal Chairman at the time, opined, "We have replaced dependency on Uncle Sam with dependency on the tribe, which is only slightly healthier," while a tribal elder who has spent most of her life on the reservation added, "We are breaking up." To my knowledge, not one among New England's bumper crop of anthropologists and indigenous studies scholars have so much as acknowledged this situation within the region's most famous Indian tribe. Has this trend of drug use and despondency deflated since the tribe's economic nosedive, which began in 2008 and soon led to the termination of generous stipends for all adult members? The academy, which seems quite content to entertain itself with visions of decolonialism, cannot be counted on to take any interest in such harsh realities.

CHAPTER SIXTEEN

THE GRAFT OF WHITE SETTLER
COLONIAL GUILT

TODAY, MANY WHITE New Englanders have descended into what appears to be a penitential stage of orientation toward Indians, which is, ironically, revitalizing racial divisions. In their explicit efforts to make racism and discrimination things of the past, or at least signify that they are no longer complicit toward such, some end up mirroring the racial paranoia that Indians have been negotiating for centuries. Racial paranoia has profound effects on the lives of contemporary people, counteracting shared racial equality goals and promoting an ignorance of the harmful duplicities of "interracial" dialogue (Jackson 2008). Naturally, it would be nice to hope for more Indians to escape its curse in the twenty-first century. But the likelihood of that happening is undermined by these white settler colonial folk who seem to believe that sympathetically indulging their own brand of racial paranoia in a misplaced show of solidarity will somehow be helpful to everyone.

I call this brand of racial paranoia white settler colonial guilt. Its rise in recent years may superficially resemble karma or poetic justice to those with leftist sensibilities. But anyone concerned with the well-being of society should recognize that it is merely yet another mechanism by which human individuality is suppressed and group preconceptions are reinforced. It throws fuel on the fires of social disintegration and Balkanization while somehow being applauded as a step forward for social progress. Concerned about where this sort of thinking may lead, a prominent French philosopher implores us to "just imagine little blond, brunette or curly headed kids coming up to each other on the playground and introducing themselves as descendants of slaves, of colonized peoples, of slave traders, of bandits, of peasants or beggars" (Bruckner 2012). But the thing is, in New England, we do not have to try very hard to imagine this outcome. We are training our children to do this in the here and now.

Ceremonial stone landscape activism draws political power from white guilt, the psychosocial phenomenon African American race relations scholar Dr. Shelby Steele describes, whereby black Americans are objectified by whites eminently concerned with dissociating from racism and claiming redemption from the nation's past sins (2006). In New England, Indians are similarly objectified from a settler colonial perspective. For instance, my neighbor, who, like me, appears undeniably white, has initiated several conversations along these lines: "Tim! Did I tell you that I visited the National Museum of the American Indian? I can't believe how badly we treated the Indians! What are we supposed to do?" Putting aside the fact that her ancestors fled to the United States to escape an Ireland that had become deeply impoverished under British colonial exploitation, her performance invites me to resolve a shared anxiety—the shame accompanying a white identity that is indexed to settler colonialism and racism. Under the right circumstances, such shame presents a sociopolitical asset that may be traded for authority, legitimacy, and power (Steele 2006).

When Indian representatives appear in formal settings, they are often welcomed as moral standard-bearers before whom white settler colonial guilt may be confessed. I have witnessed this many times, such as at a historic preservation planning meeting several years ago when a municipal representative explained to a tribal authority, in a strangely well-rehearsed manner: "You look at yourself in the river, where you see yourself with the sky and the clouds and the trees. We look into a mirror, where we only see ourselves." This was, I presume, a poetically romantic apology for the collective greed of whites that saluted Indians as possessing superior virtue. And I remember cringing at an academic conference when an Indian lecturer was implored by an audience member, his voice cracking with heartfelt urgency, "Teach me! I am here! I want to learn from you! Please!" Though we may dismiss such self-effacing, deferential rhetoric as little more than an awkward spectacle, it betrays a deep shame that often surrounds white identity when self-consciously juxtaposed to Indian identity. And, as I see things, this behavior is no less apparent among leftist white academics, who, to borrow the words of James Baldwin, habitually employ "the unfortunate tone of warm congratulation" (1963) when entering into conversation with Indian identity bearers regardless of the content of their character.

Indians are never so objectified by whites than in the weeks leading up to Thanksgiving. For instance, in 2019, students at Four Winds Middle school in Gill, Massachusetts, learned about the arrival of the Mayflower and the cultural conflict that followed. As the school's director explained, "It left all our students with this sense of European guilt, or something" (Marcus 2019). According to one student, "We kind of decided we wanted to do something about reparations," and settled on holding a walkathon fundraiser for the Mashpee Wampanoag Tribe on Indigenous People's Day (formerly Columbus Day) because "we heard they were one of the first tribes that the Pilgrims interacted with" (Spencer 2019). Another explained "If we don't try to repair what our ancestors did, the tribes will die off," adding that "We feel like it's our job, but we don't feel like it's our personal fault" (Marcus 2019). Regardless, their educational experience is telling them they are on the hook. As the centuries-old Massachusetts state seal reminds us, local settler colonists have long imagined that Indians are in desperate need of outside help.

These students appear to have internalized white settler colonial guilt and were applauded for this by teachers and administrators. The students raised over $2800 for the tribe—a mere drop in the bucket compared to the roughly $500 million the Mashpee have received in recent years from Genting (Conneller 2020). But this drop rippled with a special, domestically sourced moral virtue. The school's director touted the fundraiser as embodying "what we want to be teaching [our students] about activism and being involved in the community" (Spencer 2019). What would the Mashpee do without such interventions? Who knows, perhaps they would not be thought of as people whose good fortunes depend on the moral enlightenment of settler colonial children. What would those children do if they did not spend their time claiming to solve exceedingly complex social issues? They might gain a more competent and objective knowledge of history.

Are the teachers at this school aware that the Mashpee tribal membership has grown significantly over the past century, from approximately 250-300 in the 1930s (United States Department of the Interior 2006), to 500 in the mid-1970s, to 850 in 1989, to 1,001 in 1996, to 1,462 in 2005, and to 2,600 in 2020 (Mashpee Wampanoag Tribe 2020)? Do they teach their students that the American Indian population at large expanded so dramatically over the course of the twentieth century that it rebounded to 1492 population estimates (Shoemaker 2000)? Contrary to popular belief, there is no shortage of Indians today, only an apparent surplus of miseducated settler colonists. Regardless, the media stories presented the children, who appear to have helped solve a problem that empirically does not exist, as generally heroic, providing good optics for everyone involved.

The message that local Indians are in desperate need of outside help is also being voiced from within tribal communities. Consider Bella Noka's comparison of her tribe to an endangered species. She explained from the grounds of Rhode Island's state capitol:

> There are less than 3000 Narragansets. During this pandemic and any other time when there is less than 3000 of anything such as whales, Bengal tigers, polar bears, what we do is protect them. We put them in a class of protection. But nobody has reached out to the Narragansett Indian Tribe to protect them. (transcribed from a video posted in Ahlquist 2020)

Even if one presumes that the Narragansett Indian Tribe is sliding toward extinction, it is difficult to overlook the irony of comparing a "sovereign tribal nation" to an endangered species, a concept built on the assumption that if a particular population is critically declining, their recovery depends on outside intervention. From among the various immigrant groups famous for realizing rapid economic success in the U.S., such as East Indian, West Indian, and Chinese Americans, Noka appears to call out Jewish Americans as fitting candidates to provide assistance. She explained that they are "here in my country doing very, very, very well" and "I don't ever see one of them reach out to my people. Never." Perhaps a more useful line of inquiry would be to try and figure out how Jewish people at large have managed to arrive in so many countries with little more than the clothes on their backs yet build vibrant, upwardly mobile communities that typically outpace those of their new neighbors.

Though Steele insists that white guilt "is not actual guilt" in that "most whites are not assailed in the night by feelings of responsibility for America's historical mistreatment of minorities," I believe that many white New Englanders experience sincere, albeit generic and largely misplaced, shame when the region's colonial history is brought up. This seemed to be the case when former Rhode Island State Archaeologist Dr. Paul Robinson delivered a sermonic lecture titled, "The Foundations of Thanksgiving and the Obligations of Place: Defending the Indigenous

Homeland and All That It Holds," in November 2015. With a title like that, one might think he was an Indian. Among his holiday-themed messages was that the kind, generous, and trusting way seventeenth-century Narragansett Indians treated Rhode Island's colonists was in step with Christian values, and that the failure of many English colonists to reciprocate in kind represents an enduring, to use his exact words, "original sin" (Figure 14).

Figure 14: Paul Robinson delivering his sermon on the Mount Hope Farm in Bristol, Rhode Island, November 8, 2015. Photo by the author.

I find this rather emblematic of our race-obsessed age, when some white New Englanders no longer feel that they can be publicly seen as proverbial "good Christians" by simply being good Christians. Instead, they may emplot themselves within a drama triangle based on Christian archetype, one that casts "their people" as Roman oppressors, indigenous minorities as the original, oppressed Christians, and themselves as beleaguered apostles struggling to enlighten the former and elevate the latter toward the higher purpose of ushering in a new age of peace, balance, and harmony. It is an ideologically familiar formula by which whites may cast themselves as heroes at the center of the decolonial metanarrative without making significant personal sacrifices, such as tithing their own wealth and land to local Indians.

But Christian analogies aside, we all objectively understand that no one chooses to be born into any place or group and that people can only he held accountable for their own actions and inactions. Guilt, in principle, is simply not among the things that baby humans can inherit. However, white settler colonial guilt is a horse of a different color. I believe that as much for Robinson as for myself, it compares to a religious conviction with deep cultural roots that is highly resistant to rational challenge. Where he and I differ is how we have answered its call. He appears to have taken the path of a missionary, and I, a heretic.

CHAPTER SEVENTEEN

THE WRONG SIDE OF HISTORY

W HEN I BEGAN WORKING at the Rhode Island Historical Preservation and Heritage Commission in 2012, I was wary that
ceremonial stone landscape activists had emplotted one of our sister
agencies, the Massachusetts Historical Commission (MHC), as a villain
in the centuries-long metanarrative of Indian cultural survival. That institution was cast as such in 2008 after failing to agree with a historical interpretation endorsed by the Narragansett Indian Tribe and the
Wampanoag Tribe of Gay Head, whose respective THPOs recognized
stone heaps near the end of a linear stone structure in Montague, Massachusetts, as part of a sacred Indian ceremonial complex that they called
the Turners Falls Sacred Ceremonial Hill Site.

According to tribal authorities, the site was not a stand-alone phenomenon. They claimed it was a key place of ceremony on an ancient,
sacred alignment that extends for hundreds of miles and intercepts
another ceremonial site at Fort Drum, New York, recently reported by
government archaeologist Laurie Rush and another one on Cape Cod,
Massachusetts, identified by antiquarian James Mavor. Filmmaker Ted
Timreck of the Smithsonian Institution synthesized all of this in his
documentary, *Great Falls: Discovery, Destruction and Preservation in a
Massachusetts Town* (Timreck 2010[2008]), which was submitted to the
National Park Service to represent the views of tribal authorities.

The MHC recognized the stonework at the Turners Falls Sacred
Ceremonial Hill Site as a farmer's unfinished, and generally unremarkable, wall, replete with piles of fieldstones at the "in-progress" end.

The MHC and the THPOs had committed themselves to their incompatible positions under the oversight of the Federal Aviation Ad-

ministration, which was regulating plans to expand the Turners Falls Airport in a manner that did not destroy any National Register-eligible properties. The Keeper of the National Register of Historic Places resolved this contest by endorsing, in full, the tribal interpretation, explaining their decision in a "Determination of Eligibility" (DOE) document (NRHP 2008) that cites the book *Manitou*—the same book that hypothesizes that the Mohegan Indians of Connecticut secretly built a "prayer seat" next to a high-voltage power line so they could turbo-charge their visions using its electromagnetic field (Mavor and Dix 1989:262-264). That document also cites the previously mentioned film *Great Falls*, an anonymously authored pro-ceremonial stone landscape website called NativeStones.com, and articles posted on NEARA's website. The Turners Falls Sacred Ceremonial Hill Site was deemed so important to the continuing cultural identity of the Narragansett and Wampanoag people, in the capacity of what the National Park Service defines as a Traditional Cultural Property (see Parker and King 1990), that the airport expansion plans were altered to preserve it in place.

As Indian cultural authorities applauded the Keeper of the National Register, the MHC languished in its new moral authority vacuum. Ever since, Harris has been able to claim that the Massachusetts "SHPO has a problem" acknowledging ceremonial stones (Bellow 2017). Since 2008, I have not attended a regional archaeological conference where at least one speaker or audience member did not denounce the MHC as if to broadcast an anti-racist identity. For example, after a colleague finished delivering a conference presentation about coastal archaeology at the 2017 annual meeting of the Eastern States Archaeological Federation, he opened the floor to questions. A ceremonial stone landscape activist in the audience responded by asking the following non sequitur: "In Massachusetts our SHPO refuses to acknowledge ceremonial stone landscapes. What should we do!?" In a journal article, contract archaeologists Charity Weiss (formerly Moore) and Matthew Weiss similarly demonize the MHC, stating that "the Massachusetts SHPO continues to deny" the sacred nature of the site "despite information from several Native American tribes that it was a sacred ceremonial area," and "to the best of our knowledge, has not even assigned the area a state trinomial site number" (Moore and Weiss 2016:45). Could the MHC, somehow, justify agreeing with the THPOs to avoid becoming a ritual target of moral condemnation?

I must admit that my initial reaction to the Keeper of the National Register's determination that the Turners Falls Sacred Ceremonial Hill

Site was eligible for listing in the National Register of Historic Places could be summed up by the following question: What on earth is going on here? I would eventually gain the vision necessary to answer this question, but not by secretly hallucinating beneath power lines. Shortly after arriving at the RIHPHC in 2012, I was asked by my office's assistant director to "learn more about stone piles," which had become a contested dimension of historical landscape interpretation in southern New England under the ceremonial stone landscape paradigm. Publication of my initial research attracted a malign scrutiny that I did not anticipate, but which proved personally and professionally transformative. It forced me off the moral authority scaffolding to which so many white settler colonists reflexively cling, and after accepting my new place on solid ground, I gained a broader and more detached perspective of the drama above.

My fall went something like this. I disseminated my initial stone heap research with the 2013 publication of "Remembering Stone Piles in New England," an article that reviews documented stone piling traditions and encourages collaborations between professional archaeologists and THPOs mutually concerned with stone structure preservation (Ives 2013a). Though I thought I had treated the topic fairly, a lengthy critique that I received indicated otherwise, as this excerpt shows:

> It is distressing that you willfully ignore the documentary record of Native American stone cairns, and only manage to identify agricultural stone piles, for which there is no documentary record. None. I will be charitable and merely describe this behavior as intellectually dishonest, rather than racist as many might.

Subsequently, I published "Cairnfields in New England's Forgotten Pastures," an article hypothesizing that farmers created most of the stone heaps in New England's hills (Ives 2015a). It intended to help distinguish some of what might not be ancient ceremonial structures, presuming such information is useful for determining preservation priorities. It also confronts the likelihood, as I see it, that most stone structures in today's forests are relatively young agricultural heirlooms. This article triggered strong criticisms on a variety of fronts. Relevant quotes include:

> Your position is a jingoistic one where you are likely supporting a myth so the SHPO does not have to admit they have been wrong.

> Ives' hypothesis, sadly, is just a bunch of sketches without evidentiary

support and many logical fallacies…Ives is spinning a myth.

> Every word written in "Cairnfields" seems to deny that Indigenous
> Cultures in the Northeast, over a span of 12,000 years or more, could
> have possibly left any visible reminder of their presence on the land-
> scape.

These confirmed the very emplotment I wished to avoid, compelling me to ask unsettling questions. Do my practices indeed promote a
mythology that suppresses Indian heritage? Should I remain silent on
the topic of ceremonial stone landscapes to avoid further scrutiny? Or,
should I cleverly engineer the conditions necessary to scramble back
up that moral authority scaffolding, perhaps by discursively reinventing
myself as an Indian advocate and casting a rhetorical stone at the MHC
to certify my reformation? If my answer to any of these questions was
"yes," I would not have written this book.

Still, I ponder them mindful that my office is attached to the nineteenth-century legislative hall where my employer, the State of Rhode
Island, forcibly detribalized the Narragansett Indians (Bossevain 1956;
Hernandon and Sekatau 1997:433). Political conflict between the state
and the now federally recognized Narragansett Indian Tribe continues
(e.g. Anderson 2017; Powell 2016), and I remain shocked by images
of the 2003 Rhode Island State Police raid on the Narragansett Smoke
Shop (Adams 2003) when they resurface in the media (e.g. Davis 2013;
Mulvaney 2016). In 2016, I was named a defendant in a civil lawsuit
filed in Rhode Island's U.S. District Court by the Narragansett Indian
THPO concerning alleged improper removal of artifacts by an archaeological firm working in advance of cable installation for the Block Island
Wind Farm (Narragansett Indian Tribe v. Narragansett Electric Co.,
1:16-cv-00216-M-PAS). And in 2015, a delegation from the Federation
of Aboriginal Nations of America (FANA) and the National Association
for the Advancement of Indigenous People (NAAIP) showed up unan-
nounced at my office door seeking accountability for centuries of colonial oppression. Apparently, I am the kind of person one would appeal
to for that sort of thing. They asked me to answer twelve prepared questions on video, instructed me not to ask any of my own, and requested that I not refer to local indigenous people as Native Americans. (I
have endeavored to oblige that last request in the writing of this book.)
The alliance between FANA and NAAIP was short-lived. On behalf of
FANA, Raymond "Two Hawks" Watson renounced the NAAIP in 2017,

releasing a video claiming that its leader, Hemoc Xelup, "is a fraud!" (Watson 2017).

Anyway, "racist villain" seems to be a fitting term for the role that is reserved for a state employee who looks like me in the decolonial meta-narrative…unless I were to virtue-signal my way out, to stage a dramatic escape to "the right side of history." Perhaps the easiest way for me to do so would be to just throw in the towel and endorse ceremonial stone landscape ideology. With the release of one public statement featuring the phrase "let the landscape speak," redemption would be mine. But as you have probably guessed by now, I find cheap political bargains disgusting.

Nonetheless, evading the messiness of human emotions is not an option. My closer colleagues know that I grapple with a related, and clearly irrational, sense of shame, usually by venting through self-deprecating humor to ensure that it does not reconfigure my archaeological practices or diminish my ability to appreciate others based on what Dr. Martin Luther King Jr. called "the content of their character." And, I have found myself venting quite frequently, under ceremonial stone landscape activism's inquisition.

Harris voices some of the strongest criticisms of professional archaeology:

> Many archaeologists are not willing to let go of the paradigm that gives them their degree. This element of that paradigm in specific, they have said for decades that these are the results of colonial farm clearing. That comes out of the notion that savages could not have had a civilization that was sufficient to deal with the stars and with accounting for a celestial calendar. Those kinds of prejudices die hard. It's still a battle. (Harris 2014)

For decades, the region's professional archaeologists have indeed identified stonework as agricultural that THPOs have more recently begun qualifying as ceremonial. However, Harris' embittered charge that this practice draws upon bigoted notions of Indians as uncivilized or incapable of astronomy is neither supported by sources nor reflected in my professional experience. But this is irrelevant to his implied ultimatum, which is that professional archaeologists, much less any other settler colonial functionaries, are presumed racist if they disagree with an Indian regarding the historical evaluation of a stone structure or its surrounding landscape. Framed more broadly, ceremonial stone landscape activism compels white citizenry to prove their moral virtue by signaling support, or renew their moral bankruptcy in a narrative about Indian cultural survival. The importance of white settler colonial guilt here should not be underestimated.

One uniquely intriguing feature of ceremonial stone landscape activism is its apparent total lack of concern for developing a consensus on the functions of alleged ceremonial stone features. Of course, the question of whether a stone feature is a burial marker, a memory pile, part of an astronomical alignment, or something else sounds fundamentally concerning to the average bystander who is still wearing their thinking cap. But among activists, the question seems ancillary so long as all agree that any features in question are probably indigenous and sacred and should therefore be treated as such. One could describe the situation as exemplifying, to borrow an expression from far afield, "indifference within indignation" (*sensu* Martinez 1996).

Superficially, ceremonial stone landscape preservation campaigns present mysterious ceremonies, whereby Indian and white settler colonial activists theatrically unite to rally behind an inscrutably vague preordained position. And in defense of that position, they would seem to provoke white supremacy into existence for the expressed purpose of staging its ritual defeat. But what is this really all about? I think most ceremonial stone landscape activists are too close to what they are doing to provide an objective answer. And the stones, busy enough in their latest careers as geopolitical placeholders for human controversy, are of no help to us here either. As I see it, the answer only comes into view when one steps far enough back to distinguish the broader social landscape that we inhabit—the hyper-moralized landscape of race relations.

CHAPTER EIGHTEEN

ANATOMY OF A RACIAL BARGAIN

As I see it, ceremonial stone landscape preservation campaigns represent, to some degree, collective bargains negotiated across a strictly drawn socioracial line. Indian identity bearers gain symbolic recognition, political amplification, and volunteer labor. In turn, whites are released from the otherwise implicit stigma of settler colonial guilt. To state the latter more precisely, ceremonial stone landscape activism affords whites a mechanism by which to dissociate themselves from racism and register their moral redemption by positively indexing their identities to those of previously disgraced, but now popularly valorized, Indians. By no means do I expect most readers to readily buy into that last statement, though I hope most will be willing to at least give it serious consideration by the time they finish this chapter.

To understand what I am getting at, one must appreciate the mindset of bargainers on both sides. Though some tribal communities have quietly struggled with white-red-black internal racial tensions for centuries, they tend to identify more simply as "Indians"—the identity of their collective truth—when relating to society at large. And oppositional "Indian" versus "English/white" identities have persisted throughout New England, despite centuries of biological and cultural hybridization (DeLucia 2012). For instance, Dr. Lisa McLoughlin, a ceremonial stone landscape activist with the Nolumbeka Project, Inc., who discloses her indigenous ancestry but is "not recognized by any official tribal entity," explains that "significant, thorny, political issues" make "integration of my identity impossible" while working "with and for Native Americans" (McLoughlin 2017:71). She probably understands that local Indian Country holds no shortage of identity police ready to blow their whis-

153

tles if she asserted an Indian identity, especially if it included a claim to resources.

McLoughlin reports her Indian ancestry at 1/16th, the same ratio claimed by Richard "Skip" Hayward who resurrected the Mashantucket Pequot Tribe in the late twentieth century. Hayward led them to become a casino giant and the richest tribe in America (Benedict 2001), before withdrawing from the tribe's political affairs a few years later amid intratribal factionalism that he insists was not racially charged (Kershaw 2007). Bear in mind that the tribe regards whatever members happened to be listed on the 1900 U.S. Census, which was taken after several generations of "interracial" marriage, as their genealogical baseline. Nevertheless, McLoughlin does not seem to believe that she has a legitimate public claim to an Indian identity. Some political or cultural qualification was missing, so her identity automatically defaults to that of a white settler colonist. Ceremonial stone landscape ideologues demand racial clarity, and their followers tend to comply. This, of course, requires centuries of complicated history to collapse into oblivion. McLoughlin may as well have just stepped off the Mayflower, even though she might possess more Indian ancestry than some of the Indians to whom she has pledged her service.

This socioracial essentialism, borne on the deeply internalized tensions of a settler colonialism long invested in restricting Indian identities and scrutinizing their authenticity (Campisi 1993; Gould 2013; Hernandon and Sekatau 1997; Mandell 1998; McMullen 1994; O'Brien 2010; Thee 2006), is galvanized by what human rights scholar Dr. Lea David calls the "standardization of memory" endemic to colonized places like New England (2017). Here, historical discourse abides by the popular "Western memorial model," whereby historical groups and their descendants are cast in the role of *oppressors* or *victims*. David notes that this framework tends to perpetuate contemporary societal divisions, despite its presumed intentions of collectively confronting, and eventually transcending, historical injustices. Indeed, New England is a "land of steady habits" in that it remains bound by the falsehoods of an old system of socioracial accounting that appears hopelessly entangled with group identity.

A history of violence and discrimination against Indians weighs on these identities like the Ancient Mariner's albatross, and perhaps more heavily than ever before. Historian Dr. Christine DeLucia's question, "How do they-we conceive of ourselves as complicit in these violences, or as witnesses, victims, survivors of them?" (2012:976) may sound melodramatic, but it has become an especially important question in recent years. Reflecting on such leads many New Englanders, particularly "Yankees" descended from English colonists, to reach disturbing conclusions about their place in history. For example, NEARA's Steve DiMarzo announced at the 2017 dedication of the Manitou Hassannash Preserve that he descended from Plymouth colonist Josiah Winslow, who he qualifies as the "most hated man by the indigenous people" and possibly "the reason King Philip's War started." He added that this makes him "feel pretty bad" (as transcribed from Gage 2017b). DiMarzo, who obviously bears an Italian surname, did not mention the more recent immigrant dimension of his heritage that I am willing to guess exists. Whiteness looks bright and featureless under the spotlight of ceremonial stone landscape activism's identity politics.

Though mainstream historians and anthropologists have done a brilliant job chronicling the victimization of Indians by a white dominated colonial society (e.g., Campisi 1993; Hauptman and Wherry 1993; Jennings 1975; Mandell 1996; O'Brien 1997; PBS *American Experience* 2009; Zinn 1980), they have consistently turned a blind eye to the psychosocial impacts of that knowledge on their contemporary white majority audience. This is unsurprising, knowing that most of today's academics would probably disregard any such inquiry as "sympathy for the devil." But still, could one group's unresolved identity issue have collateral effects on the identity, and perhaps even the destiny, of another? This question, even if it is a politically incorrect question that makes mainstream scholars run for cover, deserves serious consideration, if only in "sympathy for the bedeviled."

Ceremonial stone landscape theory solves New England's white settler colonial identity quagmire by revising the region's cultural-historical metanarrative, creating space for an alternative to the troubling identity standard of *oppressor*. *Manitou* provides fundamental context by proposing that Euro-American populations always included some who quietly respected, valued, and protected the places and institutions that support Indian spirituality (1989). For instance, its authors note that the Mayflower's passengers imported pagan customs and were likely "tolerant of such practices as solstice, equinox and May Day festivals," as opposed to the "comfortable," "enterprising," and "powerful" Massachusetts Bay colonists. Dr. Ezra Stiles, eighteenth-century Congregationalist minister and scholar, is hailed as a "Gentle Puritan," distinguished from his contemporaries by his interest in local Indian spiritual places and practices. They point to the "rather Indian-like manner" of the Quakers as well as the entanglement of Shaker and Indian lives. In fact, they interpret some "ritual landscape architecture" as "the work of both Indians and Shakers, first by Indians, then by working together, and finally the Shakers." Their discussions trace a moral fault line through colonial society that mainstream researchers have not, suggesting there is room for some white New Englanders on "the right side of history."

Hailed within NEARA as the "thorn in the side of the presently-accepted history of New England" (Lonegren 1993:58), this revision holds a powerful lure before white audiences wishing to recover a positive self-concept, audiences otherwise left to imagine their predecessors as villains in a colonial nightmare. It invites them to join a purportedly ancient fraternity of socially progressive whites believed to have long subverted the colonial project to ensure Indian cultural survival. Of course, this risks promoting a "white savior complex" that eclipses recognition of less romantically appealing dimensions of Indian survivance. Nonetheless, the revision I describe invents space for another Western memorial identity, which I term *advocate*. American anthropologist Keith Basso wrote that knowledge of places "is closely linked to knowledge of the self, to grasping one's position in the larger scheme of things, including one's own community, and to securing a confident sense of who one is as a person" (1996:34). I agree, particularly regarding ceremonial stone landscapes, which create an *advocate* identity space for members of a settler colonial society wishing, to borrow the words of an Australian-based ethnographer and decolonial theorist, "to inscribe a moral presence" for themselves in the world (Rose 2014:209).

The overall social dynamic running throughout ceremonial stone landscape activism can be understood according to the model of human interaction known as the "Karpman Drama Triangle" (Johnson 2020), which maps drama-intense transactional relationships according to an interplay of three roles: oppressors (in our case, presumably ignorant white settler colonists), victims (in our case, Indians), and rescuers (in our case, presumably enlightened white settler colonists, a.k.a. *advocates*). The energy that this triangle generates has the social effect of bypassing facts and reason and escalating conflict and confusion. Psychologists subscribing to this model aim to help their patients understand it, so they may extract themselves from its machinations. Chapter 24 will present a very robust example of the Karpman Drama Triangle operating within the context of a ceremonial stone landscape preservation campaign.

Historical secrecy is a prominent feature of ceremonial stone landscape narrativity, as Harris and Robinson demonstrate:

> For many years, the locations of some special places and their cere-
> monial importance were known only to some Tribal people. In some
> cases, however, this knowledge was extended to, or held by, sympa-
> thetic families of European descent, some of whom had lived there
> since colonial times, and had learned not to disturb them. Indian peo-
> ple were reluctant to share this knowledge widely because they feared
> some people might harm the place, either physically, by vandalizing or
> destroying the features, or verbally, by ridiculing the beliefs and prac-
> tices that underlay the places. In either case, making their locations
> public might risk disrupting the spirit energies of the place. (Harris
> and Robinson 2015:141)

The above passage generally relates ideas articulated in *Manitou* twen-
ty-six years prior, contextualizing contemporary efforts to preserve Indian ceremonial landscapes as the upshot of a centuries-old tradition of
covert stewardship. By extension, older efforts to conserve such places
are presumed to have been invisible to colonial society at large, so that
few, if any, documentary traces exist for today's historians and archaeologists to scrutinize. Recent repetition of this material by Harris and
Robinson does, however, carry a novel connotation—the idea that this
hypothesized movement waited for the right moment, our current age
of social justice activism, to reveal itself to the world.

Paul Loether, after being promoted to Keeper of the National Register of Historic Places, also contributed to this narrativity while convers-
ing with Harris during a public presentation on ceremonial stone landscapes (Harris 2014). Specifically, Loether stated, "I seem to remember
there was a letter issued in the 1920s by the Massachusetts Attorney
General warning tribal people to stay away from these sites." Harris replied, "We were ardently encouraged to drop our traditional cultural and
spiritual practices in lieu of colonial practices," to which Loether added,
"It was upon bane of imprisonment." If the allegation that Loether and
Harris seem to have mutually agreed upon here is correct, would it not
have already attracted a great deal of critical commentary from anthropologists and historians? This has not been the case. Despite a lack of
evidence that the Massachusetts Attorney General ever produced such
a document, I suppose there is no way to "prove" that it never existed.

I do not think it is an accident that largely unfalsifiable, however
improbable, claims are sometimes made by ceremonial stone activists
with a quasi-religious conviction. This is done so nobody can "prove

them wrong," and to intimidate anyone who might dare contemplate an attempt. If one can tangle up historical claims with a religious position, the chances that any outsiders will be willing to attempt disentangling the two are effectively minimized. This is a fundamental tactic of ceremonial stone landscape activism, one that provides remarkably effective insurance against criticism.

Some antiquarians, in the tradition of Mavor and Dix, maintain that they still have the capacity to rediscover secret indigenous ceremonial knowledge without tribal assistance, even though local THPOs have come to insist otherwise. These conservative antiquarians appear to include research partners Mary Gage and her son, James, who are referred to in antiquarian circles simply as "the Gages." In their 2017 self-published book, *Land of a Thousand Cairns: Revival of Old-Style Ceremonies*, the Gages credit nineteenth-century farmers in Hopkinton, Rhode Island, with covertly reviving older hypothesized ceremonial stone practices, a claim based on their studies of the Manitou Hassannash Preserve and adjacent properties. Though the Gages admit that they "lack formal verification," they propose that these farmers, part of the presumably Euro-American Foster family lineage, were actually Indians who secretly passed as white to avoid persecution by a public that "no longer accepted…their ceremonies," including the "Winter Solstice, Underworld, Serpent, and Spring Rainwater" ceremonies. Their inspirational conclusion that the "Foster farms were a gathering place for the tribal community" could revolutionize mainstream New England history if that "formal verification" were ever published. As far as I know, *Land of a Thousand Cairns* has not been publicly endorsed by any of the region's THPOs. Nonetheless, it stands as a triumph of virtue signaling among ceremonial stone activists at large in that it certifies its authors as advocates deeply concerned about the welfare of endangered, though perhaps largely imagined, Indian spiritualities.

Advocate identities are established through practice, with ceremonial stone landscape activism providing a narrative context. Harris praises "non-natives who are stewards in their own community of ceremonial landscapes" (2014). Among these stewards is the previously introduced Lisa McLoughlin, a Doctor of Science and Technologies Studies (Massachusetts Land Trust Coalition 2018), whose "chance finding of a yellowing poster board advertising the New England Antiquities Research Association" started her journey to becoming the politically consequential ceremonial stone landscape researcher and activist that she is today (McLoughlin 2017). Her volunteer work includes reconnoitering landscapes, which involves preparing "photos and information to feed back to the tribes" and presenting "the stones as possible material culture to descendant communities," framing "that cultural finding in political terms that invite their engagement in the federal legal structure" (McLoughlin 2017). She also coordinates crowdfunding, having raised over $8000 (not counting possible matching donations) to support the legal costs of a ceremonial stone landscape preservation campaign in Sandisfield, Massachusetts (Climate Action Now 2017a, 2017b), and aiming to raise $5000 for the direct support of Harris to "allow Doug to continue serving the land through preservation projects" (McLoughlin 2020).

She also provides a very thought-provoking commentary on her political stature as an activist supporting the cause:

> First and foremost, I have to recognize that however much I am drawn to the Native Americans – not abstractly to their culture, but concretely, as cultural property belonging to Native American people. I have made a conscious decision to realize first that what I study is Theirs. I mean this in the most respectful way, in a way that says: This is Not Mine. That is really hard for me to do. As someone who finds spirit in nature, I had to let go of any claims I wanted to have on these structures. The way I deal with that is a realization that while I have to let go of claims, I do not have to let go of the feelings. Feelings are personal, claims are political. I keep my feelings to myself and I never 'own' them in public because (repeat it with me now) It is Theirs. (McLoughlin 2017)

As an individual who is mindful of her Indian ancestry and "finds spirit in nature," McLoughlin would seem reasonably justified in feeling entitled to include suspected ceremonial stone landscape features among her cultural patrimony. But she also realizes that she "had to let go of any claims," I presume to avoid violating the racialized political order surrounding ceremonial stone landscape activism. The racial deference she broadcasts toward her essentialized Indian subject-supervisors is unambiguous, both in the tone of her writing and in her selective capitalization of the pronoun "Their." I wonder if, at some level, McLoughlin understands that she is operating within a very questionable system of racial accounting and is willing to perform whatever intellectual gymnastics are required to mitigate the cognitive dissonance she is experiencing in the process? Within this realm of less-than-ideal tradeoffs, she would appear to bargain for whatever she can. She reports that her rewards include "this gift: outsider status" (McLoughlin 2017), which I presume refers to the approval of her tribal partners.

Since expressing that thought, she has only reinforced that system of racial accounting by re-framing Euro-American ceremonial stone landscape believers, such as herself, as comprising a distinct religious group that she calls the "US Pagans." She characterizes them as a "transplanted people" who must come to terms with the fact that they are living "uninvited" on indigenous lands. She hopes that they "can find a way to relate to…the land that avoids cultural appropriation" (McLoughlin 2019). McLoughlin insists that "political justice requires that US Pagans, being non-indigenous, somehow attempt to receive permission or recognition from Indigenous Americans." If I understand McLoughlin correctly, a formal appeal to indigenous cultural authority resulting in a positive response would seem to present a moral precondition to any spiritually legitimate worship or for the honoring of New England's ceremonial stone landscapes by "US Pagans" like herself.

To express some thoughts of my own—first, any belief system where Indians are framed as spiritual or moral gatekeepers for settler colonists does not sound like a step forward for race relations. Second, her identification of a secretive settler colonial minority long dedicated to honoring ancient indigenous stonework may sound surprising, but it is not original; it was woven throughout *Manitou's* narrative (Mavor and Dix 1989). I think it is quite possible that she is merely populating this hypothesized minority with flesh-and-blood people in the here and now, in the style of fulfilling a prophecy. Last, I remind you that all of this is downstream of her chance encounter with "a yellowing poster board advertising the New England Antiquities Research Association."

The boldest *advocate* identity assertions, in my "lived experience," come from the ceremonial stone landscape activist vanguard's white male demographic, whose practices have included sending me e-mails that do little more than pronounce opposition to me as a token enemy of Indians. Some webpage authors similarly register their innocence toward Indians by contrasting themselves against the guilty. For example, in his illustrated essay, "The Process of Pasturization: A Tale of Two Tims," a fellow Tim expresses how gratifying it feels to champion social and political values that are in polar opposition to what he suggests are mine (MacSweeney 2016). Elsewhere, he takes his criticism to the next level, imploring, "When will the time come when an archaeologist's reputation be in jeopardy for NOT recognizing Stone Features of the Sacred Ceremonial Landscape?" (Ibid. 2015). Others accuse the MHC of harboring a "deeply engrained" Eurocentrism (FlazyJ 2016), and of being "crooks" who have "done nothing to protect the archaeological resources of this state" (Concord Oral History Program 2010).

Such moral exhibitionism underscores the principle that social identities only exist in the interactions between people. DiMarzo, who served as NEARA's Rhode Island Regional Coordinator while working with his organization's dramatically named Rapid Documentation Unit of Stone Structure Researchers, illustrates as much when he defines a space for himself between the Narragansett Indian Tribe and a culturally oppressive academic regime, one in which antiquarian practices seem to present a prelude to restorative justice:

> Our work continues now in Coventry, where Todd has located, once again, another valuable area steeped in these stone structures. Only through careful documentation will the experts, both researchers and academics, be able to discern what may be indeed field clearing vs sacred/ceremonial stone structures deliberately constructed for various reasons, which we "White" people, either won't understand or will never understand. However, it is the height of elitism and disrespect for those in academia to try to tell the Narragansett Tribal Elders or for that matter any Native American Tribe what these stone structures mean! Shame on those who are still messing with the Natives 400+ years after first contact believing that they know better! We will keep you posted! (Comment posted by Steve DiMarzo, following Drummond 2015.)

From my perspective, DiMarzo and like-minded *advocates* espouse, to borrow the words of indigenous Australian lawyer Noel Pearson, "a social morality designed to rebuild moral authority by simultaneously acknowledging past racial injustices while separating themselves from those injustices" (2007) through the practice Steele calls "dissociation" (2006).

This practice, within the context of ceremonial stone landscape activism, aims to dichotomize white settler colonists into two classes—a reformed class (what I call *advocates)* that is entitled to moral authority, and an unreformed class that is not. Like that of many ceremonial stone landscape activists, DiMarzo's work seems to exemplify how representations of history are mobilized as "resources that can be used to influence what social identity becomes salient for a person, and whether that identity is perceived as positive or negative" (Dresler-Hawke and Liu 2006:133), perhaps galvanizing a perception of Indians, to borrow the words of a sociologist, "as objects capable of conferring redemption"

(Hughey 2012:229).

So we return to the ultimatum, "Which side are you on?" by taking a critical look at how certain academics demonstrate that they are on "the right side."

CHAPTER NINETEEN

A "GOOD GUYS VERSUS BAD GUYS" MINDSET

Anakin Skywalker: I've just learned a terrible truth. I think Chancellor
Palpatine is a Sith Lord.
Mace Windu: A Sith Lord?
Anakin Skywalker: Yes. The one we've been looking for.
Mace Windu: ...Then our worst fears have been realized.
—*Star Wars Episode III: Revenge of The Sith*

I AM KNOWN AMONG PEERS and serial public audience members
as someone who enjoys breaking up his own potentially boring
lectures with melodramatic spectacles, often seasoned with a compul-
sory dash of mildly regrettable self-deprecation. And I am lazy about
it, routinely mining the Star Wars franchise for material. As a fan who
is deep enough in it to commission his own custom lightsaber from a
professional machinist, and having been asked a question at my doctoral defense forwarded to my committee by George Lucas himself, what
archaeologist would be more entitled to appropriate Star Wars? So when
I discuss soil stratigraphy, do not be surprised if I include a doctored
photo showing me carving out a core sample using what appears to be a
fully operational lightsaber. And when I discuss the topic of ceremonial
stone landscapes, I may direct people to send criticisms to my office in
the Death Star's throne room.

By now, you have probably gathered that I do not actually see real
life, past or present, as a moral melodrama populated by "good guys"
and "bad guys." But I have come to understand, all too well, that many,
particularly those on the political left, faithfully cling to such a vision.

Naturally, they must imagine themselves on the side of the angels, otherwise, they lack the moral authority to enjoy whatever fortunes or advantages they possess that others may lack in the mist of what they imagine is a great battle to level humanity's playing field. Though I am willing to hold many of their feet to the hot coals of the regrettable things that they have, of their own volition, said and done in the service of advancing and protecting the ceremonial stone landscape perspective, I do not by any stretch of the imagination attempt to convince anybody else that these people are bad-natured or that they deserve to be silenced.

I have not received the same affordances in return. As someone who has unashamedly asked critical questions of ceremonial stone landscape activism, I have been called many things, including arrogant, colonial, jingoistic, racist, and evil. I have been threatened before giving a lecture, had politicians and colleagues forward me an email originating from an activist attempting to brand me as a propagandist, and been notified by journal editors that antiquarians have independently contacted them in attempts to protest and/or preempt the publication of my research. In other words, a number of ceremonial stone landscape activists have taken a "cancel culture" approach toward my presence on the scene, aiming to discredit and silence me rather than engage my ideas transparently and publicly.

The bottom line is that when people imagine they are on the side of the angels, they will do almost anything to get their way, even if that requires disregarding the ethical standards of civilized life. I presume the problem they imagine I pose justifies their means. Perhaps I am the Sith Lord the ceremonial stone landscape activists have been looking for. If so, their worst fears have been realized. But seriously, I have probably provided them with a very sturdy crutch in terms of group identity, which is clearly at the heart of all of this. What brings people together in fevered solidarity better than the threat posed by a common enemy? Seeing that these activists cannot even agree on what constitutes a ceremonial stone landscape, my looming presence on the scene as a "non-believer" would seem to hold all the more value.

Relatively speaking, such explicit melodrama is all fine and dandy as far as I am concerned. At least there is no doubt about its intentions. What I find more unsettling is how leftist scholars go about much the same work in such a seemingly innocent fashion. Of course, they cannot call people any of the aforementioned words in their publications; it is below their station. They are more subversive, and arguably, far more subtly compelling in their effect.

Their chief methods are precisely the same as those of many anti-quarians: information filtering, verbal sleight of hand, clever stigmatization of dissenters, and the galvanization of an imagination of Indians as permanent victims in need of assistance from deep thinkers such as themselves. In the balance of such antics, which tend to pass theater for scholarship, the enemy appears to be laid bare and the position of the author among "the good guys" is conveniently revealed. In Chapter 22, I show you what these practices look like, and explain why I find them concerning. But first, it bears explaining why leftist scholars have involved themselves in the ceremonial stone landscape controversy.

CHAPTER TWENTY

THE ACADEMIC SWAMP

C EREMONIAL STONE LANDSCAPE activism has attracted a modest halo of leftist scholars for reasons that run deep. To efficiently explain when and why this has occurred, I must resort to some straw-mannery. Let us begin by acknowledging that American four-year colleges and universities have been leaning far left since at least 2007, and that New England is largely responsible for swinging the national balance in that direction (Jaschik 2012, 2016, 2017). As a professor of politics who has studied this issue advises, "I cannot say for certain why New England is so far to the left. But what I can say, based on the evidence, is that if you are looking for an ideologically balanced education, don't put New England on the top of your list" (Abrams 2016). The ideological consensus among leftist professors in the humanities and social sciences provides a "safe space" to freely explore and promote a broad spectrum of untested, and potentially dangerous, ideas, unfettered by the clear principles and internally consistent cannons that inform true disciplines such as chemistry, mathematics, and physics. Simply put, the main goal of leftist scholars is to generate new ideas, primarily for an audience of their peers, to deconstruct, debate, and celebrate. Many of their publications are virtually unreadable to anyone beyond their peer circles, due to excessive verbosity and a scarcity of clear lessons that can be applied to real world phenomena. Part of what makes this all so fun is that there are no immediate consequences for being wrong.

The most extreme of such scholars behave, in many regards, like my favorite animals—frogs. These slippery, short-term thinkers are drawn to the shiniest and fastest moving targets coming into season, leaping at novel ideas and "paradigm shifts." Their data must follow their theories wherever they may happen to go. Mobility is vital to their sense of security, which involves finding new ideological pads to occupy whenever old ones start sinking. And, come springtime, they eagerly crank out a batch of younger versions of themselves who are ill-equipped to thrive beyond their natal swamp. Departments must pretend that none of this is the case if they are concerned about maintaining enrollment, which, of course, they are. How many anthropology department home pages advertise that in 2012, *Forbes* magazine determined that "Anthropology and Archaeology" was the worst major for U.S. students to pursue, provided their goal was to become economically self-sufficient adults (Goudreau 2012)?

Another important principle to keep in mind is that the career trajectories of leftist scholars are often deeply informed by moral vanities that otherwise have no influence whatsoever over those of scholars working in the parallel universe of STEM disciplines. As a University of Connecticut professor warned in 1995, too many anthropologists were abandoning the production of objective research to pursue "moral careers" whereby data is produced for sociopolitical engineering purposes on behalf of the presumably oppressed, cultivating a climate of "denunciation and rage" toward anyone who stands in their way (D'Andrade 1995). He must be spinning in his grave. As argued by anthropologist Peter Wood in his 2006 book, *A Bee in the Mouth: Anger in America Now,* American culture at large has entered into an enduring age of "New Anger" where performative outrage is expected behavior (Wood 2006). This certainly rings true in the field of archaeology, where contributions coming from sources other than the political left are often met with nothing less than "denunciation and rage."

Consider the case of *Repatriation and Erasing the Past,* the 2020 book by archaeologist Elizabeth Weiss and attorney James Springer, which endured a crowdsourced cancellation campaign for the sin of taking a "critical look at laws that mandate the return of [Native American] human remains from museums and laboratories to ancestral burial grounds." One university professor, who provided no indication of having read the book, felt sufficiently informed to proclaim in a Tweet that it was "racist garbage and needs to be pulled immediately" (Schneider 2020). Calls for book cancellations have become a disturbingly common phenomenon in the world of publishing. Anyone who is not alarmed by the growth of a contemporary mass "book-burning" movement is either supporting one or failing to recognize that such movements have always represented historically particular calls to power by particular contingents of societies.

Today, leftist scholars pursuing their moral careers are determined to recruit like-minded colleagues, and take on likeminded students. For me, this point really hit home when I was filling out job applications (ca. 2010-2012), hoping to land a tenure-track anthropology position in academia (Ives 2018). Many of the applications required a so-called "diversity statement." According to *InsideHigherEd.com*, the best topics to address in such are one's relationship to "racial oppression, sexism, homophobia, transphobia, ableism or some other commonly recognized form of oppression" (Golash-Boza 2016). In other words, diversity statements require their authors to demonstrate how compellingly they can portray themselves as victims or rescuers. I can think of no clearer testament to the ideological stranglehold the political left has on today's humanities and social sciences, or a more effective tool by which to restrict the breadth of intellectual and political diversity on today's college campuses, than a requirement for job applicants to furnish these testaments (Gilley 2017).

And it does not help that university department faculty across the U.S. have increasingly shifted their traditional teaching responsibilities to graduate students, who often lack sufficient training, knowledge, and wisdom. When dropped into this situation by tenured professors holding the keys to their academic success, many of these graduate student-instructors, some nearly as young and green as their undergraduate pupils, find themselves, quite understandably, with an intellectual deficit on their hands. But this reality, along with the self-doubt it should arouse, is easily evaded. Tethering one's pedagogy to notions of social justice and activism affords an automatic claim to moral superiority and, by extension, social legitimacy, which most undergraduate students cannot readily distinguish from intellectual competency.

A fundamental political shift has everything to do with when and why ceremonial stone landscapes transitioned from being the latest antiquarian theory ignored by leftist academics (pre-ca. 2008) to an intriguing new Indian paradigm defended by leftist academics (post-ca. 2008) (Ives 2018). The antiquarians who had gotten nowhere with all of this for so many years had been encumbered with an unsurmountable epistemological handicap. They were predominantly middle-class whites who did not fit the victimhood profile that attracts the special interests and sympathies of leftist scholars. They were automatic suspects of perpetuating romantic misconceptions about indigenous people in potentially harmful ways, which, I admit, appears close to the mark. In accordance with their special brand of hubris, leftist academics believe that only they are intellectually sophisticated enough to transcend romantic preconceptions and appropriately "handle" the presumably fragile cultural interests of indigenous people without causing them further settler colonial-induced harm. Promoting this neurotic outlook is precisely how they generate a demand for their special services.

The fact that the academy neglects to openly acknowledge the central role white antiquarians have played in the development and propagation of the ceremonial stone landscape paradigm is very much in step with the hollow nature of so-called cultural relativism as practiced by the left at large. Essentially, leftist academics feel no obligation to acknowledge the cultural appropriation of a white settler colonial ideology by Indian tribal officials. But I presume they would be extremely concerned over appropriations of Indian ideologies by white settler colonists. In other words, they are not concerned with holistically exploring the nature and position of various individuals subscribing to various group identities in the postcolonial intellectual economy; they are concerned with theatrically foregrounding the presumed, and apparently never-ending, power white settler colonists have over indigenous people. As noble as this project may sound, it effectively guarantees that white settler colonial agency will be very carefully filtered. Clearly, the world cannot rely on such academics to speak broadly and objectively on the topic of ceremonial stone landscapes, much less expect them to admit that they view objectivity as a lost cause.

The 2008 victory that southern New England THPOs claimed at the Turners Falls Municipal Airport in Montague, Massachusetts (NRHP 2008; Timreck 2010), was more than just a symbolic win for decolonialism—it set a major political shift in motion. Its significance rose to a much higher level than the town of Carlisle's decision to endorse a ceremonial stone landscape interpretation of the Benfield Parcel "A" property in 2006. The Turners Falls victory marked the political legitimization of ceremonial stone landscape ideology by the highest-ranking historic preservation authority in the U.S.—the Keeper of the National Register of Historic Places. Many professional archaeologists working in New England's cultural resource management industry were shocked. This turn would, predictably, magnify pre-existing political tensions between Indian cultural representatives and professional archaeologists who are otherwise expected to work together effectively and efficiently on federally regulated undertakings. Spaces once filled with reasonably productive cooperation and a dash of good faith shrank as the moral authority of decolonialism expanded.

Others perceived the Turners Falls victory as a beacon of light, or perhaps more of a distress signal, from the most oppressed people imaginable—small remnants of indigenous populations struggling to protect their presumably sacred patrimony from certain desecration. The "indigenization" of the ceremonial stone landscape cause created a virgin social justice front for leftist academics to colonize. And this ideological advance would not be limited to academics. Even a few professional archaeologists eager to morally one-up their colleagues have taken to casting cultural resource management archaeology as an instrument of settler colonial oppression.

But the political needle has been drifting toward ritual settler colonial self-flagellation for some time. As one northeastern archaeologist with decades of experience observed, it has become routine for "negative characterizations" to be "made of non-Native archaeologists and their relationships with Native peoples," and for indigenous cultural advocacy to "insert itself into or in some cases" supplant "scientific inquiry, a circumstance that can affect not only archaeology but other areas in contemporary American Indian Studies" (Starna 2017:122). A Canadian ethnographer recalled the decadence of his field in the late twentieth century in these terms:

> [I]n the late stages of an age of identity politics, considerable care has been invested in grooming anthropologists not so much as intellectuals but rather as practically oriented professionals who wish to proclaim their sympathies and solidarity with Indigenous peoples and to place their services at the disposal of Aboriginal leaders. (Dyck 2006)

What he describes applies to the current situation in southern New England, one where collaborative archaeologists almost appear to be working on parole for the crimes of their settler colonial ancestors and the sins of their discipline.

CHAPTER TWENTY-ONE

THE HUNT FOR REDNECK ARCHAEOLOGY

As far as I can tell, New England's archaeologists are, on balance, politically left-of-center to begin with and largely dedicated to the ideals of diversity and cultural relativism. I suppose this is what makes ceremonial stone landscape activism's apparent interest in rooting out old bigotries among them seem so conspicuously misplaced and frustratingly counterproductive. Nevertheless, this interest has inflated a "guilty until proven innocent" mentality within the field, whereby innocence from racism is readily claimed by any archaeologist willing to publicly embrace the social morality of *advocates*. What I find amazing is the fact that none seem willing to so much as acknowledge the possibility that these actions may have costs. Costs such as promoting a view of Indians as victims requiring outside help, or further entrenching a view of Indians as an exquisitely sensitive class of people whose interests must be engaged with extreme caution. Such views are, arguably, discriminatory and perhaps even reflect a subtle form of human betrayal. Of course, it would be reassuring to presume that publicly casting oneself as a "good guy," specifically in regard to Indians, is a harmless action without complicated side effects, as if society is not largely a system of complicated side effects set in motion by the actions of individuals.

Robinson, when serving as Rhode Island's state archaeologist, would seem to be a "good guy" when he coined the term "redneck archaeologist" in the 2008 documentary film *Great Falls* (Timreck 2010[2008]). Regarding the age of a particular Indian stone feature, he explained to Harris, "You'll never convince redneck archaeologists that that date's as-

171

sociated with this thing…Maybe you don't need to. Because the number of redneck archaeologists I think is getting smaller and smaller." Essentially, he points to a moral fault line dividing the archaeological profession. Socially progressive archaeologists stand safely with Robinson on one side, while a doomed generation of unreformed, and presumably racist, archaeologists stand on the other. I still do not know who any of those redneck archaeologists were or are. Until Robinson identifies them with certainty, I will continue interpreting his rhetorical nod toward them as a dissociative performance registering an anti-racist position.

Arguably, Robinson's modest reputation as an intellectual who is sympathetic toward Narragansett Indian tribal interests has long existed at the pleasure of the tribe's THPO and hereditary Medicine Man, John Brown III. Consider that Robinson's doctoral research (Robinson 1990) centered on his analysis of skeletal remains that he helped excavate from a seventeenth-century Narragansett Indian cemetery in North Kingstown, Rhode Island, registered as RI-1000. Several archaeologists made that 1983 excavation, which occurred years before the passage of the Native American Graves Protection and Repatriation Act, an object of their scholarship (Robinson, Kelly, and Rubertone 1985; Rubertone 1994, 2001; Turnbaugh 1984, 1993). At the center of that scholarship were the ancestors of contemporary Narragansetts such as Brown III, who visited the RI-1000 excavation as a young man. Robinson not only learned what it felt like to crouch over the skeletons of Narragansett ancestors who had been ravaged by malnutrition and European diseases, he learned what it felt like to do so while falling beneath the shadow of a man who embodied a moral superior, as dictated by politics, and who would eventually rise to become one of the most outspoken, influential, and administratively engaged Indian cultural authorities in New England. The US Department of the Interior's 1996 affirmation of Brown III as the Narragansett Indian Tribe's THPO effectively instituted him as Robinson's primary tribal partner in Rhode Island archaeology for the remainder of his career.

Of course, there is no way for me to know for sure if the psychosocial phenomenon known as "white guilt" influenced Robinson's professional work, but the circumstances for such a development were not exactly unfavorable. Regardless, it seems worth noting that one does not cultivate an identity as a collaborative archaeologist by disagreeing with one's advertised tribal partner on key issues and that, theoretically speaking, the work of archaeologists who do not pursue a collaborative identity is less likely to be constrained by identity politics.

Since resigning from the RIHPHC in 2011, Robinson has served as an adjunct professor of anthropology at Rhode Island College and has pursued collaborative work with Doug Harris (long-time Deputy THPO to Brown III) that advances the ceremonial stone landscape paradigm. Writing in the capacity of the former Rhode Island State Archaeologist, he listed himself as junior co-author to Harris in a *Northeast Anthropology* article titled "The Ancient Ceremonial Landscape and King Philip's War Battlefields of Nipsachuck" (Harris and Robinson 2015). It discusses an area in North Smithfield, Rhode Island, where they report "sacred ceremonial stone features" were "used by the people to participate directly in the ways of the universe" (Ibid.:140). No photographs, representations, or metrics of any stone features are included, nor are any maps or illustrations depicting the impressive list of celestial phenomena to which they are noted to articulate. Their data-free claims must be taken on faith, against a broadly woven backdrop of historical and circumstantial context that contains no complicating facts or perspectives from potentially relevant sources (e.g., Gero 1989; Leveillee 1997, 1998, 2001; Ives 2013a, 2015a, 2015b; Jones 2015; Moeller 1987; Walwer 2015).

Identity positioning has proven contagious among certain scholars whose rhetoric suggests that professional archaeology is a nefarious enterprise in need of major reform. Dr. Craig Cipolla, Associate Curator of North American Archaeology with the Royal Ontario Museum and current director of the Mohegan Archaeological Field School based out of Montville, Connecticut, casts himself as such a reformer. Self-identifying as a "Euro-American academic archaeologist" (Cipolla and Quinn 2016:119) and "a descendant of settler colonists" (Cipolla et al. 2019:128), Cipolla's potential to harm his indigenous partners would appear to be checked by the fact that his field school is "an equal partnership between the tribe and an academic archaeologist" (Institute for Field Research 2020). He clarifies that his archaeological field school is not "a traditional wolf in collaborative sheep's clothing" (Cipolla and Quinn 2016:126) and follows the general playbook of collaborative archaeologists who are preeminently concerned with, to borrow the words of a seasoned Canadian archaeologist, "mitigating the presumed negative effects of archaeological practice on the living descendants of the communities that are studied" (McGhee 2008:581). Cipolla may be following the lead of his former mentor, Dr. Stephen Silliman, who launched a collaborative archaeological field school with the nearby Eastern Pequot Tribe. Silliman conspicuously signals his harmlessness toward his Eastern Pequot partners, submitting to an independent tribal audit at the end of each field day, not to prove that he is not trying to "run off with something" but merely to assure them that "everything is okay" (Wellner 2005:38).

Cipolla's field school assumes a postmodern cultural relativist position toward stone features that they find in the woods, teaching students "to respect all such features for what they could be" (Cipolla and Quinn 2016:123-124). This appears to be in step with his stated responsibility of "introducing mechanisms for change and decolonization" of the archaeological discipline and using archaeology to "grab the assumptions you hold dearest and shake them until they fall apart" (Harris and Cipolla 2017:3).

If there are "bad guys" in archaeology, Cipolla could not be mistaken for one. He critiques professional archaeologists whom he proposes seek "comfort in the practical, perhaps safer, interpretation of all such [stone] features as related to white farming practices" (Cipolla 2018), which he suggests is aimed at "purifying" land to clear it for modern development. He applauds Indians who have risen to challenge this practice. He also encourages those who engage New England's "contested stone heritage" to embrace a "flat ontology," which I think means that every group's way of thinking about a given phenomenon deserves to be counted, and that recognizing one school of thought as more legitimate than another is potentially oppressive. To me, this sounds both elegant and forward-thinking.

And if I understand his theory correctly, the thoughts and ideas of antiquarians should be taken just as seriously as those of Indians. However, Cipolla does not appear to take antiquarians very seriously, qualifying them as little more than an "interest" group of "romantics" who sometimes have a "staunch disregard for contemporary Indigenous people" (Cipolla 2018:60). Though I generally agree with Cipolla on those points, I insist that gaining a holistic understanding of the Ceremonial Stone Landscape Movement requires taking a serious and sustained look at the rather prominent, if not central, role of those antiquarians. Perhaps an archaeologist like me, who does not advertise that he is in a committed relationship with a THPO who appears to be in a committed relationship with the movement, as evidenced by policy decisions, is freer to take that look.

Dr. Christina DeLucia, Assistant Professor of History at Williams College, appears to cast ceremonial stone landscape activism as a political advance against settler colonialism in her 2018 book, *Memory Lands:*

King Philip's War and the Place of Violence in the Northeast (2018:280-81). Therein, she shares the position that "the very questioning of ceremonial landscape claims can be seen as retrenchment of antitribal ways of thinking and seeing" (2018:280). Though this statement could be seen as sympathetic toward Indian subjects, its author's inner social detective must have at least momentarily considered the likelihood that some white readers would take it as a warning never to question a ceremonial stone landscape claim because the very act could get them branded a racist.

A frequent grievance aired by ceremonial stone landscape activists is that archaeologists at large believe that Indians never built stone structures prior to European colonization and that all stone structures standing today were created by farmers. In researching this book, I could not find a single quote from an archaeologist to substantiate this accusation. The closest thing I found was a passage from a short, obscure article published in 1973 stating that the "Indians of the Northeast did not use stone architecture" (Hall and Woodman 1973), which is, by and large, a reasonable statement. Of course, most archaeologists would probably agree that *most* stone structures on previously farmed land are likely agricultural in origin. But this is different from declaring that *all* stone structures are agricultural in origin. As I see it, ceremonial stone landscape activists have a great incentive to swap out *all* for *most* in this context. By choosing to use the term *all*, they get to promote their narrative—a narrative that archaeology is determined to erase sacred Indian heritage and needs to be redeemed.

Skeptics such as I might be willing to buy into this narrative if it were backed by facts rather than innuendos, blanket condemnations, and unsupported criticisms from the anointed. For example, take the case of Curtiss Hoffman. In his 2019 book, *Stone Prayers: Native American Stone Constructions of the Eastern Seaboard*, he states that "'rock piles' are considered by some—by Ives in particular—as all being of post-Contact Euro-American construction, while cairns might not be. I disagree with Ives about this" (Hoffman 2019:61). Hoffman seems unaware of a more fundamental issue, which is the fact that I have never, in speech or writing, ever supported such a black-and-white position, either toward "rock piles" or "cairns." But for his purposes of argumentation, it is convenient to claim that I did. To back this inaccurate claim, he cites an article that I published in 2015 (Ives 2015a) but does not include any supporting quotes (because none exist). I find it curious that Hoffman frames my contribution to the discourse on contested stone features through repeated reference to that one short article. Two other related articles that I had already published, which I presume he read (in fact, he listened to me read a version of one at a conference), do not turn up on his academic radar (Ives 2013a, 2015b). I speculate that some of the information contained in those articles, and particularly in the one titled "Romance, Redemption, and Ceremonial Stone Landscapes" (2015b), were so threatening to his ideological vision that a turning away presented a justifiable course.

Alexandra Martin, a recently-minted anthropology doctor from the College of William and Mary, has also joined the ceremonial stone landscape activist mission. She wrote her dissertation on the topic of ceremonial stone landscapes in collaboration with the THPOs of "the Mashantucket Pequot, Mohegan, Narragansett, and Wampanoag of Gay Head (Aquinnah)," who apparently required her college to enforce a moratorium on its publication until February 2, 2030 (Martin 2017). Ironically, her dissertation is listed on a website titled "W&M ScholarWorks: Open Access to Scholarly Research." At least the abstract is available, which shows that Martin has adopted the ceremonial stone landscape narrative to frame her scholarship. She premises that tribal officials "have been ignored" and that "the legacy of colonialism and the historic bias that it has instilled in New England has led to dismissal of Tribal ceremonial stone landscapes," resulting in their destruction. She claims that her work helps "maintain Tribal connections to ceremonial places" and contributes "to the new colonial history of New England." Presumably, she continues to build that "new colonial history" through her work with Ceremonial Landscapes Research, LLC, serving as the company's designated Registered Professional Archaeologist. Unfortunately, the reports her company produces for its clients, the same four THPOs she consulted with on her dissertation, are also confidential. Ultimately, Martin's archaeological research appears to be confined to a political bubble that is beyond the reach of the archaeological profession at large.

Dr. Laurie Rush, Cultural Resources Manager and Army Archaeologist stationed at Fort Drum, New York, takes a stern posture toward archaeologists who remain unconvinced of the ceremonial stone landscape paradigm's legitimacy. Her seminal research on this topic was conducted at Fort Drum, where she reports having documented sacred celestial alignments among an array of boulders (Timreck 2010[2008]). If I understand correctly, her research is beyond the full scrutiny of her peers, presumably according to its culturally sensitive nature. In a lecture for the Archaeological Institute of America titled "Ceremonial Stone Landscapes of Northeastern North America," she states the following, before listing *Manitou* as a recommended reading:

> Over the past 350 years, Europeans have systematically separated Native Americans of northeastern North America from their places of religious significance and ceremony. Disenfranchisement has taken the form of characterizing sacred places as locations of devil worship; attribution of aboriginal stone architecture to ancient European visitors; failure to appreciate Native American understanding of celestial events, and archaeological identification of aboriginal stone features as farmers' piles and root cellars. (Rush 2019)

Following her logic, calling a root cellar a root cellar might translate into much more than a "microaggression" toward Indian representatives. It might represent yet another step forward in the broader disenfranchisement of indigenous people everywhere.

One of her related presentations states that "'All cairns in New England are stone piles made by Colonial farmers' is not a true statement" (Rush 2016). But, to date, I am not aware of any researcher from New England who has ever made such a statement. In the absence of real adversaries, it appears that ceremonial stone landscape activists are in the business of inventing them. According to contract archaeologists Charity (formerly Moore) and Matthew Weiss, who insist that "archaeologists *can* [emphasis in original] learn to read the landscape and take on the responsibility of speaking on behalf of disenfranchised native peoples" (Moore and Weiss 2016:45), have stated that the Massachusetts Historical Commission's (MHC) website "claims that no Native American stone features are located in the state" of Massachusetts (Weiss and Weiss 2017). The problem is, such a statement has never appeared on their website, though it does feature the following objective and clearly written statement:

> Piles or continuous walls of fieldstones are common in rural Massachusetts wherever there are rocky soils. When historians and archaeologists have conducted thorough, professional research into such stone piles, they have invariably shown that these features are not associated with the Native American settlement of Massachusetts. (Massachusetts Historical Commission n.d.)

If and when "thorough, professional research" furnishes an example of these features being associated with Indian religious construction or practices, I, as well as MHC archaeologists, would certainly be interested. But I, for one, have no stake in becoming enlightened by an activist movement with closely guarded data. I do, however, remain open to becoming convinced of that movement's specific archaeological assertions and implications, when substantive supporting evidence is widely shared and understood within my profession.

Unfortunately, reports produced by Ceremonial Landscapes Research LLC, contribute nothing to archaeological discourse because they are kept secret from the archaeological community at large. A secret dissertation is equally useless, as are announcements of profound but largely confidential discoveries at Fort Drum by Rush. Does a stack of NEARA publications and self-published books by this organization's members, which collectively showcase highly varied and often conflicting ideas, provide a solid basis on which to form an archaeological position? No. Subtle indictments of nonbelievers by ceremonial stone landscape activists, which have apparently come to include a few archaeologists, do nothing to advance archaeological discourse. They merely raise the political temperature. I believe that, ultimately, they are performative registrations of moral superiority by people who feel compelled to serve ceremonial stone landscape activism's warrant.

Antiquarians serve this warrant in the same fashion. For instance, NEARA's Norman Muller insists:

> There is a view common among many archaeologists in the Northeast that the American Indians of the region didn't learn how to build with stone until they were taught by the colonial settlers in the seventeenth century, implying that they were somehow deficient in constructing with stone until then. (2015:29)

In his mission to "change the mindset of regional archaeologists," he overlooks the testimony of Elder Narragansett Indian Tribal Medicine Man Lloyd Wilcox, as featured in the 2008 *Stories in Stone*, a documentary film about Narragansett Indian stonemasonry that I have repeatedly viewed on public television and shown in university classrooms:

> One thing you should understand, the Narragansetts, precolonial Narragansetts, to my knowledge, did not build stone walls. Why would people—the Woodland Indians—where everything was wood and bark and cloth and squash and corn and fish and game, unless they were building a fish trap in a very small stream or something along

those lines, there would be no need. The trade was learned, not the handling of stone. Stone men we were in terms of our utensils and weapons and what not. The building in stone was, as it was told to me, learned from the English, from the English settlers. And it ends up that because we were much better related to stone, we end up exceeding the people that taught us. [transcribed from Level and Dekel 2008]

Yes, this testimony comes from the same Medicine Man that Harris points to as the spiritual father of the Ceremonial Stone Landscape Movement. Of course, if a white archaeologist so much as suggested that the Narragansett Indians had learned "building in stone…from the English," activists would swiftly condemn that archaeologist as racist.

Despite the accessibility of Wilcox's seemingly important testimony, it has never, to my knowledge, been cited by any antiquarian nor by any of the presumably well-informed scholars and professionals mentioned in this chapter. Not even Paul Robinson, whose career has centered on studying Narragansett Indian archaeology and history. This conspicuously selective silence betrays the sociopolitical aims of ceremonial stone landscape activism, which appear to be preeminently concerned with virtue signaling, stigmatizing dissenters, outsourcing moral authority to categorically oppressed "others," and checking the spread of inconvenient information—even if it comes from their movement's symbolic founder. Contrast Wilcox's testimony with the first sentence of the prologue to *Manitou*:

> The early seventeenth-century English settlers of America called the land New England because, among other reasons, it reminded them of home; they saw stone walls, standing stones and stone heaps like those of the English countryside. (Mavor and Dix 1989:1)

Essentially, Mavor and Dix premise that the stone walls and heaps that are ubiquitous throughout New England's countryside were present when the Mayflower arrived, because Native Americans had already built them. This was *their* vision.

To describe this ideological entanglement of professional and academic archaeologists, tribal authorities, and antiquarians as a bona fide conspiracy would be inaccurate. These actors are generally too far afield from, and often too deeply in competition with, one another to effectively coordinate, yet they have a powerful net effect on how the issue of ceremonial stone landscapes is presented to the world at large. Thomas Sowell describes how this sort of thing works:

It is not necessary for either individuals or a cabal to work out a plan of deliberate deception for filtering of information to produce a distorted picture that resembles the vision of the anointed rather than the reality of the world. All that is necessary is that those in a position to filter – whether they are reporters, editors, teachers, scholars, or movie-makers – decide that there are certain aspects of reality that the masses would "misunderstand" and which a sense of social responsibility requires those in a position to filter and leave out. (Sowell 2011:198)

Historian Dr. Alice Dreger once wrote "forms of 'scholarship' that deny evidence, that deny truth, that deny the importance of facts—even if performed in the name of good—are dangerous not only to science and to ethics, but to democracy. And so they are dangerous ultimately to humankind" (2011). I am not sure which is more alarming—the fact that some scholars do not seem to agree with her wisdom, or the fact that most are no longer willing to admit that they do.

CHAPTER TWENTY-TWO

THE NEW, ANTI-RACIST FACE OF NIMBYISM

T HE WORK OF NEW ENGLAND'S municipal zoning authorities has never been enviable. Among their top challenges is refereeing the popular misconception that individuals are entitled to buy or build a home in "the woods," where they may live out their days in isolated bliss. Established homeowners who subscribe to this vision often attempt to stop similarly minded folk from building their own homes within view, usually by showering zoning authorities with any number of objections. In return, such homeowners are often stigmatized as "NIMBYs" (acronym for Not-In-My-Back-Yard) by others who wish to poke fun at their often understated self-interests. All of this is expected behavior within the sphere of rural residential development. However, a more politically powerful and morally authoritative brand of NIMBYism has expanded into this sphere in the form of ceremonial stone landscape activism.

Take, for example, the 2013-14 campaign that resulted in the establishment of the Manitou Hassannash Preserve in Hopkinton, Rhode Island. This property was originally privately owned, and the owner had proposed subdividing it for development. Neighbors who were not Indians, but who were reportedly "very concerned about this property possibly being sold to a private person who would then possibly not respect the structures there" (Drummond 2015) opposed these plans. Occupying their own houses within the very same stone-structure-rich landscape, they worked with NEARA and the NITHPO to prevent others from following, framing themselves as protectors of a sacred tribal space. Anyone calling homeowners NIMBYs under such optics risks being stigmatized, in turn, as unsympathetic toward Indians, or worse. Let me be clear: I have no doubt that some pursued the preservation of that property for virtuous reasons, made personal sacrifices along the way, and perhaps even experienced some form of moral or spiritual enlightenment. I am merely pointing out that social stigma also played an important role. Otherwise, the property's original owner would not report feeling that she was "portrayed as the villain of the story" (Drummond 2014). She eventually agreed to sell the property to the Hopkinton Land Trust and moved out of state.

After the dust settled, the property was named the Manitou Hassannash Preserve. On October 17, 2017, which a number of municipal organizations agreed to recognize as Hopkinton's "Ceremonial Stone Landscapes Day," Narragansett Indian tribal representatives stood amongst the property's stone structures and blessed them in a public ceremony. Harris made the following announcement to the crowd:

> There will be, shortly, a new state historic preservation officer. The end of last month, Ted Sanderson resigned. He didn't drop his title. He's gonna still be hanging around making sure his shop is doing its job. But we're going to have to embrace the state, and get the state on board where the towns are arriving. Leadership is from the grassroots up in a democracy, and I believe that. I believe that you all will lead the state and the federal government in the path that they have to follow. (Doug Harris, transcribed from Gage 2017a)

I doubt that Harris, or anyone else present, anticipated how soon Rhode Island's State Historic Preservation Officer would get "on board."

Ten days later, at the request of my office's recently resigned Executive Director (who doubled as the soon-to-resign State Historic Preservation Officer), Edward Sanderson, I attended a meeting at the Manitou Hassannash Preserve. It was also attended by a variety of preservationists, including THPO staff from the Narragansett Indian, Mohegan, and Aquinnah Wampanoag tribes. The guest of honor was Paul Loether, who was, at the time, the Keeper of the National Register of Historic Places and a regular defender of his office's 2008 determination that the Turners Falls Sacred Ceremonial Hill Site is eligible for listing in the National Register of Historic Places. In fact, Loether had served as a key liaison between the National Park Service and tribal officials throughout that affair. And according to that history, THPO staff at this meeting doubtlessly recognized him as a powerful political ally, perhaps the most powerful they have ever had within the federal government.

Standing among the stone heaps, Loether delivered an impromptu speech, remarking, "My ancestors were New England farmers and they didn't build these structures. Who is left if you don't believe it was Irish monks?" To me, it sounded like a non-committal way of laying out the following logic: "If you, like me, are willing to dismiss the most likely explanation (i.e., field clearing) out of hand, then are we not obligated to conclude that these were built for ritual?" I decided not to speak up and add that if everyone knew what their ancestors did and did not do, the fields of archaeology and history would not exist. Lauded by ceremonial stone landscape activists (e.g., Buford 2018:9), Loether's comment proved prophetic.

Amidst the Trump administration's crusade to disrupt existing policies and processes at the National Park Service, Loether resigned to replace Sanderson as my new boss, the Executive Director of the Rhode Island Historical Preservation and Heritage Commission and State Historic Preservation Officer for Rhode Island. This is why I do not read fiction. Life provides enough surprises. Yet, even more surprising has been discovering how effectively Loether and I have worked on nearly every agency-related issue other than ceremonial stone landscapes. Yes, a top hero and a top villain of the Ceremonial Stone Landscape Movement have, for three years, been working together very productively under the same roof, with the villain answering to the hero. Of course, I would be lying if I said we pulled this feat off by our lonesome. We have been aided and abetted the whole time by honesty and civility.

Shortly after arriving, he coordinated the award of a Certified Local Government grant, which is a type of federally funded (i.e., taxpayer funded) historic preservation grant, to the town of Hopkinton to survey stone structures at the Manitou Hassannash Preserve and conduct background historical research for the property. The work was awarded to Ceremonial Landscapes Research, LLC, which was qualified by a local reporter as "a team of archaeologists" (Sullivan 2019). It would have been closer to the truth for that reporter to have qualified them as "a team of antiquarians that includes an archaeologist." Loether delivered a lecture about the project at the 2019 Annual Meeting of NEARA. I was not surprised to find that this grant-funded project was insulated from having any contact with me in its later stages. Ceremonial stone landscape activism affords no legitimacy to non-believers.

To illustrate this principle, consider the case of Harvey Buford, the Hopkinton Conservation Commission's longtime Chairman, who, after waking up to the ceremonial stone landscape cause, became NEARA's

Rhode Island Coordinator in 2017 and ascended to the organization's presidency the following year. In a published commentary on the Manitou Hassannash Preserve, he explained that it was "rescued" from development: "In spite of the state archaeologist contending the stone groupings were farmer's piles" and clarified that "all" others "involved were convinced of the Native American attribution for the site and its importance" (Buford 2017). He failed to acknowledge that I, in fact, advocated for the preservation of that property and the stone features contained thereon, recommending openly in writing to the property owner, the NITHPO, and the town of Hopkinton "that efforts to leave the stone pile features undisturbed to the greatest extent possible be incorporated into any landscape management plans for this parcel" (Ives 2013b). Though Buford was doubtlessly privy to the entirety of that letter, it appears that nothing other than my lack of agreement with NITHPO's interpretation was information fit to pass through his ideological filter. Otherwise, I could not be effectively vilified. But I suppose the identity politics surrounding the Manitou Hassannash Preserve could have been worse.

Such was the case for another recent ceremonial stone landscape preservation campaign in Shutesbury, Massachusetts. It opposed construction of a six-megawatt solar array on a 30-acre parcel of forest on Pratt Corner Road that was privately owned by W.D. Cowls, Inc. (Merzback 2017a, 2017b, 2017c, 2018a, 2018b; Murray 2016; Serreze 2016a, 2016b, 2016c, 2016d, 2016e, 2017b). Projected to produce "more power than the entire town of Shutesbury uses" and generate "$50,000 a year in property taxes," the solar project looked like a win-win for both the 87% forested town (Shutesbury 2012) and the developer, Lake Street Development of Chicago (Merzback 2018b).

Most of the related discourse took place in municipal planning board meetings, the minutes of which are available online and serve as the factual basis of much of the following two chapters (Shutesbury Planning Board 2015-17). These records demonstrate, beyond any shadow of a doubt, that this campaign was solicited to prop up a NIMBYism that had already played its usual hands to no avail. And they also illustrate the tendency for certain white New Englanders to seemingly become deeply concerned about the spiritual welfare of Indians, whatever that may happen to consist of, after learning that their rural vistas are under threat, and to build their case against development on whatever Indian identity holders can be drawn to the table. The movement to preserve ceremonial stone landscapes was born out of NIMBYism, as this book has already established, and continues to be leveraged for that purpose.

But this new variant of NIMBYism, like so many of today's political endeavors, is passed through the prism of race relations because of the instant moral gravity of the resulting projection, which, in turn, increases the chances that the prism-holders will prevail. And even if they do not prevail, they can still revel in the self-righteous attention that they draw.

CHAPTER TWENTY-THREE

A STORM GATHERS

WHEN THE SOLAR PROJECT was initially presented to the Planning Board in the spring of 2015, Miriam DeFant, a near-abutter, opposed it for the next year. She responded with a list of concerns over such things as wetlands, slopes, buffer cut lines, erosion, and wildlife habitat. She pushed for a municipal moratorium on solar farm development, which, according to another abutter, should be passed because "she moved here for the woods." DeFant later presented herself as spokeswoman for the Alliance for Appropriate Development, an organization founded to engage the project by leveraging zoning, wetlands, and endangered species regulations. But the moratorium was never realized, and DeFant's concerns may have begun to sound trivial. According to March 2016 planning board meeting notes, DeFant "doesn't feel there is nothing that can be done to satisfy her and that she is feeling encouraged that we are getting closer." Later in the meeting, she conceded to the planning board that the project "is much better" and that "we are not as worried as we were six months ago." It seemed she had tried opening every possible door of protest. But, in the eleventh hour, one more would appear.

Opportunity knocked when Sarah Kohler, a New Salem resident and "amateur researcher," approached the planning board in April to report "the possible presence of a burial mound" on the property, which someone had desecrated by "stomping on a ceremonial stone." To my knowledge, she did not claim Indian ancestry or identity, though she did carry experience in the ceremonial stone landscape arena. She had opposed the construction of a solar array in the town of New Salem in 2014, while serving on their planning board, claiming that the project area contained "sacred stone circles" (Serreze 2016d). She would later explain that her unauthorized visit to this Shutesbury property was "not a trespass," because she was simply taking "advantage of its cultural features...that attest to their presence in the landscape" (Merzbach 2016). From my perspective, Kohler had come before the planning board to mobilize the age-old American trope described by Native American Studies scholar Melanie Benson Taylor, the view of Indians as "irresistible victim-symbols for anybody who wants to join a struggle against colonial-capitalist aggression" (Taylor 2017). The prospect of joining that struggle would prove irresistible to many locals.

Planning board meetings became a theater for pan-Indian politics beginning in May 2016, and attracted a diversity of personalities, including Loril MoonDream, a resident of nearby Wendell, who worked as a wildlife rehabilitator, and cultural promoter. Her May 2020 obituary identifies her as a "White Mountain Apache from New Mexico" who "grew up on a reservation with her grandparents who taught her the ways of her people and the importance of all animals on the planet through stories, teachings and song" (Legacy.com 2020). Tribal affiliations of other attendees recorded in the minutes include the Mohawk Nation of New York, the Arawak Taino Nation of Puerto Rico, the Aquinnah Wampanoag of Massachusetts, and the Narragansett Indian Tribe of Rhode Island. Doug Harris was identified to the planning board as someone "who could perform the function of all relevant tribes for this site," despite a resident specifying that the Nipmucs are more local. All of this brings to mind the politically incorrect observation of a Mashpee Wampanoag tribal member who stated that when it comes to Indian representation, "White people don't give a damn who's in charge...long as they get what they want" (ReelWamps.com 2011).

In addition to the "ceremonial stone" reported by Kohler, the project area also contained a number of pit and mound features that some found concerning. At the planning board's request, the property owner hired a professional archaeology firm to determine whether those features might represent Indian burials. The resulting report was made public as part of the municipal proceedings (SWCA Environmental Consultants 2016). It concluded that those features merely represent the ordinary, tell-tale scars left by wind-toppled trees whose trunks had long since rotted away. Nevertheless, an independent review of the report by Dr. Eric Johnson, Director of the since-disbanded University of Massachusetts Archaeological Services, suggested that the reporting itself did not quite meet industry standards.

But concerns over the thoroughness of an archaeology report disappeared beneath the shadow of a more politically contentious issue. The property owner had refused to allow Narragansett and Aquinnah Wampanoag THPOs to participate in that archaeological survey. In fact, they issued a no trespass order to those THPOs. The property was privately owned and there were no state or federal "hooks" that could be used to compel tribal access and consultation. As far as the ceremonial stone landscape activists were concerned, this no trespass order signified nothing less than a racist offence to Indians everywhere. This was the justification they needed to throw everything they could at the highest authority available—the local municipal government. The following drama, which, to borrow a phrase, featured an "almost recreational quest to take umbrage on behalf of people other than white" (McWhorter 2018), appears to have been squarely aimed at leveraging white settler colonial guilt, illustrating Thomas Sowell's oft-quoted observation that "many on the political left are so entranced by the beauty of their vision that they cannot see the ugly reality that they are creating in the real world."

CHAPTER TWENTY-FOUR

PEACE, BALANCE, AND HARMONY COME TO TOWN

As you read the following chapter, digest this thought from the late Indian activist-poet John Trudell. During a 1999 interview, he explained:

> Anyone who goes around claiming to be the spiritual master, the spiritual teacher, the spiritual anything, anyone who goes around waving that banner about how spiritual they are, see how responsibly they behave. (Bencorbett.net 2018)

The ceremonial stone landscape spiritual banner was metaphorically marched into the Shutesbury Town Hall at the August 17 planning board meeting (Figure 15). Let us see how its bearers behaved.

A variety of personalities arrived with strong, though not necessarily consistent or compatible, opinions on how the town should proceed. Nor did they even agree as to precisely what they were there to protect—an endangered burial ground, ceremonial ground, archaeoastronomical site? Unified by moral outrage, they did not need to agree on any specifics to promote their agenda, which seemed to center on little more than the collective seizure of political power. Doomed before it started, the meeting's agenda included considering the findings of the archaeological survey report.

MoonDream was not convinced that falling trees make those features. According to the minutes, she explained: "I went to the site of the mounds. All uniform in length and size and height, I had a very spiritual feeling. It will be a bad spiritual feeling place if you do not do this. I am wearing my hair down in mourning." She did not mention whether she had permission to enter the property.

Figure 15: The scene outside (top) and inside (bottom) the August 17 planning board meeting. Used with permission. (Serreze 2016b)

Curtiss Hoffman, noted in the minutes as an archaeologist "held in high esteem," did not support the tree-throw explanation, either. Via correspondence, he submitted the possibility that the mounds resulted from a mass interment of Indians who succumbed to a European-introduced epidemic in early colonial days. In my opinion, this was alarmist virtue signaling aimed at registering himself as sensitive to the gravest Indian concerns imaginable. And perhaps it was, in part, a display intended to win back the favor of Harris who appears to have dropped his ties to Hoffman several years back. Hoffman had fought for Harris a decade before in Carlisle at Benfield Parcel "A," and signaled his willingness to fight for him again.

Harris was not inclined to afford legitimacy to any archaeological opinions on the property—not even from his former ally. True to his position that ceremonial stone landscape activism must defer to indigenous authority, Harris advised the planning board that "It is a ceremonial stone landscape, so you must use a technique developed by the tribe in 2008. You've got blinders on!" He warned them that they were inviting a lawsuit (Serreze 2016b) (Figure 16). As transcribed in the minutes, Harris explained:

> What you and the town and the citizens are taking responsibility for is the ancient relationship. You are the conscience of the town officials. They, the town officials, are being pressured by project proponents. Even though no federal agents are here now. The ceremonial stones are indicative of a ceremonial area, burial area or not, their remains may have been moved but their spirits are being honored by the ceremonial stones, when a great imbalance has occurred. If you honor that before you it will honor you.

Essentially, Harris conceded that he could not exert any legal power over the project because he could not get Uncle Sam on the regulatory hook. So he appears to have leveraged the rhetoric of white settler colonial guilt for its proven capacity to influence municipal politics.

Figure 16: Doug Harris at the August 17 planning board meeting. Used with permission. (Serreze 2016b)

This meeting presented a prime opportunity to stir up racial anxiety. Defant asked the planning board "to make a motion to not approve of discrimination" and require the developer to grant THPOs property access (Figure 17). Deliberating to boos, hisses, and yells from the audience, the planning board acknowledged its lack of legal standing to do so. The town counsel (attorney) clarified that the planning board "does not have the authority to order the private property owner to allow the THPO onto their private property. We hoped at first THPO could go on the property. That does not change the fact that the town has no authority." But it was too late for rational excuses. The evening's identity politics had effectively stripped the planning board of its moral authority and, by extension, social legitimacy.

Figure 17: Miriam DeFant at the August 17 planning board meeting. Used with permission. (Serreze 2016b)

A previously unknown activist revealed himself during this meeting (Figure 18). In the previous year, Shutesbury resident Rolf Cachat-Schilling was acknowledged by the planning board as "a professional ecologist" and "author of ecology texts" who brought forestry-related concerns to the table. According to November 2015 planning board minutes, he submitted "testimony about the timing of mowing to protect nesting animals." And as of March 2016, he had emailed the planning board to recommend substituting "more of a wildflower seed mix" for the "standard solar seed mix." But the texture of Cachat-Schilling's engagement with this solar project would change significantly, and within only a matter of weeks. By August of 2016, his concerns over "nesting animals" and "seed mix" appear to have become eclipsed by his concerns over a ceremonial stone landscape. At this August 2016 meeting he engaged the planning board as more than an interested ecologist. One may wonder if he experienced an awakening of sorts.

Jumping backward, consider that in 2010 he was listed as "Dr. Rolf Schilling, Botanist and Environmental Director, Garden in the Woods, Framingham, MA" in the *Code of Ethics for Botanical Artists Working in the Field* published by the American Society of Botanical Artists (2010), while advertising his services online as a local "Buddhist mentor" (Cachat-Shilling 2010). After 2016, Cachat-Schilling qualified his title as "Rolf Cachat-Schilling, M.S." (Cachat-Schilling 2017a) and included "Chair, Western Chapter, Massachusetts Archaeological Society" on his curriculum vitae (Cachat-Schilling 2018a). For the record, as explained to me by one of the society's officials in 2019, the Western Chapter was disbanded many years ago and had still not been reinstated. He is also among the founders of the "Massachusetts Ethical Archaeology Society." Its website is remarkably critical of mainstream archaeologists—especially those at the Massachusetts Historical Commission (Massachusetts Ethical Archaeology 2018). Cachat-Schilling is also editor and ethnographer for the Oso:ah Foundation. Its website explains that Oso:ah means "planting a tree in the name of peace" (Merzbach 2017) and is dedicated to the pursuit of "more cultural recovery and more healing, more exchange and understanding, between people divided into groups" (Oso:ah.org). This was not necessarily the effect that Cachat-Shilling would have at this planning board meeting.

Figure 18: Rolf Cachat-Schilling at the August 17 planning board meeting. Used with permission (Serreze 2016b).

He addressed the planning board, announcing that a lawsuit had already been filed. Before the meeting, he and co-plaintiffs James Schilling-Cachat, Michael Suter, Sarah Kohler, and Alejo Zacarias had filed a civil rights lawsuit in U.S. District Court against Lake Street Development's Martin Lebovits and Zachary Schulman and Shutesbury Planning Board members Jeffrey Lacey and Deacon Bonnar (*Rolf*

Cachat Schilling et al vs. Shutesbury Planning Board and Lake Street Development, 3:16-cv-30144-MGM). Claiming membership in a religious group called the "Syncretic Spiritualists of the Northeast," the plaintiffs demanded property access to perform stone-related ceremonies and determine whether any human burials exist thereon. They also claimed that their alienation from this property and various unspecified others throughout Shutesbury could lead to negative health outcomes including *death*. Cachat-Schilling exited the meeting before it concluded, yelling "liars" and throwing down his sign that read "Turn Vehement Anger into Lasting Peace" (Serreze 2016b). This is the same individual who, only five months prior, expressed concern over the composition of the seed mix the developer planned to use.

Racial fireworks continued to fly after the meeting adjourned as activists targeted the demoralized planning board. Kohler shouted at them, "This is native land and you are abusing your authority!" (Sereeze 2016b). DeFant asked them, "To what do you attribute your belief that [THPOs] are unqualified, except that they are a different color, race, and religion?" (Serreze 2016b). This drama graced a local media report. Titled "Solar Foes Claiming Indian Burial Mounds Raise Ruckus at Shutesbury Meeting," it featured a picture of Doug Harris shouting at the planning board (see Figure 16) and other photos showing activists holding signs that read "Sac-RED-land."

At the next planning board meeting, Harris requested that the board pay him $500 to walk the property, explaining "my skills are not psychic…but those who have those skills might be able to see more deeply into what's happening and the ancestors who may or may not be in the ground" (Merzbach 2016). On behalf of the Aquinnah Wampanoag Tribe, Bettina Washington added, "You're not going to get your answer unless the tribes are involved," pointing to the fact that soliciting the informed opinion of a THPO on a given property requires granting said THPO property access. The project proponent had declined to do so and offered no signal that the issue was being reconsidered.

From that point forward, the Narragansett and Aquinnah Wampanoag THPOs appear to have left the campaign largely in the hands of Cachat-Schilling and his husband, James Schilling-Cachat. They crowdsourced funding for the federal religious lawsuit through a Petition Site page titled "Regional Tribes Banned from Inspecting Suspected Burial Ground Slated for Destruction" (Cachat-Schilling 2016) and a GoFundMe page titled "Suspected Burial Ground Rescue" (Schilling-Cachat 2016). The latter states that the solar farm property includes:

[A] suspected burial ground that 2 Federally-recognized tribes were banned from inspecting. Lake Street Development is looking to dig up this burial ground without allowing any Tribal official to see the site, and without performing tests for human remains. 5 local private citizens have filed for a Federal injunction to allow Tribal Historic Preservation Office inspection and proper assessment. The suspected burial site also contains probably ceremonial stone relics that the Tribes were prevented from inspecting. So far, we have gone it alone and paid out of our pockets. Now, we need your help...fighting for our rights and those of others in Federal court against a multi-million bankster scheme. (Schilling-Cachat 2016)

One of the donors posted, "Let's participate in our own Standing Rock! We can preserve the sacred site against big money!" Cachat-Schilling represented the plaintiff pro se as proceedings continued into the fall (Sereeze 2016d), and was reprimanded by the judge for failing to follow court rules (Serreze 2016e).

Months later, Cachat-Schilling and fellow activists submitted a petition titled, "Resolution to Preserve Native American Historical Sites and Traditional Cultural Properties, Including Ceremonial Stone Landscapes" (Merzbach 2017) to the town under the auspices of the "Friends of Shutesbury" and the "Oso:ah Foundation," calling for the acknowledgment of local avocational archaeologists and various southern New England tribal cultural experts as the town's cultural resource management authorities (Town of Shutesbury 2017). The petitioners almost acquired this municipal-level power. After becoming a warrant article, this resolution was narrowly defeated by a 54-52 paper ballot in the spring of 2017 (Viles 2017). As reported, opponents felt that the petition was "poorly worded, called for the involvement of too many agencies and did not rely enough on consultation with professional archaeologists."

Meanwhile, objections to the solar project continued to appear in the media. For instance, on behalf of several residents of Shutesbury (Ezzell Floranina, Leslie Cerier, Miles Tardie, Rolf Cachat-Schilling, James Schilling-Cachat and Jade Alicandro), Mary Lou Conca published the following piece on May 2, 2017:

We wish to offer a perspective not often presented in the media. The humans whose remains lie beneath a sizable burial mound on this sacred hill inhabited this area for thousands of years before any of us were ever even here. We feel the urgency to honor their existence. We do not agree with the disturbance of the souls resting there or the

decimation of places of worship and ceremonial stone landscapes....
Long before any development or high-rise buildings, Native Americans nourished our land and lived in harmony with nature. We must
not ever forget this fact. The environmental damage, and damage to
the Native American souls lying in their final resting place, has not
been taken into account. Religious practice is being trampled... The
trees will be readily sliced up by huge, destructive machines, the earth
dug up and torn apart with human remains being thrown in every direction with total and absolute disregard. Ceremonial stone structures
will be tumbled and crushed by heavy machinery. (Conca 2017)

A millennial Shutesbury resident, Eric Thompson-Martin, published a noteworthy opposing opinion on May 8, 2017, titled "Baffled by
Opposition to Solar Project," shortly thereafter:

I am baffled by the strong opposition to the plan to install a solar array
off Pratt Corner Road. I was dismayed to see a letter...[claiming] that
the location is a Native American burial site. Maybe it is because as a
high school student I know that I personally will be affected by global
warming for my entire life, but it is clear to me that solar power is
necessary to prevent the destruction of nature. Why are the 30 acres
near our homes more important than the millions upon millions of
acres of coastline all around the world that are under the constantly
growing threat of destruction with every passing storm? These coasts
were often the home of Native Americans as well. In the past few decades, Native American groups have been major advocates of all efforts
to fight climate change, especially solar, and Shutesbury as a town has
also been generally supportive of environmental issues. I call out to
all of Shutesbury that it is our responsibility to help this global fight.
People all around America are refusing to do their part because they
do not want to make some small, everyday sacrifices. Some don't want
to give up driving their Hummer and others don't want to give up 30
acres of forest in their town, but we all must realize that the whole
Earth requires these sacrifices in order to prevent massive destruction
of the natural world. (Thompson-Martin 2017)

The federal religious lawsuit was dismissed in August 2017, allowing
the permitting of the solar project to proceed. Cachat-Shilling concluded that the Massachusetts courts were "completely contaminated" (Serreze 2017b) and led an intertribal memorial service for the property on
the Shutesbury Town Common the following month.

The Shutesbury campaign offered low-hanging fruit for academic
identity positioning. At the nearby University of Massachusetts, Am-

herst, anthropology scholars passed. However, Drs. Henry Geddes and Martín Valdiviezo of the communications department did not, coauthoring "Struggles Against Colonization in the U.S.A: Mohicans in Massachusetts" in the online "investigative journal" *Intercontinental Cry* (Geddes and Valdiviezo 2017). Their February 2017 article, which claims to defend the "cultural property rights of the Mohican people," does not reference any specific individuals or groups who identify as Mohican. Perhaps their perfunctory representation of Mohicans as voiceless victims requiring scholarly defense seems justifiable to inspire readers "to fight against the Eurocentric order," advance "decolonization of the Americas" and fulfill "the democratic ideals of freedom, equality and solidarity," as mentioned.

But so long as such scholars, or anyone for that matter, continue broadly defaulting to white settler colonial guilt to explain generalized Indian grievances, their rhetoric of decolonization, equality, and solidarity should be recognized for what it is—an exhibition of moral vanity that is of little or no practical use for resolving complex, real-world social problems. Thomas Sowell once wrote that modern American racism is "kept alive by politicians, race hustlers and people who get a sense of superiority by denouncing others as 'racists'" (2012b). I believe this ceremonial stone landscape preservation campaign illustrates his point.

While Cachat-Schilling survived his alienation from the solar farm property, the following communication suggests he emerged from that experience with an oppositional posture toward certain public servants. The April 3, 2018 minutes of the select board document its unanimous passage of a motion to "protect town employees and volunteers from continued abuse via email from Rolf Cachat-Schilling by approving the blocking and filtering of email communication to town employees and volunteers." But beyond the municipal stage, Cachat-Schilling has realized rapid success in the field of anthropology, reporting that he was trained by his late great-aunt in ceremonial practices involving stones. Presuming nothing less than honesty on his behalf, the anthropological perspective is obligated to register his related memories and insights as ethnographic truths. His works have appeared in the *Bulletin of the Archaeological Society of Connecticut*, the *Massachusetts Archaeological Society Bulletin*, and the peer-reviewed journal, *Northeast Anthropology* (Cachat-Schilling 2016, 2018b, 2018c), and are regarded by many as important contributions to the expanding genre of ceremonial stone landscape studies.

Solar farm issues aside, Harris and his associates have continued to advance the ceremonial stone landscape agenda in Shutesbury through the municipal historical commission, which DeFant joined as a member. The commission's minutes from May 7 and June 18, 2018, show that Harris provided a local screening of the *Great Falls* film (Timreck 2010[2008]) and would be compensated $350 from the commission's funds. The commission discussed the possibility of reaching out to property owners to solicit ceremonial site locations, as well as the possibility of signing an Memorandum of Understanding with various THPOs on behalf of Shutesbury to protect such properties. They noted Lisa McLoughlin as someone who should speak to the commission, and Eva Gibavec, one of the founding members of Ceremonial Landscapes Research, LLC, as someone who might be able to lead a local educational forest walk. At their February 7, 2019, meeting, DeFant requested $500 in funds from the commission to pay Harris "to continue discussion of Indigenous Ceremonial Stone Landscapes in the Northeast." All voted in favor.

CONCLUSION:

EXITS ARE LOCATED
ON EITHER SIDE
OF THE THEATRE

CHAPTER TWENTY-FIVE

THE THEORY THAT DARE NOT SPEAK
ITS NAME

T HE IDENTITY POLITICS of ceremonial stone landscape activism
are in no way mysterious, nor are they confined to New England.
If you are an American who reads the news regularly, you understand
these politics very well. They are cut from the cloth of a nationwide
ideological trend that is disintegrating multicultural America before our
very eyes. These are the politics of what the University of Toronto psychology professor and public speaker Dr. Jordan Peterson (in)famously
refers to as "postmodern neo-Marxism," or "Cultural Marxism" when he
is inclined to conserve syllables.

Unhelpfully, leftists have ardently sought to publicly suppress any
thoughtful discussion of Cultural Marxism through their favorite and
most cost-effective political tactic—stigmatizing it as racist to ward off
all potential interest. And they have been quite successful, seeing that
it is widely presumed that people using the term are, at best, "pseu-
do-intellectuals" (Singleton 2020) and, at worst, right-wing extremists
attempting to promote white supremacist agendas and anti-Semitic
ideology (e.g., Berkowitz 2003; Berlatsky 2019; Moyn 2018). Having no
stand-alone index for Cultural Marxism, Wikipedia features "Cultural Marxism conspiracy theory" on a page that prominently features a
photograph of the far-right terrorist and convicted mass murderer An-
ders Behring Breivik. And who would risk being associated with him?
Nobody, of course. Accordingly, it is no wonder that the term Cultural
Marxism is effectively banned from discussion in today's left-leaning
university classrooms, despite a tacit understanding that its principles

firmly govern social and political life throughout surrounding campus communities. Still, as compellingly argued by a conservative political writer, regardless of the fact that "the term 'Cultural Marxism' has been appropriated by some bigots and conspiracists, the existence of the ideology is a matter of historical record" (Zubatov 2018). I insist that the ceremonial stone landscape phenomenon is most effectively understood in the context of today's populist Cultural Marxism, which I see as a relatively young phenomenon that is far removed from early twentieth-century Frankfurt School intellectualism and has nothing to do with anti-Semitism.

Bear in mind that one does not encounter self-declared Cultural Marxists. They are labeled from without, much as New England's indigenous people were labeled "Indians" by seventeenth-century Europeans, and much as the descendants of those Europeans were labeled "WASPs" by a Jewish American in the 1950s (Kaufmann 2006:239). Cultural Marxism in the U.S., as I would define it, is a post-Civil Rights Era trend that leftist scholars and public intellectuals developed "from Marxist theory in the 1970s and 80s as a framework for explaining the repressive functions of the capitalist state" (Pettegrew 2020). But about one decade into the new millennium, Marxism's spirit of revolutionary empowerment in the name of mass social justice discovered a perfect medium in which to flourish—an increasingly hyper-informed, morally preoccupied, and racially paranoid American public that had become atomized by the rise of secularism, the decline of the nuclear family, and the insecurity of a post-industrial economy. Smartphones provided anchors, allowing new social networks to materialize and identities to be groomed and registered. Naturally, many choose to register as heroes, readily finding one another in the collapsed geography of cyberspace where radical voices dominate. Smartphones allowed anyone to casually participate in the nationwide "interruption" of any perceived form of oppression, including not only the old standby of capitalism, but ableism, ageism, classism, ethnocentrism, Eurocentrism, nationalism, scientism, racism, and sexism. Perhaps Cultural Marxism's greatest fiat is having provided a single ideological platform for a diverse spectrum of radical critical theorists and like-minded citizens to gather and amplify their calls for societal deconstruction and reformation.

The seduction of the Cultural Marxist worldview is that it appears to offer a share of collective power to the seemingly "disadvantaged" individual with one hand while using the other to unburden them of responsibility for their place in the world, though at the risk of producing "a quite depressed and dysfunctional personality" (Watts 2018). Today's Cultural Marxism at large merely demands that one hold faith in a sweeping vision of reality that operates according to these presumptions:

- Each individual is bound to the collective destiny of their intersectional group identity, which is a politically constructed composite of various essential group identities drawn primarily from such categories as ethnicity, gender, sex, and race.
- Intergroup disparities, both real and perceived, across indices such as crime, incarceration, education, health, and wealth, exist because less powerful groups are continually oppressed by more powerful groups through systemic discrimination pervading all traditional institutions.
- Until equalities of outcome are realized among all groups, society at large will remain illegitimate and moral authority will remain an exclusive property of oppressed groups that is hierarchically distributed in accordance with the apparent magnitude of their respective victimhood claims.

I must concede that to call this a theory, in an academic sense, gives it more credit that it is due. Academic theories are characterized by intellectual rigor, demanding to be tested and refined in relation to the sorts of evidence they claim to make sense of. Cultural Marxism is more accurately qualified as a mass social ideology, or perhaps even a mass theology. It thrives on consensus, assumes the veracity of its propositions, disregards unsupportive information, and experiences unwanted questions as forms of "intellectual violence." Tragically, this has become the dominant ideological thread in American education and popular media.

In the balance, Americans find themselves practicing a rather eccentric social morality. This morality explains why Uncle Ben, Aunt Jemima, and a certain Indian "butter maiden" lost their jobs in 2020, but that a brand of salsa using the racially derogatory term "gringo" remains gainfully employed. It explains why there are widespread complaints about the lack of racial diversity on American soccer fields, but not on the National Basketball Association's courts. It also explains why actor Jussie Smollett hired a pair of Nigerian brothers to pose as white hate crime perpetrators who yelled bigoted and homophobic (i.e., racially and sexually intersected) messages at him, and probably why Cook County prosecutors initially armed with overwhelming evidence, and to the shock of legal experts at large, dropped all criminal charges. It explains why so many academic visionaries prescriptively refer to all American Latinos as "Latinx" despite that population's overwhelming majority preference to the contrary (Ne-Bustamante et al. 2020). It explains why university professors Rachel Dolezal (formerly of Eastern Washington University) and Dr. Jessica Krug (formerly of George Washington University) enjoyed vibrant careers under "appropriated" non-white identities, until fellow academics and journalists outed (i.e., racially delegitimized) them as "white," and why there is no corresponding social warrant to root out "non-white" individuals who take on a "white" identity, which is probably a more prevalent phenomenon (Williams 2019:20). It explains why a younger Elizabeth Warren took the liberty of identifying as "American Indian" on a registration card for the State Bar of Texas and as a minority law professor in a Harvard directory, and why the viability of her 2020 presidential candidacy required her to publicly reverse the polarity of her identity after tribal authorities demanded that she relinquish her claim to American Indian-ness (Elmahrek 2020). So she apologized and confessed herself to be merely a "white woman." It explains why presidential candidate Joe Biden, immediately after choosing Kamala Harris as his vice-presidential running mate, strategically proclaimed that "all across the nation, little *girls* woke up, especially little *black and brown girls* [italics mine] who often feel so overlooked and undervalued in our communities," to see themselves "as the stuff of presidents and vice presidents," broadcasting his faith in a popular intersectional moral hierarchy of race and gender. It is the same moral hierarchy alluded to by former Georgia gubernatorial candidate, Stacey Abrams, when she explained that she wants Americans to recognize the political importance of "women of color, and white women who have entered the space where they are" because "men seem to be men no matter which race they are in" (Comedy Central 2020).

Seeing that politically correct food producers, sports fans, an otherwise fine actor and his public prosecutors, socially prescriptive academics, racially nimble professors, and leading leftist politicians already follow the rules of Cultural Marxism so effectively, despite never using the ideology's unwanted *nom de plume*, it seems reasonable to concede that these rules, in fact, exist and have propagated into mainstream American sociocultural programming. They are followed and enforced in accordance with a new social morality that incentivizes individuals to defer to the authority of group identity and claim—or conspicuously defer to—a collective victimhood status whenever possible. Unfortunately, the chief product of this morality appears to be mass social dysfunction as evidenced by the inflation of racial ideology, extreme political polarization, the decline of free speech, the public displacement of facts by feelings, and the general erosion of our otherwise great multicultural democracy—a democracy that is worth fighting to save and might require great bravery to save.

This decline, largely a casualty of the uncompromising ideological crusade Cultural Marxists feel compelled to wage against non-believers, ostensibly in the name of social justice, is occurring across the country on many scales. And its second order effects may prove disastrous. The rise of Cultural Marxism at this point in American history may be nothing less than a white supremacist demagogue's dream come true. What could more effectively draw impoverished whites, who number 14.2 million in 2020 according to the U.S. Census Bureau, into a dangerously frustrated racial solidarity than a standing national accusation that they are members of a class that was born racist and irredeemably advantaged? I speculate that white supremacist organizers no longer require cohesive recruitment strategies or a nuanced knowledge of propaganda when they need only wait in dark corners of cyberspace with open arms, as books such as Ibram X. Kendi's *How to Be an Antiracist* (2019) and Robin DiAngelo's *White Fragility* (2018) dominate best-seller lists and social media threads. If America's political left wants to "get real" about ensuring that Donald J. Trump is not re-elected to the U.S. presidency in 2024, it would start dealing with this situation, a situation largely of its own making, immediately.

Essentially, ceremonial stone landscape activism represents a regional front where the standard of Cultural Marxism has advanced, which I propose is evidenced by numerous lines of reasoning that I have explored throughout this book. Consider that antiquarians seeking to preserve an alleged ceremonial landscape in 1996 were not recognized as legitimate sources of information by the town officials of Carlisle, Massachusetts, but that antiquarians seeking to preserve a strikingly similar landscape in the same municipality a decade later were recognized as legitimate sources of information by town officials, after it became clear that they had tribal allies. Consider that antiquarians who preached about the importance of preserving what would eventually be called ceremonial stone landscapes were ignored by academics for years, but that several academics signaled their defense of the ceremonial stone landscape paradigm after Indian authorities registered their endorse-

ment. Consider that antiquarian Peter Waksman found himself unceremoniously ferried to the margins of the very movement he worked to
create while Doug Harris substituted Lloyd Wilcox for James Mavor and
Byron Dix as the movement's ideological patron. Consider Craig Cipolla's suggestion that fellow archaeologists should, as a rule, hold Indian
interpretations of stone phenomena equal to their own, while generally
disregarding the interpretations of antiquarians. Consider how activist
Lisa McLoughlin publicly sacrificed the Indian dimension of her identity (not unlike Elizabeth Warren), demonstrating the depth of her deference to the Indian cultural authorities who hold the power to confer
upon her that "gift" of "outsider status." Consider that landowners hoping to stop development on adjoining properties have learned to solicit
the "voices" of Indian identity bearers to increase their chances of success. As I see it, a common principle is quietly but powerfully operating
behind all of these phenomena: a tendency for whites to see Indians as
special bearers of moral authority and social legitimacy.

I remain unconvinced that the Ceremonial Stone Landscape Movement is effectively working to transcend racial divides or meaningfully
enlighten the public regarding history and heritage, though many within the movement may insist that those goals are indeed being effectively
served. Rather, I have come to suspect that this movement has become
a vehicle for a supply and demand economy, one where Indian identity
bearers preside over the supply of a certain intangible commodity that is
in great demand among contemporary whites. Let me break this down
within the context of Cultural Marxism. Within Cultural Marxism's political economy, moral authority, and, by extension, social legitimacy is
presumed to be a heritable property of Indian identity bearers in accordance with their transhistorical position at the apex of America's racial
victimhood hierarchy. Its members are, as a rule, born with a moral authority surplus that naturally flows into them from somewhere in the
deep past. White identity bearers, on the other hand, are presumed to be
oppressive since birth and perhaps before. They are born with a moral
authority deficit, with guilt flowing into them from somewhere in the
deep past. The quality of their upbringing and the content of their character, unfortunately, count for little to nothing at this point in time—a
discouraging development marking the popular abandonment of the
late Dr. Martin Luther King Jr.'s philosophy. But whites can solve their
moral authority deficit problem quite easily, by publicly associating with
Indians and agreeing with them on major issues. And, regardless of the
extent of genetic and cultural commonalities resulting from centuries

of regional cohabitation, publicly identifying as part white and part Indian, or neither, does not make for a politically viable moral authority trader on this scene. That is why the trade deserves to be examined critically—it depends on upholding and leveraging a strict system of racial accounting that crystallized when New England was a collection of British colonies. This is not a dimension of our collective heritage worth preserving.

How did this situation come to develop in New England? I see it as fitting within a greater nationwide trend. It seems that moral authority became a progressively scarce psychosocial resource for white Americans at large, after the Civil Rights Movement compelled their collective admission of racial guilt on a nationwide scale (Steele 2006). In recent years, the value of that resource, from the white racial perspective, has appreciated enough to merit active pursuit. In New England, under the implicit stigma of "whiteness," many citizens who may otherwise have little in common find themselves aligned by their motivation to acquire moral authority—the philosopher's stone of modern American politics—so that they might reap its dividends. The easiest way to do this is to acquire moral authority by proxy—by conspicuously deferring to members of presumably oppressed or disadvantaged groups. I believe the Ceremonial Stone Landscape Movement is tangled up in all of this, because it clearly involves a relationship between those who are self-consciously white and those who are recognized as unambiguously Indian.

And, as in so many situations where a proverbial carrot is being pursued, there is also a proverbial stick being evaded. Failing to support, or at least acquiesce to, Cultural Marxist agendas, which include ceremonial stone landscape activism, renders one an automatic suspect of anything and everything they promise to remedy. And the overarching condition that the Ceremonial Stone Landscape Movement at large promises to remedy is racial ignorance toward Indians, so who would risk being publicly seen as anything less than supportive? Maintaining so much as a token grip on ceremonial stone landscape activism's moral high ground offers white identity bearers a sense of immediate political safety and moral superiority, but the prospect of letting go may be discouraged by a fear that is as deep as it is silent. And Indians who realize just how terrified today's leftist whites have become at the prospect of being called racist doubtlessly understand that that phenomenon can be harnessed as a source of political power.

I know many of the individuals whose words and actions I have critiqued in this book, and I believe they are all fundamentally good people. In fact, some played key roles in my training and development as an archaeologist. I was once Dr. Kathleen Bragdon's student at the College of William and Mary (1997-2001), when I was enrolled in the anthropology department's graduate program in historical archaeology. This was years before she took on Alexandra Martin as a student and signed off on her confidential dissertation with a handful of co-advisors that included Paul Robinson. I revered Bragdon when I was her student, though I do not remember her ever mentioning ceremonial stone landscapes. Nor does she mention any in her award-winning 1999 book, *Native People of Southern New England, 1500-1650,* or in her outstanding 2009 sequel, *Native People of Southern New England, 1650-1775,* which acknowledges my service to her as a research assistant. So what happened?

I was also a student of her husband, Dr. Marley Brown, III, who has long taught courses in the same historical archaeology program, signed off on my master's thesis, and later signed off on Martin's dissertation. Brown, III, is, hands down, the most brilliant and critically thinking mind I have ever seen in action. I marveled at his ability to efficiently and gleefully break down the faulty assumptions of his students (myself included) and found his capacity to provoke critical and productive audience discussions following conference papers delightful. But he also never said anything about ceremonial stone landscapes. Yet, he chose to put his signature to Martin's dissertation—her "new colonial history of New England"—which appears to be based on the ceremonial stone landscape paradigm. So what happened?

And then there is Curtiss Hoffman, who I have long regarded as a charismatic and pioneering out-of-the-box thinker. He has taken the time and care to correspond with me about a variety of archaeological issues over the years, and I always felt privileged simply to receive a message from him. And, I have been actively supportive of his mission to conduct a large-scale study of stone structures up and down the Eastern Seaboard. Unfortunately, in my opinion, his resulting publication, the beautifully illustrated book, *Stone Prayers: Native American Constructions of the Eastern Seaboard* (Hoffman 2019), reveals the depth of his commitment to the ceremonial stone landscape paradigm. Of course, I support his right to free speech and encourage others to consider his findings for themselves, despite his characterization of my contributions to related discourse as little more than "an attempt to fabricate a forgotten eighteenth-century farm use" (Hoffman 2019:251) for stone heaps.

Why have these arguably great minds of the archaeological world voluntarily underwritten the ceremonial stone landscape paradigm? I speculate that it is because they are committed to supporting Cultural Marxist ideology wherever it may lead, even if it leads into questionable territory. I would be reassured to presume that they have taken this path to pursue social justice for indigenous people at large. But having seen what I have seen, and having learned what I have learned, I am left wondering if they have merely added their voices to an ideological echo chamber for the political benefit of a few? Telling people what they want to hear may not help them in the long run, though it usually helps the tellers in the short run. This is common sense. But many of today's academics do not think and act like common people.

So, any archaeologists who suffered their way through this book and prefer never to thumb through it again, just highlight this paragraph of takeaways. First, ceremonial stone landscapes are not an archaeological paradigm. Second, if you engage the Ceremonial Stone Landscape Movement, do so with both eyes open and consider the broader social consequences. Third, this movement, insofar as it involves Indians, is a twenty-first-century ethnographic phenomenon that you are probably underqualified to study, one that presents an unsound foundation on which to build a lasting revisionist history.

Recognizing today's politically perilous climate, I doubt that any ethnographers will rise to the challenge of studying the Ceremonial Stone Landscape Movement. But should any feel up to this task and fail to critically examine the interests and involvement of white settler colonial stakeholders, they will probably do little more than propagate the Cultural Marxist wave. Just imagine what might happen if we all allowed this wave to dissipate. We could begin appreciating individuals according to the content of their character, have honest conversations, broaden our children's horizons, harness intellectual diversity, and stop helping ourselves by presuming to help other people. Seriously, white people have been doing that last bit for centuries. Is this pattern truly unbreakable?

CHAPTER TWENTY-SIX

BALDWIN WAS RIGHT

A ND THERE I GO AGAIN, ranting about "white" identity, a histor-ically ever-shifting social construction that I have allowed to flourish between the covers of this book. I have taken no pleasure in writing this final chapter, which pours acid over the mortar of "race talk" holding much of the preceding material together. It centers on an anecdote from a family dinner table—my own.

Though I try to avoid discussing work-related issues over dinner, I admit that on more than a few occasions I have expounded on various ironies and absurdities boiling out of the Ceremonial Stone Landscape Movement in front of my wife and children, who have learned better than to solicit any details. And one evening, feeling as full as my stomach, I went so far as to compliment myself on how much I believed I had learned about the topic. Without missing a beat, someone added, "You're also more racist." After an awkward silence, I donned my poker face and carefully replied, "That's an interesting thing to say. What do you mean?" to which they replied, "You never used to talk about people as 'white' or 'Indian' very much. But you do it all the time now and it sounds racist."

The evidence had been stated, and I saw no possibility of escape. I had been shoring up the centuries-old white-Indian identity wall in front of my own young, impressionable children by incessantly indulg-ing in "race talk." To say that I felt embarrassed would have missed the mark. I was frozen. Apparently, my family had watched me sleepwalk into a darker place. This should have been avoidable. I had long consid-ered ceremonial stone landscape activism to be fundamentally racist, and assumed, in my hubris, that any criticism I directed toward it was, by nature, antiracist, even if I did not advertise it as such. But perhaps I had come to fit my subject like a hand carefully worked into a glove. Perhaps we were only promoting our own versions of antiracism, willfully ignorant to the truth that antiracism itself, despite its politically correct veneer, is a top enforcer of racial ideology.

Staring at my empty plate, stripped of my poker face and vestigial leftist impulse to rhetorically dodge all criticism, the words "yes, I think you're right" escaped my lips as naked truth. I obsessed over that exchange for several days. It reminded me of an idea the late American novelist James Baldwin posed in various ways over the course of his career: "As long as you think that you are white, there is no hope for you" (Thorsen 1989). Perhaps equally relevant is that he never said, "As long as you think that you are an antiracist white, there is some hope for you." The absolutist wisdom of Baldwin's statement had finally registered.

Being confronted with a mirror can make you freeze, especially if you see yourself unconsciously slogging along on the racism treadmill. And I suppose that is my greatest criticism of ceremonial stone landscape activism's identity politics. Regardless of whether one is for or against these politics, otherwise well-intentioned people in prolonged contact with them may find that they have allowed themselves, as have I, to become needlessly reinvested in race constructions in ways they did not see coming, and at a time in our collective societal development when we could fundamentally undermine racism simply by failing to indulge it. And to think I self-identified as a white settler colonist for the duration of this book. No good could possibly come of that. Life is too precious to spend as a projection of someone else's imagination, be it their worst or best.

In the fashion of an alcoholic hitting rock-bottom, perhaps it is high time for Americans to confront a dangerous paradox that has been hanging in our collective blind spot for far too long: how do we pour over race, day in and day out, without unwittingly internalizing its ideology? How do we continue having so many "conversations" about "peoples of color" without practicing what sociologist Dr. Karen E. Fields and historian Dr. Barbara J. Fields call "racecraft" (*sensu* Fields and Fields 2014)? Does today's antiracist training not rely on the performative revival of yesterday's racialized modes of thought? What good are the media's incessant reminders that the U.S. will have a minority white population by 2050, as if that trend should signify anything more than a passing curiosity? Will all of this lead us to the promised land, or will it divide us beyond reconcile? Though nobody knows for sure, it seems worth considering Thomas Sowell's warning that "our children and grandchildren may yet curse the day we began hyping race and ethnicity" and that "there are countries where that has led to slaughters in the streets but you cannot name a country where it has led to greater harmony." There has never been a better time to seriously explore other ways of thinking.

In his recent book, *Self-Portrait in Black and White: Family, Fatherhood, and Rethinking Race* (2019), Thomas Chatterton Williams proposes that American conceptions of race, all of which on the broad scale of human history are relatively recent inventions, are guaranteed to persist among us so long as we continue making them objects of constant attention. Rather than engaging contemporary racial discourse as a hard social reality without an expiration date, he soberly deliberates over its insidiously viral qualities and the tragic limitations that it imposes on the minds and, by extension, life trajectories of individuals in the here and now. Why? As a young father in a so-called "mixed-race" family, building productive and sustainable futures for his children has become his top priority. He decided that learning to think and move outside of the racial box, or to "unlearn race," is a risk worth taking, testifying to how an individual can commit to a radical reformation of self-image and worldview, even against powerfully popular currents, to serve a greater good for future generations. And that greater good appears to be the liberation of the ultimate minority—the individual. Get his book if you want to read something fearless, radical, and hopeful.

And hopefulness is something this book sorely lacks, which I did not realize until I finished drafting it. Of course, it probably did not help that I drafted it in 2020. But writing is a path that leaves the writer transformed, so I have left the history of this path, an artifact of its time and place, unrevised to bear witness. Only now, after having written a book orbiting the topic of race relations, have I truly begun to understand the promise to humanity of breaking that orbit. I imagine that for every individual who figures out how to divest from racial ideology, a tiny hole might appear in the common fuel tank of racial demagoguery. And if enough of us divest, that fuel might run out, leaving radicals of the left and the right politically isolated on the extreme fringes of public discourse where they belong…until they have calmed down enough to productively rejoin civilization. Now that seems like a vision worth pursuing.

BIBLIOGRAPHY

Abrams, Samuel J.
2016 "There Are Conservative Professors, Just Not in These States." 01 July. *New York Times.* www.nytimes.com/2016/07/03/opinion/sunday/there-are-conservative-professors-just-not-in-these-states.html.

Acciardo, Linda A.
1983 "Burial Site Claims Could Divert Power Lines." 03 November. *The Observer: News and Picture Weekly for North Providence, Johnston, Smithfield, Scituate, Foster, Glocester, Lincoln, Cumberland, North Smithfield and Burrillville. Greenville, Rhode Island* 29(30):1,27.

Adams, Jim
2003 "Spotlight on R.I. Smoke Shop Raid." *Indian Country Today.* indiancountrymedianetwork.com/news/spotlight-on-ri-smoke-shop-raid/.

Adams, Myron
1842 "Plowing and Drawing." *New England Farmer and Horticultural Register.* 7 December 21(23):177 Joseph Breck & Co., Boston.

Advisory Council on Historic Preservation (ACHP)
2017a *Improving Tribal Consultation in Infrastructure Projects.* www.achp.gov/docs/achp-infrastructure-report.pdf.
2017b *Meeting, Native American Affairs Committee.* March 22.

Ahlquist, Steve
2020 "Indigenous People's Day Open Mic at the State House." *Uprise RI.* https://upriseri.com/2020-10-13-indigenous-peoples-day.

Allport, Susan
1994 *Sermons in Stone: The Stone Walls of New England and New York.* W.W. Norton and Co., Inc., New York.

Anderson, Benedict
1983 *Imagined Communities: Reflections on the Origin and Spread of Nationalism.* Verso, New York.

Anderson, J.S.
1883 "Breeding, Fedding and Management of Livestock." 19 February, Pg. 4, *Vermot Phoenix,* Brattleboro, Vermont.

Anderson, Patrick
2017 "Narragansett Tribe Seeks Injunction to Stop Work on

Providence Viaduct." *Providence Journal.*
www.providencejournal.com/news/20170403/narragansett-
tribe-seeks-injunction-to-stop-work-on-providence-viaduct.

Andrade, Kevin G.
2018 "R.I. Narragansetts Raising Their Own Food, Connecting to
the Land Again." 26 August. *Providence Journal.* Accessed June
2, 2020. www.providencejournal.com/news/20180826/ri-nar-
ragansetts-raising-their-own-food-connecting-to-land-again.

Andrews-Maltais, Cheryl
2005a Letter to Bob DeSista, ACOE. 10 May.
2005b Letter to Carlisle Board of Selectmen. May 9.

Baffoni, Anita
2020 'FBI Asks for Tips, Footage from Last Week's Riots in
Providence.' 8 June. *WPRI.com.* Accessed June 30, 2020. www.
wpri.com/news/local-news/providence/fbi-investigating-vio-
lent-riot-in-providence/.

Baker, Andrew, and Holly Paterson
1988 "Farmer's Adaptations to Markets in Early-Nineteenth-
Century Massachusetts." *In The Farm: Annual Proceedings of
the 1986 Dublin Seminar for New England Folklife*, edited by P.
Benes, pp. 95-108. Boston University Press, Boston.

Baldwin, James
1963 *The Fire Next Time.* Dial Press.

Ballard, Edwin C.
1999 "For Want of a Nail: An Analysis of the Function of Some
Horseshoe or 'U'-Shaped Stone Structures." *Bulletin of the
Massachusetts Archaeological Society* 60(2):38-54.

Ballard, Edwin C., and James W. Mavor, Jr.
2006 "A Case for the Use of Above Surface Stone Constructs in a
Native American Ceremonial Landscape in the Northeast."
New England Antiquities Research Association Journal 40(1):33-
45.

Banda, Queen
2020 "Mashpee Student Qualifies for State Seal Test for Wampanoag
Biliteracy." 19 July. WCAI, Local NPR for the Cape, Coast &
Islands. Accessed July 24, 2020. www.capeandislands.org/post/
mashpee-student-qualifies-state-seal-test-wampanoag-bilitera-
cy#stream/0.

Banks, Charles E.
1911 *History of Martha's Vineyard.* G.H. Dean, Boston.

Barber, John W.

1836 *Connecticut Historical Collections.* A. Willard, Hartford.

Barre Evening Telegram

1900 "Getting Rid of Stones on the Farm." 17 February. Pg. 2. *Barre Evening Telegram.* Barre, Vermont.

Basso, Keith H.

1996 *Wisdom Sits in Places: Landscape and Language among the Western Apache.* University of New Mexico Press, Albuquerque.

Bay State Banner

2014 "Black Native Americans Beginning to Assert Identity." 30 December. *BayStateBanner.com.* www.baystatebanner.com/2014/12/30/black-native-americans-beginning-to-assert-identity/.

Bell, Michael M.

1989 "Did New England Go Downhill?" *Geographical Review* 79(4): 450-466.

Bell, Vikki

1999 "Performativity and Belonging: An Introduction." In *Performativity and Belonging,* edited by Vikki Bell, pp.1-10. Sage, London.

Bellow, Heather

2017 "Tennessee Gas Pipeline May 'Bulldoze' Sacred Native American Sites." *The Berkshire Edge.* theberkshireedge.com/tennessee-gas-pipeline-may-bulldoze-sacred-native-american-sites/.

Bencorbett.net

2018 "Native Voice: Interview with American Indian Activist-Poet John Trudell." 19 January. Downloaded April 18, 2020. bencorbett.net/index.php/2018/01/19/native-voice-interview-with-american-indian-activist-poet-john-trudell/.

Benedict, Jeff

2000 *Without Reservation: How a Controversial Indian Tribe Rose to Power and Built the World's Largest Casino.* Harper Collins.

Berkowitz, Bill

2003 "'Cultural Marxism' Catching On." *Intelligence Report.* Summer Issue, August 15. Southern Poverty Law Center. www.splcenter.org/fighting-hate/intelligence-report/2003/cultural-marxism-catching.

Berlatsky, Noah
  2019 "The Lethal Antisemitism of 'Cultural Marxism.'" 3 May.
        Jewish Currents. jewishcurrents.org/the-lethal-antisemi-
        tism-of-cultural-marxism/#:~:text=RIght-wing%20self-
        help%20guru%20Jordan%20Peterson%2C%20for%20exam-
        ple%2C%20has,what%20he%20sees%20as%20North%20
        American%20cultural%20rot.

Bidwell, Percy W.
        1921 "The Agricultural Revolution in New England." *The
        American Historical Review* 26(4):683-702.

Bidwell, Percy W., and John I. Falconer
  1941 *History of Agriculture in the Northern United States 1620-1860*.
        Peter Smith, New York.

Bingham, Amelia B.
  1970 *Mashpee: Land of the Wampanoags*. Mashpee Centennial
        Committee, Mashpee, MA.

Blancke, Shirley and Arthur E. Spiess
  2006 "The Flagg Swamp Rockshelter, Marlborough, MA: A
        Summary." *Bulletin of the Massachusetts Archaeological Society*
        67(1):2-24.

Boissevain, Ethel
  1956 "The Detribalization of the Narragansett Indians: A Case
        Study." *Ethnohistory* 3(3):225-245.

Borg, Linda
  2016 "Watson to Use $300K Innovation Fellowship to Expand
        Cultural Tourism in R.I." *Providence Journal*. 13 April. www.
        providencejournal.com/article/20160413/news/160419791.

Boston Journal
  1903 "Reported Gold Find Sets Farmers Wild." 29 March, Pg. 10.
        Boston Journal. Boston.

Boston Sunday Globe
  1898 "Abandoned Farms Made Edens." 9 January. Pg. 29.
        Boston Sunday Globe. Boston.

Boudillion, Daniel V.
  2001 *The Boxborough Esker. Field Report*. New England Antiquities
        Research Association website. www.neara.org/images/pdf/
        esker.pdf.

Bourne, S.
  1830 "Map of Plymouth Settled in 1620." Pendleton's Lithograpy
        Boston.

Bragdon, Kathleen J.

1999 *Native People of Southern New England, 1500-1650.* University of Oklahoma Press, Norman.

2009 *Native People of Southern New England, 1650-1775.* University of Oklahoma Press, Norman.

Brewster Standard

1892 No Title. 20 May. Pg. 3. *Brewster Standard.* Brewster, New York.

Brown III, John B., and Paul A. Robinson

2006 "'The 368 Years' War:' The Conditions of Discourse in Narragansett Country." In *Cross-Cultural Collaboration: Native Peoples in Archaeology in the Northeastern United States,* edited by Jordan E. Kerber, pp. 59-75. University of Nebraska Press, Lincoln.

Brown, Raymond H.

1958 "The Housatonic Indians, the Original Inhabitants of Southern Berkshire County." *Bulletin of the Massachusetts Archaeological Society* 19(3):44-50.

Brown, Simon (editor)

1853 *The New England Farmer.* Volume 5. Raynolds & Nourse, Boston, MA.

Brown University

2017 "Brown Pokanoket Agree on Plan for Preservation and Inclusive Tribal Access to Bristol Land." Brown.edu. www. brown.edu/news/2017-09-25/agreement.

Bruckner, Pascal

2012 *The Tyranny of Guilt: An Essay of Western Masochism.* Princeton University Press.

Burge, Kathleen

2012 "Mysterious Cave Now part of New Upton Heritage Park." *Boston Globe.* www.bostonglobe.com/metro/regionals/ west/2012/07/11/mysterious-cave-now-part-new-upton-heri- tage-park/I7a1puzdb6z9iAYTG9AZvJ/story.html.

Bullion, Brenda

1988 "The Agricultural Press: 'To Improve the Soil and the Mind.'" In *The Farm: Annual Proceedings of the 1986 Dublin Seminar for New England Folklife,* edited by P. Benes, pp. 74-94. Boston University Press, Boston.

Buel, J.

1836 "Industry: An Address to the Young." 12 July. Pg. 1. *Rutland*

Herald. Rutland, Vermont.

Buford, Harvey

2017 "Coordinators' Report: Rhode Island." *New England Antiquities Research Association Transit* 29(1):7-8.

2018 "Coordinators' Report: Rhode Island." *New England Antiquities Research Association Transit* 30(1):8-9.

Burl, Aubrey

1979 *Rings of Stone: The Prehistoric Stone Circles of Britain and Ireland.* Frances Lincoln, London.

Burlington Free Press

1855 "Items for Farmers." 4 May. Pg. 1. *Burlington Free Press.* Burlington, Vermont.

Burns, Thomas A, Lloyd Wilson, and Alberta Wilson

1979 "Interview with Lloyd Wilcox and Alberta Wilcox about Stone Wall Building, Narragansett Indians, Medicine Men, Growing Up in Charlestown, Rhode Island," Parts 1 through 3. Putnam, Connecticut, 1979. Audio. Retrieved from the Library of Congress. www.loc.gov/item/afc1991022_afs22328/.

Busby, Elanor

2019 "Far-Right Activities at Universities Rising as Young People Deny Holocaust, Experts Warn." 27 January. *The Independent.* www.independent.co.uk/news/education/education-news/far-right-holocaust-memorial-day-denial-universities-jew-ish-students-antisemitism-extremism-a8747181.html.

Butler, Eva L.

1946 "The Brush or Stone Memorial Heaps of Southern New England." *Archaeological Society of Connecticut Bulletin* 19(3):44-50.

Cabot, Dan

2008 "DAR Restores Historic Mayhew Memorial." *The Martha's Vineyard Times.* June 12.

Cachat, James

2016 "Suspected Burial Ground Rescue." *GoFundMe.com.* www.gofundme.com/NatAmerBurials.

Cachat, Rolf

2016 "Regional Tribes Banned From Inspecting Suspected Burial Grounds." *Care2Petitions.com.* www.thepetitionsite.com/928/325/407/regional-tribes-banned-from-inspect-ing-suspected-burial-ground-slated-for-destruction/.

Cachat-Schilling, Rolf

2010 "A Better Understanding of Trees & Their Ecology." www.ecolandscaping.org/03/trees/trees-a-challenge-of-per-spective/.

2016 "A Quantitative Assessment of Stone Relics in a Western Massachusetts Town." *Bulletin of the Massachusetts Archaeological Society* 77(2).

2017a "Native Sacred Spaces: Groundbreaking Study Shows Ritual Use of Sacred Stone Sites." *Oso:ah.org.* http://oso-ah.org/custom.html.

2017b "Stone Prayers of the Naśaué Nipmuk: A Quantitative Assessment of Stone Relics in a Western Massachusetts Town." *New England Antiquities Research Association 53rd Annual Meeting Program.*

2018a CV. *GrassRootsFund.org.* grassrootsfund.org/sites/default/files/attachments/grow-grant/cachat-schilling_rolfcv_0.pdf.

2018b "Assessing Stone Relics in Western Massachusetts Part II: Patterns of Site Distribution." *Bulletin of the Archaeological Society of Connecticut.*

2018c "Éli Luweyok Nek Kikayunkahke." *Northeast Anthropology* 85-86:21-45.

Campisi, Jack

1993 *Mashpee Indians: Tribe on Trial.* Syracuse University Press.

Caranci, Paul F.

2013 *The Hanging and Redemption of John Gordon. The True Story of Rhode Island's Last Execution.* The History Press.

Carini, Frank

2020 "Green New Deal Lacks Color." 2 February. *EcoRINews.* www.ecori.org/social-justice-archive/2020/2/19/green-new-deal-lacks-color.

Carocci, Max

2009 "Written Out of History: Contemporary Native American Narratives of Enslavement." *Anthropology Today* 25(2):15-19.

Carlson, Suzanne

2004 "Big Dig in Bingham: Maine Cairn Field Study." *New England Antiquities Research Association Journal* 38(2):32-42.

Carroll, Nicole

2020 "The language had gone quiet. Remarkably, she brought it back, saving far more than just words." 27 August. *USA*

Today. www.usatoday.com/in-depth/life/women-of-the-cen-
tury/2020/08/17/19th-amendment-jessie-little-doe-baird-
brings-back-lost-language/5476098002/.

Caulkins, Frances M.
  1866 *History of Norwich, Connecticut: From its Possession by the
         Indians to the Year 1866*. Hartford.

Ceremonial Landscapes Research, LLC
  2016 *Technical Report: Ceremonial Stone Landscape Survey
         Avoidance Plan*. waylandrec.com/wp-content/up-
         loads/2017/01/Avoidance-Plan-Memorandum-Dud-
         ley-Woods.pdf.
  2017 About Us. Ceremonial Landscapes Research, LLC.
         www.clresearch.org/about/.

Chomsky, Noam
  2002 *Media Control: The Spectacular Achievements of Propoganda*.
         Second Edition. Seven Stories Press.

Cipolla, Craig N.
  2018 "Earth Flows and Lively Stone. What Differences Does
         'Vibrant Matter' Make?" *Archaeological Dialogues* 25(1):49-70.

Cipolla, Craig N., and James Quinn
  2016 "Field School Archaeology the Mohegan Way: Reflections on
         Twenty Years of Community-Based Research and Teaching."
         Journal of Community Archaeology and Heritage. 3(2):118-134.

Clark, Emily
  2020 "Judge Rules in Favor of Mashpee Tribe." 9 June.
         Carver.WickedLocal.com. carver.wickedlocal.com/
         news/20200609/judge-rules-in-favor-of-mashpee-tribe.

Clifford, Ernest S.
  2008 "Our Native American Heritage: Hiding in Plain Sight." *New
         England Antiquities Research Association Journal* 42(1):24-26.

Climate Action Now
  2017a "Indigenous Ceremonial Stone Landscape Protection." 05
          June. *YouCaring.com*. www.youcaring.com/indigenousceremo-
          nialstonelandscapeprotection.
  2017b "Indigenous Ceremonial Stone Landscape Protection."
          Fundrazr.com. fundrazr.com/21Nzl2?ref=ab_4QbRfDsBdY-
          94QbRfDsBdY9.

Cole, Arthur H.
  1926 "Agricultural Crazes. A Neglected Chapter in American
         Economic History." *The American Economic Review* 16(4):622-

639.

Collins, David

2018 "Pequot Police Department is Overseen by a Criminal." 01
May. *The Day*. www.theday.com/article/20180501/
NWS05/180509955.

Comedy Central

2021 "Stacey Abrams: Flipping Georgia Blue & The 'Magic' of Black
Women." 21 January. *The Daily Social Distancing Show*. Comedy Central.

Conca, Mary Lou

2017 "Opposed to Installing Solar Array in Shutesbury: Opinion."
02 May. *Gazette.net*. www.gazettenet.com/Shutesbury-so-
lar-project-moving-forward-9681199.

Concord Oral History Program

2010 *The Language of Ancient Stones*.
www.concordlibrary.org/scollect/fin_aids/OH_Texts/Waks-
man.html.

Conneller, Philip

2019 "Aquinnah Wampanoag Tribe Attacks Bill to Restore
Reservation and Casino Hopes to Sister Tribe, Mashpee." 30
January. *Casino.org*. www.casino.org/news/wampanoag-aquin-
nah-tribe-attacks-bill-to-restore-mashpee-reservation/.

2020 "Mashpee Wampanoag Tribe Faces Power Struggle After
Failed Casino Bid Leaves It $500 Million in the Red." *Casino.
org*. www.casino.org/news/mashpee-wampanoag-tribe-pow-
er-struggle-after-failed-casino-bid/.

Contreras, Russell

2009 "Ex-Mashpee Wampanoag Chairman Pleads Guilty to Fraud."
South Coast Today. www.southcoasttoday.com/arti-
cle/20090212/News/902120386.

Cote, Jackson

2020 "Cedric Cromwell, chair of Mashpee Wampanoag Tribe,
accused of extorting thousands in bribes with architecture
firm owner in connection with Taunton casino project." 13
November. *Masslive.com*. www.masslive.com/casinos/2020/11/
cedric-cromwell-chair-of-mashpee-wampanoag-tribe-ac-
cused-of-extorting-thousands-in-bribes-with-architecture-
firm-owner-in-connection-with-taunton-casino-project.html.

Cothren, William

1854 *History of Ancient Woodbury*. Bronson Brothers, Waterbury,

CT.

Coughtry, Jay
1981 *The Notorious Triangle: Rhode Island and the African Slave Trade, 1700-1807.* Temple University Press.

Country Gentleman
1860 "What Shall be Done for Our Pastures?" *Country Gentleman.* 14 June, 15(24):379. Albany, New York.

Critic
1893 "Abandoned Farms." 10 June. Pg. 386. *The Critic: A Weekly Review of Literature and the Arts.* New York.

Crosby, Constance A.
1993 "The Algonkian Spiritual Landscape." In *Algonkians of New England: Past and Present,* edited by Peter Benes, pp. 35-41. Boston University, Boston.

Cronon, William
1983 *Changes in the Land: Indians, Colonists and the Ecology of New England.* Hill and Wang, New York.

Curtain, Edward V.
2016 "Archaeologists and Anthropologists Gather for Regional Conferences, Spring 2016." Curtain Archaeological Consulting, Inc. http://www.curtinarch.com/blog/spring2016.

Curtis, Chris
2014 "Battle or Massacre? Turners Delays Vote on Study Grant Proposal." 09 January. *The Recorder.* https://www.recorder.com/Archives/2014/01/BattlefieldGrantSkirmish-GR-010114.

Dafoe, Taylor
2020 "Most Paintings on Princeton's Campus Are of Dead White Men. But One Artist is Adding Equally Grand Portraits of Its Cooks and Cleaners." 08 January. *News.ArtNet.com.* news.artnet.com/exhibitions/mario-moore-portratis-princeton-1748637.

D'Andrade, Roy
1995 "Moral Models in Anthropology." *Current Anthropology* 36(3):399-408.

David, Lea
2017 "Against Standardization of Memory." *Human Rights Quarterly* 39:296-318.

Davis, Paul
2013 "Narragansetts Still Angered by Smoke Shop Raid on 10th Anniversary." *Providence Journal.* www.providencejournal.

com/breaking-news/content/20130714-narragansetts-still-an-gered-by-smoke-shop-raid-on-10th-anniversary.ece.

The Day

1898 "Leffingwell and Uncas, Descendant of the Former Speaks on the Perils of Mohegan Indian Warfare." 21 November. *The Day.*

Day, Clarence A.

1954 *A History of Maine Agriculture, 1604-1860.* University Press, Orono, Maine.

De Forest, John W.

1853 *History of the Indians of Connecticut from the Earliest known Period to 1850.* W.J. Hamersley, Hartford.

DeLucia, Christine

2012 "The Memory Frontier: Uncommon Pursuits of Past and Place in the Northeast after King Philip's War." *Journal of American History* 98(4):975-997.

2018 *Memory Lands: King Philip's War and the Place of Violence in the Northeast.* Yale University Press, New Haven, CT.

Den Ouden, Amy

2012 "We Still Live Here – Âs Nutayuneân." *American Anthropologist* 114(4):691-693.

Devine, Charles M.

1984 "Megalithic America and the Neudorfer Approach." *New England Antiquities Research Association Journal* 19(1&2):21-24.

Dexter, Franklin B.

1916 *Extracts from the Itineraries and Other Miscellanies of Ezra Stiles, D.D., LL.D., 1755-1794.* Yale University Press, New Haven.

DiAngelo, Robin

2018 *White Fragility: Why It's So Hard for White People to Talk About Racism.* Beacon Press.

DiMarzo, Steve

2015 "Coordinator's Report: Rhode Island." *New England Antiquities Research Association Transit* 27(1):7-8.

2017 "Why and How to Document Manitou Hassannash." Lecture presented at the October 7 dedication of the Manitou Hassannash Preserve. *Hopkinton Historical Association.* http://www.hopkintonhistoricalassociation.org/2017/11/08/manitou-hassannash-preserve/.

Dix, Byron E., and James W. Mavor, Jr.

1980 "Possible Astronomical Alignments, Date and Origins of the Pearson Stone Chamber." *Early Sites Research Association Journal* 16(1).

1981 "Two Possible Calendar Sites in Vermont." In *Archaeoastronomy in the Americas,* edited by Ray Williamson. Ballena Press Anthropological Papers No.22. Ballena Press, Los Altos, CA.

1982a "Heliolithic Ritual Sites in New England." *New England Antiquities Research Association Journal* 16 (3).

1982b "Stone Chambers, Indians and Astronomy." *Vermont History* 50(3).

1983 "Progress Report on New England Archaeoastronomy." *Bulletin Early Sites Research Society* 10(2):13-24.

1987 "New England Cedar Wetlands in Native American Ritual." In *Atlantic White Cedar Wetlands,* edited by Aimlee D. Laderman. Westview, Boulder, CO.

Dix, Byron E., James W. Mavor, Jr., and June W. Potts

1980 "Progress Report on the Calendar I Area in Central Vermont." *Archaeoastronomy* 3(1).

Donahue, Brian

2007 "Another Look from Sanderson's Farm: A Perspective on New England Environmental History and Conservation." *Environmental History* 12(1):9-34.

Dreger, Alice

2011 "Darkness's Descent on the American Anthropological Association: A Cautionary Tale." *Human Nature* 22(3):225-246.

Dresler-Hawke, Emma and James H. Liu

2006 "Collective Shame and the Positioning of German National Identity." *Psicología Política* 32:131-153.

Drummond, Cynthia

2014 "Field of Rock Cairns Complicates Plan for Proposed Hopkinton Subdivision." *Westerly Sun.* www.thewesterlysun.com/news/latestnews/4081122-129/field-of-rock-cairns-complicates-plan-for-proposed-hopkinton-subdivision.html.

2015 "Hopkinton Land Trust Saves Land Valued for Artifacts." *Westerly Sun.* www.thewesterlysun.com/news/latest-news/6375120-129/hopkinton-land-trust-saves-land-valued-for-its-artifacts.html.

Dwight, Timothy
1823 *Travels in New England and New-York.* W. Baynes and Son, and Ogle, Duncan & Co., London.

Dyck, Noel
2006 "Canadian Anthropology and the Ethnography of 'Indian Administration.'" In *Historicizing Canadian Anthropology,* edited by Julia Harrison and Regna Darnell, pp. 78-92. University of British Columbia Press, Vancouver.

Eil, Phil
2020 "The Curious Case of Rhode Island Historian Pat Conley." 27 October. *UpriseRI.com.* upriseri.com/2020-10-27-patrick-conley/.

Eldred, Mike
2009 "Mysterious Whittingham Site May be Native American 'Henge.'" *Deerfield Valley News.* www.dvalnews.com/pages/full_story_obits/push?article-Mysterious+Whitingham+site+may+be+Native+American+%E2%80%9Chenge%E2%80%9D%20&id=3179491.

Elmahrek, Adam
2020 "Elizabeth Warren Is Again Pressed on Past Claims of Native American Heritage." 26 February. *Los Angeles Times.* www.latimes.com/politics/story/2020-02-26/elizabeth-warren-again-is-pressed-on-past-claims-of-native-american-heritage.

Emery, Kenneth O.
1969 "Review of *Manitou* by James W. Mavor, Jr. and Byron E. Dix." woodsholemuseum.org/oldpages/sprtsl/v4n2-Manitou.pdf.

Farmer's Monthly Visitor
1839 "Farming in Merrimack County." *Farmer's Monthly Visitor.* 15 March, 1(3):42-43. Concord, New Hampshire.

Farrell, Richard T.
1977 "Advice to Farmers: The Content of Agricultural Newspapers, 1860-1910." *Agricultural History* 51(1):209-217.

Falkner, Tim
2016 "Group of Rhode Island Native Americans File Lawsuit against State for Reparations." 14 November. *EcoRINews.* www.ecori.org/social-justice-archive/2016/11/14/reparations-sought-for-providence-indian-tribe.
2017 "Brown, Pokanoket Tribe Reach Deal to End Occupation." *EcoRI.com.* www.ecori.org/social-justice-archive/2017/9/25/brown-pokanoket-tribe-reach-deal-to-end-occupation.

Fast, Anita
1993   "Stone 'Walls' or Stone 'Rows'?" 23 April. *Carlisle Mosquito.*
Federal Writers Project for the State of Connecticut
1938   *Connecticut: A Guide to Its Roads, Lore, and People.* Houghton Mifflin Company, Boston.
Feder, Kenneth L.
1990   *Frauds, Myths, and Mysteries: Science and Pseudoscience in Archaeology.* Mayfield Publishing, Mountain View, CA.
2010   *Encyclopedia of Dubious Archaeology: From Atlantis to the Walam Olum.* Greenwood Publishing Group, Santa Barbara, California.
Fessenden, Thomas G. (editor)
1835   *New England Farmer.* Vol.13. Geo. C. Barrett, Boston.
Fields, Karen A., and Barbara J. Fields
2014   *Racecraft: The Soul of Inequality in American Life.* Verso, London and New York.
Flazy, J.
2016   "Native American Ceremonial Stone Landscapes in New England: Fact or Myth?" *Daily KOS.* www.dailykos.com/stories/2016/3/19/1503933/-Native-American-Ceremonial-Stone-Landscapes-in-New-England-Fact-or-Myth.
Fletcher, Andrew, Kate Kenney, and John G. Crock.
2016   "End of Field Letter Report for an Archaeological Reconnaissance Survey and Non-Invasive Documentation of the West Hill Cairns in the Green Mountain National Forest, Rochester, Windsor County, Vermont." *UVM Consulting Archaeology Program Report* No. 1028. Burlington, Vermont.
Fohl, Timothy
2003   "Confessions of a Professional Rockpopper." *New England Antiquities Research Association Journal* 37(2):15.
2010   "Integrated Wetland-Dry Land Features with Astronomical Associations." *Bulletin of the Massachusetts Archaeological Society* 71(1).
Fohl, Timothy and Kenneth C. Leonard, Jr.
2006   "Similarities of Ceremonial Structures in New England and Mesoamerica." Paper presented at the 73rd Annual Meeting of the Eastern States Archaeological Federation, Fitchburg, MA.
Fohl, Timothy, Doug Harris, Curtiss Hoffman, and Peter Waksman
2005   *Survey Report of Indian Ceremonial Structures on Benfield Parcel "A" Property in Carlisle, Massachusetts.* Report submit-

ted to the Carlisle Board of Selectmen.

Foster, David R.

1992 "Land-Use History (1730-1990) and Vegetation Dynamics in Central New England, USA." *Journal of Ecology* 80(4): 753-771.

1999 *Thoreau's Country: Journey through a Transformed Landscape.* Harvard University Press, Cambridge, Massachusetts.

Fortier, Marc

2020 "Mashpee Wampanoag Tribe Chairman Indicted for Bribery Scheme Involving $1B Casino Plan." 13 November. *NBC10 Boston.* www.nbcboston.com/news/local/chairman-of-mash-pee-wampanoag-tribe-indicted-for-bribery-scheme/2230939/.

Freeman's Journal

1820 "The Vermont Murder." 17 January. Pg. 2. *Freeman's Journal.* Cooperstown, New York.

Frum, David

2014 "The Impossibility of Reparations. Considering the Single Most Important Question About Racial Resstitution: How Would It Work?" 3 June. *The Atlantic.* www.theatlantic.com/business/archive/2014/06/the-impossibility-of-repara-tions/372041/.

Gage, James E.

2009 "Acknowledging Rock Piles – Some Thoughts from James Gage." *Rockpiles.* rockpiles.blogspot.com/2009/10/acknowledg-ing-rock-piles-some-thoughts.html.

2017a "Manitou Hassanash Preserve Dedication." *YouTube.com.* www.youtube.com/watch?v=hf2tbBC-_jI&feature=youtu.be

2017b Steve DiMarzo CSL Day Talk. *YouTube.com.* www.youtube.com/watch?v=MPb2Ku3AGg4&feature=youtu.be.

Gage, Mary E., and James E. Gage

2011 *A Handbook of Stone Structures in Northeastern United States, Revised First Edition.* Powwow River Books, Amesbury, Massachusetts.

2014 "Field Clearing: Stone Removal and Disposal Practices in Agriculture and Farming, With a Case Study of Stone Removal Activities in Joshua Hempstead's Diary." *Bulletin of the Archaeological Society of Connecticut* 76: 33-81.

2015a "How to Identify and Distinguish Native American Ceremonial Stone Structures from Historic Farm Structures." *Bulletin of the Connecticut Archaeological Society* 77:17-40.

2015b "Stone Chambers: Root Cellars, Ice Houses, or Native American Ceremonial Structures?" *Bulletin of the Connecticut Archaeological Society* 77:69-100.

2017   *Land of a Thousand Cairns: Revival of Old Style Ceremonies.* Powwow River Books, Amesbury, Massachusetts.

Gage, James E., Mary Gage, and Steve DiMarzo, Jr.
2012   "Exploring and Reporting Stone Structure Sites in Rhode Island." *New England Antiquities Research Association Journal* 46(2):21-27.

Galanopoulos, A.G. and Edward Bacon Galanopoulos
1969   *Atlantis: The Truth Behind the Legend.* kirkusreviews.com/book-reviews/a/a-g-and-edward-bacon-galanopoulos/atlantis-the-truth-behind-the-legend/.

Geddes, Henry and Martín Valdiviezo
2017   "Struggles Against Colonization in the U.S.A.: Mohicans in Massachusetts." *Intercontinental Cry.* intercontinentalcry.org/struggles-colonization-u-s-mohicans-massachusetts/.

Gero, Joan M.
1989   "Producing Prehistory, Controlling the Past: The Case of New England's Beehives." In *Critical Traditions in Contemporary Archaeology: Essays in the Philosophy, History, and Socio-politics of Archaeology*, edited by Valerie Pinsky and Alison Wylie, pp. 96-103. Cambridge University Press, Cambridge.

Gilbert, Colgate
2006   "Standing Stones, Observatories, Hill Farms and Indian Agroforestry: A Look at the Sweetser and Thayer Sites of Franklin County, MA." Paper presented at the 73rd Annual Meeting of the Eastern States Archaeological Federation, Fitchburg, Massachusetts.

Gilley, Bruce
2017   "Diversity Oaths: Another Step Away From Honest Scholarship." 04 April. *MindingtheCampus.org.* www.mindingthecampus.org/2017/04/04/diversity-oaths-another-step-away-from-honest-scholarship/.

2020   "The Cancel Mob Comes Back for More." 8 October. *Wall Street Journal.* https://www.wsj.com/articles/the-cancel-mob-comes-back-for-more-11602091733.

Golash-Boza, Tanya
2016   "The Effective Diversity Statement." *InsideHigherEd.com.* https://www.insidehighered.com/advice/2016/06/10/

how-write-effective-diversity-statement-essay.

GoLocalProvNewsTeam

2020 "RI Republican Splinter Group Urges Voters to Keep 'Providence Plantations' in State Name." 12 October. *GoLocalProv.com*. www.golocalprov.com/politics/ri-republican-splinter-group-urges-voters-to-keep-providence-plantations-in.

Goodby, Robert G., Sarah Tremblay and Edward Bouras

2014 "The Swanzey Fish Dam: A Large, Pre-Contact Native American Stone Structure in Southwestern New Hampshire." *Northeast Anthropology* 81-82:1-22.

Goudreau, Jenna

2012 "The 10 Worst College Majors." 11 October. *Forbes*. www.forbes.com/sites/jennagoudreau/2012/10/11/the-10-worst-college-majors/#dcb5222586c8.

Gould, Rae

2013 "The Search for Real Indians in New England in the 'Historical' Period." In *The Death of Prehistory*, edited by Peter R. Schmidt and Stephen A. Mrozowski, pp. 241-266. Oxford University Press, Oxford.

Grady, Constance

2019 "How to Publish Classic Books that Aren't Just by Dead White Men." 21 May. *Vox.com*. www.vox.com/culture/2019/5/21/18564266/modern-library-torchbearers-penguin-classics-asian-american-heritage.

Green-Mountain Freeman

1856 "The Orphan and the Fairy: A Story for Children." 27 March. Pg. 1. *Green-Mountain Freeman*. Montpelier, Vermont.

Grosvenor, Amanda M.

2016 "A Big Award for the Tomaquag Museum." 26 October. *RhodyBeat.com*. rhodybeat.com/stories/a-big-award-for-the-tomaquag-museum,22171?.

Guthrie, James L.

2006 "The Climate is Changing." *New England Antiquities Research Association Journal* 40(1):3-7.

Hadavas, Chloe

2020 "Confederate Groups Are Thriving on Facebook. What Does That Mean for the Platform?" 31 July. *Slate*. slate.com/technology/2020/07/confederate-groups-facebook-hate-speech.html.

Halbwachs, Maurice

1992 *On Collective Memory*. University of Chicago Press.

Hall, Jonathan and Eric Woodman

1973 "Beehive-Shaped Stone Structures: Ancient or Recent Origin?" *Man in the Northeast* [now *Northeast Anthropology*] 5:60-62.

Handsman, Russell G.

2008 "Landscapes of Memory in Wampanoag Country – and the Monuments Upon Them." In *Archaeologies of Place Making: Monuments, Memories, and Engagement in Native North America*, edited by Patricia E. Rubertone, pp. 161-194. Left Coast Press, Walnut Creek, California.

Harker, Harley

1891 "To the City. And the Sad Home-Coming of a Wayward Boy." 24 July. Pg. 3. *Waterbury Evening Democrat*. Waterbury, Connecticut.

Harris, Doug

2012 "Walking Together: Detection and Protection of Ancient Ceremonial Landscapes in Modern New England." A presentation sponsored by the Wayland Historical Commission. www.wayland.ma.us/Pages/WaylandMA_BComm/Historicalcom/walking.pdf.

2014 "Ceremonial Stone Landscapes." Presentation for the National Center for Preservation Technology and Training, National Park Service. Posted online by Ryan Ware on May 4, 2017. www.ncptt.nps.gov/blog/ceremonial-stone-landscapes/.

2016 Letter to Walter Ramsey, Planning and Conservation Department, Town of Montague. www.montague-ma.gov/files/Narragansett_Tribal_Statement.pdf.

Harris, Doug, and Doug Jones

2018 "Ceremonial Stone Landscapes of New England and Developing Best Practices to Assess Submerged Paleocultural Landscapes." In *Proceedings from the Maritime Cultural Landscape Symposium*, October 14-15, 2015, University of Wisconsin-Madison, Vol. 1, Presentation Papers, edited by Barbara Wyatt, pp. 147-153. National Park Service, U.S. Department of the Interior. www.nps.gov/nr/publications/guidance/NRLI/presentations/MCLS-Proceedings-vol1-final.pdf.

Harris, Doug and Paul A. Robinson

2015 "The Ancient Ceremonial Landscape and King Philip's War Battlefields of Nipsachuck." *Northeast Anthropology* 83-84:133-149.

Harris, Oliver J. T., and Craig N. Cipolla
2017   *Archaeological Theory in the New Millenium.* Routledge, New York.

Harris, Sam
2016   "Why You Should Avoid Identity Politics." *Sam Harris' Waking UP Podcast*, #45 Ask me Anything #5, September 2016. samharris.org/podcast/item/ask-me-anything-5.

Hartford Courant
1898   "To Reclaim Abandoned Farms: Corporation Formed to Buy Up New England Land." 3 January. Pg. 1. *Hartford Courant.* Hartford, Connecticut.

Hasho, Sarah L.
2012   "Bound in Stone: A Landscape and Architectural Analysis of the Eastern Pequot Tribal Nation Reservation, Connecticut." Masters thesis, University of Massachusetts, Boston. www.easternpequottribalnation.com/wp-content/uploads/2017/03/Hasho-Sarah-Thesis-on-Eastern-Pequot-UMB-2012.pdf.

Hauptman, Laurence M., and James D. Wherry (editors)
1993   *The Pequots in Southern New England: The Fall and Rise of an American Indian Nation.* University of Oklahoma Press, Norman.

Haueisen, Kathryn
2019   "Twelve Generations After the Mayflower." *HowWiseThen.com.* howwisethen.com/twelve-generations-after-mayflower/.

Hawley, Gideon
1835   "A Letter from Rev. Gideon Hawley of Marshpee, Containing an Account of his Services among the Indians of Massachusetts and New-York, and a Narrative of his Journey to Onohoghgwage." 31 July, 1794. *Massachusetts Historical Society Collections* 1(4): 50-67.

Hayes, Willet M.
1912   *Farm Development: An Introductory Book in Agriculture.* Orange Judd Company, New York.

Hays, Ted
2017   "Pokanokets Protest at Burr's Hill: Local Tribe Upset They Were 'Shut Out' of Formal Repatriation Ceremony by Cape-Vineyard Confederation. 17 May." *Rhody Beat.* rhodybeat.com/stories/pokanokets-protest-at-burrs-hill,25013.

Heaney, Sally
2005   "Indian Tribes Say Carlisle Site Bears Signs of the Ancient

Past." 15 May. *The Boston Globe.* archive.boston.com/news/lo-
cal/articles/2005/05/15/indian_tribes_say_carlisle_site_bears_
the_signs_of_sacred_past/.

Helmer, Thomas A.

2013 "The Fisher Property's Indigenous Presence." *Hopkinton
Historical Association.* www.hopkintonhistoricalassociation.
org/page88.html.

2014 "Seeing the Narragansett Presence." *Hopkinton Historical
Association.* www.hopkintonhistoricalassociation.org/page41.
html.

Henry, Ray

2007 "Tribal Purging Growing in U.S." 27 October. Associated Press,
The Oklahoman. oklahoman.com/article/3158153/purging-
tribal-rolls-a-national-trend.

2008 "Tribe, Developer Battle Over Rock Mounds." Associated
Press, *San Francisco Gate.* www.sfgate.com/news/article/Tribe-
developer-battle-over-rock-mounds-3204465.php.

Hernandon, Ruth W., and Ella W. Sekatau

1997 "The Right to a Name: The Narragansett People and Rhode
Island Officials in the Revolutionary Era." *Ethnohistory*
44(3):433-462.

Hill, Jessica

2020a "Grand Jury Subpoenas More Documents from Mashpee
Tribe." 1 September. *South Coast Today.* www.southcoasttoday.
com/news/20200901/grand-jury-subpoenas-more-documents-
from-mashpee-tribe.

2020b "Twin Sisters Sue Wampanoag Tribe Over Disputed
Membership." 27 September. *Cape Cod Times.* www.cape-
codtimes.com/news/20200927/twin-sisters-sue-wampano-
ag-tribe-over-disputed-membership.

2020c "Mashpee Wampanaog Tribal Council Chairman Indicted,
Removed From Post." 13 November. *Cape Cod Times.*
www.capecodtimes.com/story/news/2020/11/13/mash-
pee-tribal-council-chairman-arrested-extortion-brib-
ery-charges/6277244002/.

Hirsch, Adam J.

1988 "The Collision of Military Cultures in Seventeenth-Century
New England." *The Journal of American History* 74(4):1187-
1212.

Hobsbawm, Eric, and Terence Ranger (eds.)
1992 *The Invention of Tradition.* Cambridge University Press.
Hoffman, Curtiss R.
2004 "Analysis of Stone Features: The Ridges at Deer Lake Housing Development Property, Killingworth, Connecticut." On file at the Connecticut Historical Commission Hartford, Connecticut.
2015 "A Quantitative Analysis of Stone Features at the Buell Hill Site in Killingworth, Connecticut." *Bulletin of the Archaeological Society of Connecticut* 77: 123-149.
2018 "Stone Prayers: Native American Stone Constructions of the Eastern Seaboard." *America Through Time.*
Holman Bible
1890 *Holy Bible.* A.J. Holman & Co., Philadelphia.
Hoet, Gerard
1728 *Figures de la Bible.* P. de Hondt, The Hague.
Holstein, Harry
2012 "Comparison of Stone Structures at West Bolton, Vermont, With Those Found at Sites in the Southeast: Preliminary Observations Based on an Initial Visit to West Bolton." *New England Antiquities Research Association Journal* 46(1):4-33.
Hopkinton (Town of)
2016 Comprehensive Plan. www.hopkintonri.org/wp-content/uploads/2018/07/Hopkinton-Comprehensive-Plan-for-website.pdf.
Hopkinton Area Land Trust, Inc.
2018 "Ceremonial Stones in the Landscape." December. *Hopkinton Area Land Trust, Inc. Newsletter (Fall-Winter).* hopkinton-landtrust.org/wp-content/uploads/2019/07/2019-12-Newsletter.pdf.
Hosmer, F.A.
1885 "Chapter II: The Town of Great Barrington." In *History of Berkshire County, Massachusetts, with Biographical Sketches of its Prominent Men.* J.B. Beers & Co., New York.
Houghton, Sam
2019 "Recall Petition Filed Against Tribal Leaders." 25 April. *The Mashpee Enterprise.* www.capenews.net/mashpee/news/recall-petitions-filed-against-tribal-leaders/article_e81c6d79-0b09-5723-9040-8ae07f322f35.html.

Howell, John

2019 "Pisaturo Suggests Abandoning Drilling for Bayside Sewers." 13 August. *Warwick Beacon* Online. warwickonline.com/stories/to-cut-costs-speed-work-pisaturo-suggests-abandoning-drilling-for-bayside-sewers,144624.

Howes, Matthew

2016 "They Already Knew? Going Along to Get Along/Sacred Geography/Sacred Remains." *Native New England Stones.* nativenewenglandstones.blogspot.com/2016/07/they-already-knew-going-along-to-get.html.

Hughey, Matthew W.

2012 "Stigma Allure and White Antiracist Identity Management." *Social Psychology Quarterly* 75(3):219-241.

Hutchins, Francis G.

1979 *Mashpee: The Story of Cape Cod's Indian Town.* Amarta Press, West Franklin, New Hampshire.

Indianz.com

2015 "Mashpee Wampanoag Tribe Celebrates Land-Into-Trust Decision." 18 September. *Indianz.com.* indianz.com/News/2015/09/18/mashpee-wampanoag-tribe-celebr.asp.

Institute for Field Research

2020 "US-CT:Mohegan Summer 2020, Overview." *Institute for Field Research.* ifrglobal.org/program/us-ct-mohegan/.

Ives, Timothy H.

2009 "Expressions of Community: Reconstructing Native Identity in Seventeenth-Century Central Connecticut Through Land Deed Analysis." In *The Journey: An Algonquian Peoples Seminar*, edited by Shirley W. Dunn, pp. 25-38. New York State Museum Bulletin 511, Albany.

2013a "Remembering Stone Piles in New England." *Northeast Anthropology* 79-80:37-80.

2013b "Letter from Timothy H. Ives, Principal Archaeologist at the Rhode Island Historical Preservation and Heritage Commission, to Ms. Joyce Devine." 12 December. On file at the Rhode Island Historical Preservation and Heritage Commission.

2015a "Cairnfields in New England's Forgotten Pastures." *Archaeology of Eastern North America* 43:119-132.

2015b "Romance, Redemption, and Ceremonial Stone Landscapes." *Bulletin of the Archaeological Society of Connecticut* 77:151-164.

2018 "The Hunt for Redneck Archaeology: Disentangling 'White

Guilt,' Ceremonial Stone Landscape Activism, and Professional Archaeology in New England." *Northeast Anthropology* 85-86: 47-72.

(forthcoming) "Historical Accounts of Forgotten Stone Heaping Practices on Nineteenth Century Hill Farms." *Northeast Historical Archaeology* 49.

Jackson, Cassi

2020 "'We're more than just the Trail of Tears and Thanksgiving and Columbus Day': What it means to be Indigenous in Connecticut." 27 November. *Hartford Courant.* www. courant.com/news/connecticut/hc-news-indigenous-heritage-day-20201127-hc5jmqepbjcrvjh4vkqrm4ugbq-story.html.

Jackson, John L., Jr.

2008 *Racial Paranoia: The Unintended Consequences of Political Correctness.* Basic Books, New York.

Jaschik, Scott

2012 "Moving Further to the Left." 24 October. *InsideHigherEd.com.* www.insidehighered.com/news/2012/10/24/survey-finds-professors-already-liberal-have-moved-further-left.

2016 "Professors, Politics, and New England." 05 July. *InsideHigherEd.com.* https://www.insidehighered.com/news/2016/07/05/new-analysis-new-england-colleges-responsible-left-leaning-professoriate.

2017 "Professors and Politics: What the Research Says." 27 February. *InsideHigherEd.com.* https://www.insidehighered.com/news/2017/02/27/research-confirms-professors-lean-left-questions-assumptions-about-what-means.

Jennings, Francis

1975 *The Invasion of America: Indians, Colonialism and the Cant of Conquest.* University of North Carolina Press, Chapel Hill.

Jett, Stephen C.

1994 "Cairn and Brush Travel Shrines in the United States Northeast and Southeast." *Northeast Anthropology* 48:61-68.

John Milner Associates, Inc.

2012 "Archaeological Site Examination for the Upton Chamber Masonry Rehabilitation and Drainage Improvement Project, 18 Elm Street (Assessor's Parcel 28), Town of Upton, Worcester County, Massachusetts." Prepared for the Town of Upton, Massachusetts. www.uptonma.gov/sites/uptonma/files/uploads/upton_chamber_report_-_2012.pdf.

Johnson, Skip R.
2020 "Escaping Conflict and the Karpman Drama Triangle." 3 January. *BPDFamily.com*. bpdfamily.com/content/karpman-drama-triangle.

Jones, Brian D.
2015 "Interpreting Cultural Stone Landscapes in Southeastern Connecticut." *Bulletin of the Archaeological Society of Connecticut* 77: 53-67.

Kaplan, Karen
2018 From the Archives: "DNA Testing Raises a Delicate Question: What Does it Mean to be a Native American?" 16 October. *Los Angeles Times*. www.latimes.com/science/la-sci-dna-testing-native-americans-archive-20181016-story.html.

Kaufmann, Eric
2006 "The Dominant Ethnic Moment: Towards the Abolition of 'Whiteness'?" *Ethnicities* 6(2):231-266.

Keene, Adrienne J.
2013 "Revisiting Love in the Time of Blood Quantum." *Native Appropriations*. 5 September. nativeappropriations.com/2013/09/revisiting-love-in-the-time-of-blood-quantum.html.
2017 "The Pokanoket Encampment in Bristol, RI." 25 August. *Native Appropriations*. nativeappropriations.com/2017/08/the-pokanoket-encampment-in-bristol-ri.html.
2020 Curriculum vitae. *Vivo.Brown.edu.* https://vivo.brown.edu/docs/a/akeene_cv.pdf?dt=310515037.

Kendall, D. George
1974 *The Place of Astronomy in the Ancient World: A Joint Symposium of the Royal Society and the British Academy*. Oxford University Press for the British Academy.

Kendall, Edward Augustus
1809 *Travels through the Northern Parts of the United States in the Years 1807 and 1808*. Vol. 2. L. Riley, New York.

Kendi, Ibram X.
2019 *How to Be An Antiracist*. One World, New York.

Kershaw, Sarah
2007 "Family Behind Foxwoods Loses Hold in Tribe." 22 June. *New York Times*. www.nytimes.com/2007/06/22/nyregion/22pequot.html.

Kirakosian, Katharine, and Tomaquag Museum

2020 "Narragansett Food Sovereignty Initiative." 04 June. *Rhode Tour*. rhodetour.org/items/show/302.

Kreisberg, Glenn

2017 "Mass Forest Rescue Seminar Report." *New England Antiquities Research Association Transit* 29(2):1-2.

Kruk-Bochowska, Zuzanna

2018 "Transnationalism as a Decolonizing Strategy? 'Trans-Indigenism' and Native American Food Sovereignty." *Studia Anglica Posnaniensia* 53:413-423. sciendo.com/article/10.2478/stap-2018-0020.

Kuffner, Alex

2017 "Pokanoket Nation Takes Step Forward in Struggle for Identity, Ancestral Lands." 8 October. *Providence Journal*. www.providencejournal.com/news/20171008/pokanoket-nation-takes-step-forward-in-struggle-for-identity-ancestral-lands.

Lavin, Lucianne

2013 *Connecticut's Indigenous Peoples: What Archaeology, History, and Oral Traditions Teach Us About Their Communities and Cultures.* Yale University Press: New Haven and London.

Lawton, Bessie L., Anita Foeman, and Nicholas Surde

2018 "Bridging Discussions of Human History: Ancestry DNA and New Roles for Africana Studies." *Genealogy* 2(1):5. www.mdpi.com/2313-5778/2/1/5/htm.

Leary, Daniel

1988 "Field Cairns: A Study of 18th and 19th Century Field Clearing Techniques – A Homogenous Study and Analysis." *New England Antiquities Research Association Journal* 22(3&4):33-45.

Legacy.com

2020 Loril MoonDream. *Legacy.com*. www.legacy.com/obituaries/recorder/obituary.aspx?n=loril-moondream&pid=196172445&fhid=6739.

Leonard, Kenneth C., Jr.

2010 "Identification and Preliminary Analysis of a Late Woodland Ceremonial Site in Southeastern New England." *Bulletin of the Massachusetts Archaeological Society* 71(1):26-43.

Lepinoka, Mary E., and Mark Carlotto

2015 "Evidence of a Native American Solar Observatory on Sunset Hill in Gloucester, Massachusetts." *Bulletin of the Mas-*

sachusetts Archaeological Society 76(1):27-43.

Levitt, Marc and Lilack Dekel

2008 *Stories in Stone*. Transformation Films and Levittation Production.

Leveillee, Alan, and Burr Harrison

1995 "Technical Report: Reconnaissance Archaeological Survey, Conant Land Parcel." Public Archaeology Laboratory, Inc. Report #632.

1997 "When Worlds Collide: Archaeology in the New Age – The Conant Parcel Stone Piles." *Bulletin of the Massachusetts Archaeological Society* 58(1):24-30.

1998 "Archaeological Investigations of Stone Pile Features Within The Orchard Valley Estates Subdivision, Cranston, Rhode Island." *Bulletin of the Massachusetts Archaeological Society* 59(1):14-24.

2001 "Public Archaeology, The New Age, and Local Truths." *Bulletin of the Massachusetts Archaeological Society* 62(1):23-28.

2005 "Archaeological Assessment of Selected Stone Piles Within the Benfield Farm, Carlisle, Massachusetts." Public Archaeology Laboratory, Inc. Report.

Leveillee, Alan A., and Joseph N. Waller

2005 "Intensive (Locational) Archaeological Survvey, Benfield Parcel A Project Area, Carlisle, Massachusetts, Submitted to the Town of Carlisle." Public Archaeology Laboratory, Inc.

Lightman, David

1993 "Trump Criticizes Pequots, Casino." 6 October. *Hartford Courant*. www.courant.com/news/connecticut/hc-xpm-1993-10-06-0000003863-story.html.

Lin-Sommer, Sam

2016 "Mashapaug Nahaganset Tribe Files Lawsuit Charging R.I. and U.S. Governments with Environmental Racism." *EcoRI News*. www.ecori.org/social-justice-archive/2016/7/13/mashapaug-nahaganset-tribe-sues-ri-and-us-governments.

Lipman, Andrew

2008 "'A means to knit them together': The Exchange of Body Parts in the Pequot War." *William and Mary Quarterly* 65(1):3-28.

List, Madeline

2020 "Providence Mayor Signs Order to Pursue Truth, Repara tions for Black, Indigenous People." 16 July. *Providence Journal*. www.providencejournal.com/news/20200716/

providence-mayor-signs-order-to-pursue-truth-repara-
tions-for-black-indigenous-people.

Lonegren, Sig
1993 "In Memory of Byron E. Dix." *New England Antiquities
Research Association Journal* 27(3/4):57-58.

Long, Tom
1998 "Mark Strohmeyer, 45, Amateur Archaeologist And
Ex-Bethlemeite." July 14. *The Boston Globe*. articles.mcall.
com/1998-07-14/news/3217026_1_native-american-bos-
ton-public-housing-mark-strohmeyer.

Ludlum, David M.
1939 *Social Ferment in Vermont, 1791-1850.* Columbia University
Press, New York.

MacSweeney, Timothy
1999 "The Indian Cave." *New England Antiquities Research
Association*. www.neara.org/images/pdf/cave.pdf.
2010 "Game Drive." *Waking Up On Turtle Island*.
wakinguponturtleisland.blogspot.com/2010/09/game-drive.
html.
2015 "Forgotten and Ignored Sacred Indigenous Landscapes."
Waking Up On Turtle Island. wakinguponturtleisland.blogspot.
com/2015/11/forgotten-and-ignored-sacred-indigenous.html.
2016 "The Process of Pasturization: A Tale of Two Tims." *Waking Up
On Turtle Island*. wakinguponturtleisland.blogspot.
com/2016/03/the-process-of-pasturization-tales-of.html.

Maher, Savannah
2018 "The Difficult Math of Being Native American."
7 February. *National Public Radio*. www.npr.org/sections/
codeswitch/2018/02/07/583665568/love-and-blood-quantum-
buy-in-or-die-out.

Maine Board of Agriculture
1860 Fifth Annual Report of the Secretary of the Maine Board of
Agriculture. Vol. 5. Stevens & Sayward, Augusta, Maine.

Maine Farmer
1891 "Abandoned Farms." *Maine Farmer* 59(14): 1.

Mancini, Jason R.
2008 "Beyond Reservation: Indians, Maritime Labor, and
Communities of Color from Eastern Long Island Sound, 1713-
1861." In *Gender, Race, Ethnicity, and Power in Maritime America*, edited by Glenn S. Gordinier, pp. 23-46. Mystic Seaport

Museum, Inc., Mystic, Connecticut.

Mandell, Daniel R.

1996 *Behind the Frontier: Indians in Eighteenth-Century Massachusetts.* University of Nebraska Press, Lincoln.

1998 "Shifting Boundaries of Race and Ethnicity: Indian-Black Intermarriage in Southern New England, 1760-1880." *The Journal of American History* 85(2):466-501.

Marcelo, Philip

2020 "Mass. Tribes Dispute Reservation Where A $1B Casino Is Planned." 9 December. *WBUR.com.* www.wbur.org/ news/2020/12/09/mashpee-wampanoag-mattakeeset-massa-chuset-land-dispute.

Marcus, Max

2019 "Four Winds Students Raise Money for Mashpee Wampanoag Tribe." 15 October. *Greenfield Recorder.* https://www.recorder. com/Four-Winds-walkathon-29356121.

Martha Lyon Landscape Architecture, LLC, Fannin-Lehner Preservation Consultants, CME Associates, Inc. and Carlisle Arboriculture

2016 *Central Burying Ground, Carlisle, Massachusetts, Preservation Master Plan.* Prepared for the Town of Carlisle Historical Commission. www.carlislema.gov/Pages/CarlisleMA_HC-NA/0588BAE3-000F8513.

Martin, Alexandra G.

2017 "Mapping Ceremonial Stone Landscapes in the Narragansett Homelands: 'Teâno Wonck Nippée Am, I Will Be Here By and By Again.'" Doctoral Dissertation, Department of Anthropology, College of William and Mary. scholarworks.wm.edu/ etd/1530192339/.

Martin, Frederick W., and Elizabeth F. Martin

2012 "A Midsummer Sunbeam Site in New England." In *Viewing the Sky Through Past and Present Cultures,* edited by Todd W. Bostwick and Bryan Bates, pp. 287-296. Proceedings of the Oxford VII International Conference on Archaeoastronomy. Pueblo Grande Museum Anthropological Papers No. 15. City of Phoenix Parks and Recreation Department.

Martin, Frederick W., Elizabeth F. Martin, Polly Midgley, and Walter Wheeler

2012 "Archaeo-Astronomical Prospecting at the Moose Hill Stone Chambers." *Archaeology of Eastern North America* 40:145-162.

Martinez, Samuel
  1996   "Indifference within Indignation: Anthropology, Human Rights, and the Haitian Bracero." *American Anthropologist* 98(1):17-25.

Mashpee Wampanoag Tribe
  2020   Homepage. mashpeewampanoagtribe-nsn.gov/.

Massachusetts Ethical Archaeology
  2018   Massachusetts Ethical Archaeology Homepage. www.ethicarch.org/our-mission.

Massachusetts Historical Society Collections
  1846   "A Description of Mashpee in the County of Barnstable, September 16, 1802." *Massachusetts Historical Society Collections* 3(2):1-12.

Massachusetts Historical Commission
  n.d.   Review and Compliance. www.sec.state.ma.us/mhc/mhcrevcom/revcomidx.htm.

Massachusetts Land Trust Coalition
  2018   "Biographies of Today's Presenters." *Massland.org.* massland.org/sites/default/files/uploads/2018mlcc_speakerbios.pdf.

Matties, Zoe
  2016   "Unsettling Settler Food Movements: Food Sovereignty and Decolonization in Canada." *Cuizine* 7(2). www.erudit.org/en/journals/cuizine/1900-v1-n1-cuizine02881/1038478ar/.

Mavor, James W., Jr., and Byron E. Dix
  1989   *Manitou: The Sacred Landscape of New England's Native Civilization.* Inner Traditions International, Rochester, VT.
  1982   "Ritual Stones of Cape Cod." *Cape Cod Naturalist* 2(1):2-12.

Mavor, James W., Jr.
  1969   *Voyage to Atlantis.* Putnam, New York.
  1986   "Stone Mounds and Stone Rows." In *The Book of Falmouth,* edited by Mary L. Smith. Falmouth Historical Commission.
  1994   "In Memoriam: Byron E. Dix (1942-1993)." *Bulletin of the Massachusetts Archaeological Society* 55(1):43.

McBride, Kevin, David Naumec, Ashley Bissonnette and Noah Fellman
  2016   *Technical Report: Battle of Great Falls/Wissantinneqag-Peskeomskut (May 19 1676), Pre-Inventory Research and Documentation Plan. GA-2287-14-012.* National Park Service, American Battlefield Protection Program.

McDonald, Matt
    2019   "Brown University is on Occupied Territory and Is Part of the Problem, About-to-Be-Tattooed New Graduate Tells Fellow Graduates." May 26. *NewBostonPost.com*. newbostonpost. com/2019/05/26/brown-university-is-on-occupied-territory-and-is-part-of-the-problem-about-to-be-tattooed-new-gradu-ate-tells-fellow-graduates/.

McGhee, Robert
    2008   "Aboriginalism and the Problems of Indigenous Archaeology." *American Antiquity* 73(4):579-597.

McLoughlin, Lisa A.
    2017   "Semiotic Stone Mysteries." *Journal of Community Archaeology and Heritage* 4(1):69-72.
    2019   "US Pagans and Indigenous Americans: Land and Identity." *Religions*. 10(3):152. www.mdpi.com/2077-1444/10/3/152/ htm.
    2020   "Doug Harris, Stone Landscape Preservationist." 16 December. *GoFundMe.com*. www.gofundme.com/f/indige-nous-ceremonial-stone-landscapes.

McMullen, Ann
    1994   "What's Wrong With This Picture? Context, Conversion, Survival, and the Development of Regional Native Cultures and Pan-Indianism in Southeastern New England." In *Enduring Traditions*, edited by Laurie L. Weinstein, pp. 122-150. Bergin and Garvey, Westport, Connecticut.

McPherson, Robert S.
    1994   "Review. *Manitou: The Sacred Landscape of New England's Native Civilization.*" *Forest & Conservation History* 38(1):37-38.

McWhorter, John
    2018   "The Virtue Signalers Won't Change the World." 23 2018. *The Atlantic*. www.theatlantic.com/ideas/archive/2018/12/why-third-wave-anti-racism-dead-end/578764/.
    2020a "The Dehumanizing Condescension of *White Fragility.*" 15 July. *The Atlantic*. www.theatlantic.com/ideas/archive/2020/07/ dehumanizing-condescension-white-fragility/614146/.
    2020b "John McWhorter – Reparations Has Been Defeated." 20 December. *YouTube*. www.youtube.com/watch?v=tXi1vZ-cem_8.

Melish, Joanne Pope

2016 *Disowning Slavery: Gradual Emancipation and 'Race' in New England*. Cornell University Press.

Menta, John

1994 "Cultural Conflict in Southern New England: A History of the Quinnipiac Indians." Master's Thesis, Southern Connecticut State University.

Merzbach, Scott

2016 "Solar Site in Shutesbury Still Controversial." *Daily Hampshire Gazette*. www.gazettenet.com/Survey-of-solar-project-in-Shutesbury-questioned-3388012.

2017a "Solar Project Advances Despite Claims Shutesbury Property was Once a Burial Ground." *Daily Hampshire Gazette*. www.gazettenet.com/Shutesbury-solar-project-moving-forward-9681199.

2017b "Opponents Continue War of Words About Shutesbury Solar Project." *Greenfield Recorder*. www.recorder.com/shutesbury-residents-continue-push-back-on-solar-array-9738845.

2017c "Judge Tosses Lawsuit Over Shutesbury Solar Project." *Greenfield Recorder*. www.recorder.com/Civil-rights-lawsuit-related-to-Shutesbury-solar-project-dismissed-11868224.

2018a "Solar Project in Shutesbury Moves Ahead." 21 January. *Daily Hampshire Gazette*. www.gazettenet.com/Solar-project-underway-in-Shutesbury-15006061.

2018b "Shutesbury Solar Project Kicks Off." 22 January. *Greenfield Recorder*. www.recorder.com/shutesbury-solar-project-moved-forward-15050576.

Michigan Farmer

1898 "New England's Abandoned Farms." *Michigan Farmer* 33(4): 70.

Miller, G. Wayne

2015 "Race in R.I.: Since the Days of Roger Williams, Native Americans Have Suffered One Devastating Blow After Another." *Providence Journal*. www.providencejournal.com/article/99999999/news/151029773.

Moeller, Roger W.

1987 "Stone Walls, Stone Lines, and Supposed Indian Graves." *Bulletin of the Archaeological Society of Connecticut*. 50: 17-22.

Moore, Charity M. and Matthew Victor Weiss

2016 "The Continuing 'Stone Mound Problem': Identifying and

Interpreting the Ambiguous Rock Piles of the Upper Ohio Valley." *Journal of Ohio Archaeology* 4:39-72.

Moyn, Samuel

2018   "Opinion: The Alt-Right's Favorite Meme is 100 Years Old." 13 November. *New York Times*. www.nytimes.com/2018/11/13/ opinion/cultural-marxism-anti-semitism.html.

Muhall, Joe

2018   "Holocaust Denial is Changing – The Fight Against it Must Change Too." 21 November. *The Guardian*. www.theguardian. com/commentisfree/2018/nov/21/holocaust-denial-chang-ing-antisemitism-far-right.

Mukayshsak Weekuw

2020   New Student Application. www.transparentclassroom.com/s/1272/schools/1272/online_ applications/new?locale=pt.

Muller, Norman

1999   "Stone Rows and Boulders: A Comparative Study. Field Report." *New England Research Association*. www.neara.org/ images/pdf/stonerows.pdf.

2003   "The Cairns in Our Midst: Historic or Prehistoric?" *New England Antiquities Research Association Journal* 37(2):5-12.

2008   "Accenting the Landscape: Interpreting the Oley Hills Site." In *The Archaeology of Semiotics and the Social Order of Things*, edited by George Nash and George Children, pp. 129-138. Archaeopress, Oxford.

2009   "Stone Mound Investigations as of 2009." *New England Antiquities Research Association Journal* 43(1):17-23.

2015   "The Stone 'Fort' at Lochmere, NH: A History." *New England Research Association Journal* 349(1):29-42.

Mulvaney, Katie

2013   "Narragansett Tribe's Ex Director of Housing Sentenced to One Year for Embezzlement." 5 October. *Providence Jour-nal*. www.providencejournal.com/article/20131005/ NEWS/310059941.

2016   "Narragansett Chief Sachem: No Hard Feelings Over Assumpico's Role in 2003 Smoke Shop Raid." *Providence Journal*. www.providencejournal.com/news/20161103/narra-gansett-chief-sachem-no-hard-feelings-over-assumpicos-role-in-2003-smoke-shop-raid.

2017   "PJ Fox: The Man in the Middle Who Helped Defuse

Narragansett Tribal Standoff." 1 January. *Providence Journal.* www.providencejournal.com/news/20170101/pj-fox-man-in-middle-who-helped-defuse-narragansett-tribal-standoff.

Murray, Stephanie
2016 "Shutesbury OKs Permit for Controversial Solar Project." *Daily Hampshire Gazette.* www.gazettenet.com/Shutesbury-Planning-Board-approves-special-permit-for-30-acre-solar-installation-2661555.

National Register of Historic Places
1980 Nomination Form, Queen's Fort. March.
2008 "The Turners Falls Sacred Ceremonial Hill Site. Determination of Eligibility Notification," National Park Service, Washington, D.C. Redacted. www.achp.gov/sites/default/files/2018-05/National%20Register%20of%20Historic%20Places%20determination%20of%20eligibility%20of%20the%20Turners%20Falls%20Sacred%20Ceremonial%20Hill%20Site-Redacted1.pdf.

National Park Service
2017 *Acknowledging Landscapes: Presentations from the National Register Landscape Initiative.* National Register Landscape Initiative. www.nps.gov/nr/publications/guidance/nrli/presentations/acknowledging-Landscapes-2017-07.pdf.

Newell, Margaret Ellen
2003 "The Changing Nature of Indian Slavery in New England 1670-1720." In *Reinterpreting New England Indians and the Colonial Experience*, edited by Colin Calloway and Neal Salisbury, pp. 106-136. The Colonial Society of Massachusetts.

New England Antiquities Research Association (NEARA)
2004 "FAQ: Forty Years and Still Asking Questions." *New England Antiquities Research Association Journal* 38(1):20-28.
2014 "50 Years Past and Present–Now Comes the Future." *New England Antiquities Research Association Journal* 48(2):38-44.

Neudorfer, Giovanna
1979 "Vermont's Stone Chambers: Their Myth and Their History." *Vermont History* 47(2):79-147.
1980 *Vermont's Stone Chambers: An Inquiry Into Their Past.* Vermont Historical Society, Montpelier.

New York Herald
1844 "Silas Wright." 11 July. Pg. 2. *New York Herald.* New York.

New York Sun
  1886 "Magnificent Politics." 1 August. Pg. 3. *New York Sun*. New York.

Nichols, Tom
  2017 *The Death of Expertise: The Campaign Against Established Knowledge and Why It Matters*. Oxford University Press.

Niedowski, Erika
  2011 "RI Governor Pardons Irish Man Hanged in 1845." 29 June. *Boston.com* (Associated Press). web.archive.org/web/20110702114523/http://www.boston.com/news/local/rhode_island/articles/2011/06/29/ri_governor_pardons_irish_man_hanged_in_1845/.

Noe-Bustamante, Luis, Loren Mora, and Mark Hugo Lopez
  2020 "About One-in-Four U.S. Hispanics Have Heard of Latinx, but Just 3% Use It." 11 August. *Pew Research Center*. www.pewresearch.org/hispanic/2020/08/11/about-one-in-four-u-s-hispanics-have-heard-of-latinx-but-just-3-use-it/.

Norton, Henry Franklin
  1923 *Martha's Vineyard: History, Legends, and Stories*. The Author, Hartford.

Norwich Bulletin
  2016 "Tribe Behind Foxwoods Rehires Ex-Leader Convicted of Theft." Associated Press. www.norwichbulletin.com/article/20160122/news/160129823.

O'Brien, Jean M.
  1997 *Dispossession by Degrees: Indian Land and Identity in Natick, Massachusetts, 1650-1790*. Cambridge University Press.
  2001 "Changing Conditions of Life for Indian Women in Eighteenth-Century New England." In *Major Problems in American Indian History: Documents and Essays*, edited by A.L. Hurtado & P. Iverson, Second Edition. Houghton Mifflin, New York.
  2006 "Vanishing Indians in Nineteenth-Century New England: Local Historians' Erasure of Still-Present Indian People." In *New Perspectives on Native North America: Culture, Histories, and Representations*, edited by Jean O'Brien, Sergei Kan and Pauline Turner Strong, pp. 414-32. University of Nebraska Press.
  2010 *Firsting and Lasting: Writing Indians Out of Existence in New England*. University of Minnesota Press, Minneapolis.

O'Connor, Devin
2020 "Former Mashpee Chairman Indicted on Several Charges, Asks Tribe for Legal Costs." 25 December. *Casino.org*. www. casino.org/news/former-mashpee-chairman-indicted-asks-tribe-to-cover-legal-costs/.

Ogdensburg Advance and St. Lawrence Weekly Democrat
1902 "City Locals." 17 July. Pg. 5. *Ogdensburg Advance and St. Lawrence Weekly Democrat*. Ogdensburg, New York.

Orcutt, Samuel
1882 *History of the Towns of New Milford and Bridgewater, Connecticut, 1705-1882*. Case, Lockwood, and Brainard Company, Hartford.

Orleans County Monitor
1874 "Poor Economy." 31 August. Pg. 4. *Orleans County Monitor*. Barton, Vermont.

Oxford Democrat
1910 "Greenwood." 1 February. Pg. 2. *Oxford Democrat*. Paris, Maine.

Ouimette, Kate
2019 "'Bringing Back the Songs We Need': The Narragansett Food Sovereignty Initiative." Student Thesis. Mount Holyoke College. ida.mtholyoke.edu/xmlui/bitstream/handle/10166/5688/Thesis%20Narragansett.pdf?sequence=1&isAllowed=y.

Parker, Patricia L. and Thomas F. King
1990 "Guidelines for Evaluating and Documenting Traditional Cultural Properties." *National Register Bulletin* 38. U.S. Department of the Interior, Washington, D.C.

Pattee, S. C.
1886 "Our Forests."19 February. Pg. 4. *Vermont Phoenix*. Brattleboro, Vermont.

Paul, Tom
2001 "Hammonasset Line Chapter 1: A Summer Solstice Sunrise." Field Report. *New England Antiquities Research Association*. www.neara.org/images/pdf/Hammonasset01.pdf.

PBS *American Experience*
2009 "We Shall Remain: America Through Native Eyes." Video Series. PBS Home Video, Arlington.

Pearson, Noel
2007 "White Guilt, Victimhood and the Quest for a Radical Centre." *Griffith REVIEW Edition 16: Unintended Consequences*. www.

capeyorkpartnerships.com/downloads/noel-pearson-papers/white-guilt-victimhood-and-the-quest-for-a-radical-centre-010607.pdf.

Peters, Paula
2016 *Mashpee Nine: A Story of Cultural Justice.* SmokeSygnals, Mashpee, Massachusetts.

Pett, Sarah
2015 "It's Time to Take the Curriculum Back from Dead White Men." 08 May. *TheConversation.com.* theconversation.com/its-time-to-take-the-curriculum-back-from-dead-white-men-40268.

Pettegrew, Lloyd
2020 "Cancel Culture Spells the Demise of Academic Freedom." 4 November. *The Jewish Voice.* thejewishvoice.com/2020/11/cancel-culture-spells-the-demise-of-academic-freedom/.

Plane, Ann Marie
2002 *Colonial Intimacies: Indian Marriage in Early New England.* Cornell University Press.

Pfaff, Alexander S. P.
2000 "From Deforestation to Reforestation in New England, United States." In *World Forests from Deforestation to Transition?*, edited by M. Palo and H. Vanhanen, pp. 67-82. World Forests Book Series, Vol. 2. Springer, Dordrecht, Netherlands.

Plymouth Antiquarian Society
2012 "Plymouth Antiquarian Society: Historic Sites." Plymouthantiquariansociety.org/historic.htm.

Poli, Domenic
2017 "Wendell, Tribes Combine Forces to ID Ceremonial Sites." *Greenfield Recorder.* www.recorder.com/Working-to-preserve-Native-American-sites-in-Wendell-13328361.

Potter, Parker B., Jr.
1989 "The NEARA Approach and Current Archaeological Method and Theory." *New England Antiquities Research Association Journal* 24(1/2):14-22.

Powell, Christine
2016 "Tribe Can't Block Work on Wind Farm in Preservation Suit." *Law360.* www.law360.com/articles/796533/tribe-can-t-block-work-on-wind-farm-in-preservation-suit.

Prince, J. Dyneley
1907 "Last Living Echoes of the Natick." *American Anthropologist*

6(1):18-45.

Providence Journal

1884 "The Franklin Society Botanical Trip to 'The Blunders.'" 2.
Sept. Pg. 8. *Providence Journal*. Providence, Rhode Island.

1888 "What Shall We Do With It? To the Editor of the Journal." 30
January. Pg. 8. *Providence Journal*. Providence, Rhode Island.

1895 "A Paper Roof: Up on East Thompson There is a Peculiar
Looking House." 2 September. Pg. 1. *Providence Journal*. Providence, Rhode Island.

2014 "Former URI Instructor Charged with Faking Degree."
www.providencejournal.com/breaking-news/con-
tent/20140409-retired-uri-professor-charged-with-faking-de-
gree.ece.

Putnam County Courier

1873 'Picking Stones." 9 August. Pg. 1. *Putnam County Courier*.
Carmel, New York.

Ranslow, Mandy

2014 "Tribal Consultation and the Role of the State Agency: The
View from the Connecticut Department of Transportation."
Paper presented at the Conference on New England Archaeol-
ogy, May 17.

Rapkin, Rachel

2016 "Local Tribes Create Team to Document Ceremonial Sites
Near Pipeline Path." *Greenfield Recorder*. www.recorder.com/
Archives/2015/11/tribaldocumentation-GR-111115.

Raup, Hugh M.

1966 "The View from John Sanderson's Farm: A Perspective for the
Use of the Land." *Forest History* 10(1):2-11.

ReelWamps.com

2011 "Barnstable Judge Throws Cassie Out of Court." 29 January.
reelwamps.com/archives/2011/01.

2017 "She Come by it Honest." 16 October.
reelwamps.com/archives/she-come-by-it-honest.

2020 "Course Correction." 29 November.
reelwamps.com/archives/2020/11.

Reynard, Elizabeth

1934 *The Narrow Land: Folk Chronicles of Old Cape Cod*. Houghton
Mifflin Company.

Rhode Island Historical Preservation and Heritage Commission

2001 *Historic Landscapes of Rhode Island*. Herald Press.

2002 *Native American Archaeology in Rhode Island*. Rhode Island Historical Preservation & Heritage Commission.

Richie, Chip

2004 *Black Indians: An American Story*. Rich-Heape Films.

Ricoeur, Paul

2006 *Memory, History, Forgetting*. University of Chicago Press.

Robinson, Paul

1990 "The Struggle Within: The Indian Debate in Seventeenth-Century Narragansett Country." Doctoral dissertation, Binghamton University.

2015 "The Foundations of Thanksgiving and the Obligations of Place: Defending the Indigenous Homeland and All That It Holds." 8 November. Presented for the Mount Hope Farm Lecture Series, Bristol, Rhode Island.

Robinson, Paul A., Marc Kelly and Patricia E. Rubertone

1985 "Preliminary Biocultural Interpretations from a Seventeenth-Century Narragansett Indian Cemetery in Rhode Island." In *Cultures in Contact: The Impact of European Contacts on Native American Cultural Institutions, A.D. 1000-1800*, edited by William Fitzhugh, pp. 107-130. Smithsonian Institution Press.

Rose, Deborah Bird

2014 "Decolonising the Discourse of Environmental Knowledge in Settler Societies." In *History, Power, Text: Cultural Studies and Indigenous Studies*, edited by Timothy Neale, Crystal McKinnon, and Eve Vincent, pp. 208-228. University of Technology Sydney ePress. utsepress.lib.uts.edu.au/site/chapters/e/10.5130/978-0-9872369-1-3.n/.

Rothovius, Andrew

1990 "Our Sacred Stones." *New England Antiquities Research Association Journal* 24(3/4):90-91.

Rubertone, Patricia E.

1994 "Grave Remembrances: Enduring Traditions Among the Narragansett." *Connecticut History Review* 35(1):22-45.

2001 "Grave Undertakings: Archaeology of Roger Williams and the Narragansett Indians." Smithsonian Institution, Washington, D.C.

2020 *Native Providence: Memory, Community, & Survivance in the Northeast*. University of Nebraska Press.

Rural New Yorker
  1918 "Some Questions from New Hampshire." Vol. 77. *The Rural New Yorker*. Rural Publishing Co., New York.
Rush, Laurie
  2016 "Native American Sacred Sites and the Federal Government: A Training for Federal Employees and Contract Staff Developed under the Sacred Sites Memorandum of Understanding." www.justice.gov/file/952031/download.
  2019 "Ceremonial Stone Landscapes of Northeastern North America." Archaeological Institute of America. www.archaeological.org/lecturer/laurie-rush/.
Ruttenber, Edward Manning
  1872 *History of the Indian Tribes of Hudson's River*. J. Munsell, Albany.
Saltzman, Dale
  2008 "Hiding in Plain Sight Part II." *New Antiquities Research Association Journal* 42(2):36-38.
Schieldrop, Mark
  2011 "State's Last Executed Man Finally Gets a Proper Burial." 9 September. *Patch.com*. patch.com/rhode-island/cranston/states-last-executed-man-finally-gets-a-proper-burial.
Schneider, Christian
  2020 "Scholars Denounce Attempt to Ban their Archaeology Book After Being Accused of Racism Against Native Americans." 23 December. *The College Fix*. www.thecollegefix.com/scholars-denounce-attempt-to-ban-their-archeology-book-after-being-accused-of-racism-against-native-americans/.
Schultz, Spencer
  2019 "SPEAK Report Reveals Lack of Political Diversity in University Speakers." 25 April. *The Brown Daily Herald*. www.browndailyherald.com/2019/04/25/speak-report-reveals-lack-political-diversity-university-speakers/.
Schwartz, Doug
  2004-5 "Did Celts from Europe Build the Northeastern U.S. Stone Ruins?" *Native Stones*. nativestones.com/celts3.htm.
Serreze, Mary C.
  2016a "Shutesbury Solar Farm Opponents Say Site May Contain Native American Burial Ground." *Mass Live*. www.masslive.com/news/index.ssf/2016/08/shutesbury_solar_opponents_say.html.

2016b "Solar Foes Claiming Indian Burial Mounds Raise Ruckus at Schutesbury Meeting." *Mass Live.* www.masslive.com/news/index.ssf/2016/08/solar_foes_claiming_indian_bur.html.

2016c "Solar Foes Claiming Indian Burial Mounds File Federal Civil Rights Lawsuit Naming Town Officials, Developer." *Mass Live.* www.masslive.com/news/index.ssf/2016/08/shutesbury_solar_farm_foe_file.html.

2016d "Lawyer for Shutesbury Solar Farm Developer Says Opponents' Civil Rights Lawsuit has No Merit." *Mass Live.* www.masslive.com/news/index.ssf/2016/09/lawyer_seeks_dismissal_of_fede.html.

2016e "Federal Judge Tells Shutesbury Solar Foes to Start Following Rules of the Court." *Mass Live.* www.masslive.com/news/index.ssf/2016/12/federal_judge_to_shutesbury_so.html.

2017a "Kinder Morgan Wins OK to Construct Connecticut Expansion Pipeline." *Mass Live.* www.masslive.com/news/index.ssf/2017/04/kinder_morgan_wins_ok_to_start.html.

2017b "Shutesbury Solar Foes Claiming Native American Burial Mounds Take Parting Shot at Planning Board." *Mass Live.* www.masslive.com/news/index.ssf/2017/08/disappointed_by_lawsuit_dismis.html.

Shoemaker, Nancy

2000 *Native American Population Recovery in the Twentieth Century.* University of New Mexico Press.

2015 *Native American Whalemen and the World: The Contingency of Race.* Chapel Hill: University of North Carolina Press.

Shutesbury Planning Board

2015-17 Meeting Minutes. www.shutesbury.org/minutes/search?tid=20&field_meeting_date_value%5Bmin%5D=&field_meeting_date_value%5Bmax%5D=&items_per_page=50.

Shutesbury, Town of

2012 "Open Space and Recreation Plan Update, 2012-2019." www.shutesbury.org/sites/default/files/offices_committees/open_space_cmte/plan/FINAL%20SHUTESBURY%20OPEN%20SPACE%20PLAN%20May%202015final.pdf .

Silliman, Stephen W.

2020 Stephen W. Silliman, Faculty, University of Massachusetts Boston. www.faculty.umb.edu/stephen_silliman/.

Silverman, David J.

2001 "The Impact of Indentured Servitude on the Society and Culture of New England." *New England Quarterly* 74(4):622-666.

Simmons, William S.

1986 *Spirit of the New England Tribes: Indian History and Folklore, 1620-1984.* University Press of New England, Hanover, New Hampshire.

Singleton, Olly

2020 "The Problem With Peterson's 'Cultural Marxism.'" 21 July. *The Independent.* www.indiependent.co.uk/the-problem-with-petersons-cultural-marxism/.

Smithfield, Town of

2016 Comprehensive Community Plan. smithfieldri.com/pdf/planner/Comprehensive_Community_Plan.pdf.

Society for American Archaeology's Archaeological Record

2020 Issue 4 (September), Volume 20. onlinedigeditions.com/publication/?i=674270.

Sotirakopoulos, Nikos

2020 "The Alt-Right: Identity Politics on Steroids." 1 May. *SpikedOnLine.com.* www.spiked-online.com/2020/05/01/the-alt-right-identity-politics-on-steroids/.

Sowamsheritagearea.org

2017 "Pokanoket Tribal History." sowamsheritagearea.org/wp/pokanoket-tribal-history/.

Sowell, Thomas

2011 *Intellectuals and Society. Revised and enlarged edition.* Basic Books, New York.

2018 *Discrimination and Disparities.* Basic Books, New York.

Spencer, Ryan

2019 "Central Massachusetts School Holds Fundraiser for Mashpee Wampanoag Tribe." 11 December. *The Mashpee Enterprise.* www.capenews.net/mashpee/news/central-massachusetts-school-holds-fundraiser-for-mashpee-wampanoag-tribe/article_554afb07-4148-57b6-958f-32768fda4194.html.

2020a "Vice Chairwoman of Mashpee Tribe To Receive Governor's Award in the Humanities." 2 October. *The Mashpee Enterprise.* www.capenews.net/mashpee/news/vice-chairwoman-of-mashpee-tribe-to-receive-governors-award-in-humanities/article_4a97aa30-bc50-5027-8bfe-f40e9fb7dd6d.html.

2020b "FEMA: Mashpee Wampanaog Tribe Winning Against COVID." 4 December. *CapeNews.net*. www.capenews.net/mashpee/news/fema-mashpee-wampanoag-tribe-winning-against-covid/article_541f0b85-bc05-51b0-ad37-62a141564cf1.html.

Stanton, Anthony Dean

2019 "Splinter Groups." 1 February. NarragansettIndianNation.org. narragansettindiannation.org/office-of-the-chief-sachem/.

Starna, William A.

1990 "The Pequots in the Early Seventeenth Century." In *The Pequots in Southern New England*, edited by Laurence M. Hauptman and James D. Wherry, pp. 33-47. University of Oklahoma Press.

2017 "After the Handbook: A Perspective on 40 Years of Scholarship since the Publication of the Handbook of North American Indians, Vol. 15, Northeast." *New York History* 98(1)112-146.

Stening, Tanner

2018 "Mashpee Wampanoag Tribe Language Program Awarded $1.4M Grant." 18 September. *Cape Cod Times*. www.capecodtimes.com/news/20180918/mashpee-wampanoag-tribe-language-program-awarded-14m-grant.

Strohmeyer, Mark

1996 "On Seeing the Sacred: Three Massachusetts Stonework Sites." Abstract of paper presented at the 1996 New England Antiquities Research Association Fall Meeting, North Falmouth, Massachusetts.

Speck, Frank G.

1928 *Territorial Subdivisions and Boundaries of the Wampanoag, Massachusetts and Nauset Indians, Indian Notes and Monographs, No.44*. Heye Foundation, New York.

1945 "The Memorial Brush Heap in Delaware and Elsewhere." *Bulletin of the Archaeological Society of Delaware* 4:17-23.

Spencer, Susan

2012 "New Park Preserves Upton Stone Structure." *Telegram and Gazette*. www.telegram.com/article/20120414/NEWS/104149854/1116.

Steele, Shelby

2006 *White Guilt: How Blacks and Whites Together Destroyed the Promise of the Civil Rights Era*. Harper Collins, New York.

Stening, Tanner
2019 "Newspaper Finds Access to Tribal Records Irregular." 10 March. *SouthCoastToday.com*. www.southcoasttoday.com/ news/20190310/newspaper-finds-access-to-tribal-records-ir-regular.

Streich, Catherine
2020 "Op/Ed: The State of Rhode Island and Problematic Plantations." 18 June. *East Greenwich News*. eastgreenwich-news.com/op-ed-the-state-of-rhode-island-and-problematic-plantations/.

Strohmeyer, Mark
1996 "On Seeing the Sacred: Three Massachusetts Stonework Sites." Abstract of paper presented at the 1996 NEARA Fall Meeting, North Falmouth, Massachusetts.

Strong, Roslyn
1990 "Chapter News: Maine." *New England Antiquities Research Association Transit* 1(2):5-6.

Sturges, Mark
2014 "Fleecing Connecticut: David Humphreys and the Poetics of Sheep Farming." *The New England Quarterly* 87(3):464-489.

Sullivan, Kelly
2019 "History in the Making." 12 October. *The Chariho Times*. www.ricentral.com/chariho_times/news/local_news/ history-in-the-making/article_9a6ff540-ec42-11e9-9f36-23305c78a5f9.html.

SWCA Environmental Consultants
2016 "Phase IA Archaeological Pedestrian Survey, Shutesbury, Franklin County Massachusetts." Submitted to Martin Lebo-vits, Managing Director and Co-Founder, Lake Street Devel-opment Partners LLC.

Sydney Peace Foundation
2011 "City of Sydney Peace Prize Lecture by Prof Noam Chomsky." 3 November. *In Peace Blog*. sydneypeacefoundation.org. au/2011-city-of-sydney-peace-prize-lecture-by-prof-noam-chomsky/.

Szep, Jason
2007 "Piles of Rocks Spark an American Indian Mystery." Reuters. www.reuters.com/article/us-usa-indians-rhodeisland/ piles-of-rocks-spark-an-american-indian-mystery-idUSN1625947520070518.

Tantaquidgeon, Gladys
  1935 "Location, History, Government, Language, Etc. of the Mashpee Indians." Office of Indian Affairs. Typescript.
Taylor, Cathy
  2008 "The Great Trail." *New England Antiquities Research Association Journal* 42(1):19-23.
Taylor, Charles J.
  1882 *History of Great Barrington, Massachusetts.*
Taylor, Melanie Benson
  2017 "The Convenient Indian: How Activists Get Native Americans Wrong." 9 April. *Los Angeles Review of Books.* lareviewofbooks.org/article/the-convenient-indian-how-liberals-get-native-americans-wrong/.
Taylor, Paul S. and Anne Loftis
  1981 "The Legacy of the Nineteenth-Century New England Farmer." *The New England Quarterly* 54(2):243-254.
Thee, Christopher J.
  2006 "Massachusetts Nipmucs and the Long Shadow of John Milton Earle." *New England Quarterly* 79(4):636-654.
Thistlethwaite, Frank
  1967 *The Great Experiment: An Introduction to the History of the American People.* Cambridge University Press, London.
Thom, Alexander, and Archibald S. Thom
  1978 *Megalithic Sites in Britain and Brittany.* Clarendon Press, Oxford.
Thompson-Martin, Eric
  2017 "Baffled by Opposition to Solar Project in Shutesbury: Opinion." 07 May. *Gazette.net.* www.gazettenet.com/Eric-Thompson-Martin-supports-solar-project-in-Shutesbury-8962823.
Thorsen, Karen (Director)
  1989 *James Baldwin: The Price of the Ticket.* USA.
Thorson, Robert M.
  2002 *Stone by Stone: The Magnificent History in New England's Stone Walls.* Walker and Company, New York.
  2005 *Exploring Stone Walls.* Walker and Company, New York.
  2018 *Stone Therapy.* Stone Wall Initiative. stonewall.uconn.edu/2018/07/27/stone-therapy/.
Timreck, Ted
  2010 [2008] *Great Falls: Discovery, Destruction and Preservation in*

a Massachussetts Town. Film produced by Ted Timreck and
Peter Frechette. Hidden Landscapes, LLC, New York.

Tomison, Bill

2020 "New Walking Tour Shows Early Black History of Providence."
30 January. *WPRI.com.* www.wpri.com/news/local-news/
providence/new-walking-tour-shows-early-black-history-of-
providence/.

Town of Shutesbury

2017 Warrant Article Petition, Filed March 22, 2017, 2:15 PM.
"Resolution to Preserve Native American Historical Sites and
Traditional Cultural Properties." www.shutesbury.org/sites/
default/files/170322%20Preserve%20Native%20American%20
Historical.pdf.

Town of Montague

2012 Selectmen's Meeting Minutes, December 17.

Trumbull, James H.

1881 *Indian Names of Places, etc., in and on the Borders of
Connecticut.* Case Lockwood and Brainard Co., Hartford.

Tucker, Luther

1834 "Hints to Farmers." *Genesee Farmer and Gardener's Journal.*
10 May. 4(19):150. Luther Tucker & Co., Rochester, New York.

Tuoti, Gerry

2013 "Mashpee Wampanoag Tribe Official Issues Apology for
Remarks Made at Taunton Casino Hearing." 6 December.
Taunton Daily Gazette. www.tauntongazette.com/x915450732/
Mashpee-Wampanoag-tribe-official-issues-apology-for-re-
marks-made-at-Taunton-casino-hearing.

Turnbaugh, William A.

1984 *The Material Culture of RI-1000: A Mid-17th Century
Narragansett Indian Burial Site in North Kingston, Rhode
Island.* Department of Sociology and Anthropology. University
of Rhode Island Press, Kingston.

1993 "Assessing the Significance of European Goods in Seventeenth
Century Narragansett Society." In *Ethnohistory and Archaeology: Approaches to Postcontact Change in the Americas,* edited
by J. Daniel Rogers and Samuel M. Wilson, pp. 133-162. Ple-
num Press, New York.

Turner, Camilla

2018 "Schools Must Look Beyond 'Dead White Men' to Make the
Curriculum More Diverse, Teacher Union Chief Says."

The Telegraph. 08 June. www.telegraph.co.uk/educa-tion/2018/06/08/schools-must-look-beyond-dead-white-men-make-curriculum-morediverse/.

Turner, Frederick J.
1919 “Greater New England in the Middle of the Nineteenth Century.” *American Antiquarian Society* 29:222-241.

United South and Eastern Tribes, Inc.
2003 “Sacred Landscape within Commonwealth of Massachusetts.” USET Resolution #2003:22, United South and Eastern Tribes, Inc., Nashville, TN.
2007 “Sacred Ceremonial Stone Landscapes Found in the Ancestral Territories of United South and Eastern Tribes, Inc.” USET Resolution #2007:037, United South and Eastern Tribes, Inc., Nashville, TN.
2014 “Requesting the Federal Energy Regulatory Commission to Initiate Tribal Consultation.” USET Resolution #2014:056, United South and Eastern Tribes Inc., Nashville, TN.

Union and Easton Journal
1837 13 March. *Union and Easton Journal*. Biddeford, Maine.

United States Department of the Interior
2006 “Summary Under the Criteria for the Proposed Finding on the Mashpee Wampanoag Tribal Indian Council, Inc.” United States Department of the Interior, Office of Federal Acknowl-edgement MWT-V001-D005. www.bia.gov/sites/bia.gov/files/assets/as-ia/ofa/petition/015_mashpe_MA/015_pf.pdf.

Urban, Cori
2020 “Turners Falls May be Renamed Because of Association with Native American Massacre.” 16 July. *Masslive.com*. www.masslive.com/news/2020/07/turners-falls-may-be-re-named-because-of-association-with-native-american-massa-cre.html.

Vaughn, Lawrence M.
1929 “Abandoned Farmland in New York”. *Journal of Farm Economics* 11(3): 436-444.

Verplanck, Johnston
1968[1822] *A Knickerbocker Tour of New York State, 1822: Our Travels, Statistical, Geographical, Mineorological, Geological, Historical, Political and Quizzical*. Edited by Louis Leonard Tucker. DigitalCommons@University of Nebraska-Lincoln. digitalcommons.unl.edu/etas/61/.

Vermont Farmer
1872   "Removing Stones from Tillage Land." 6 Dec. *Vermont Farmer.* Newport, Vermont.

Vermont Phoenix
1848   "The Farm of E. Phinney, Esq." 19 May. Pg. 1. V*ermont Phoenix.* Brattleboro, Vermont.

Vermont Transcript
1864   "Farmer's Department." 1 September. Pg. 4. *Vermont Transcript.* St. Albans, Vermont.

Vermont Watchman
1883   3 October. *Vermont Watchman.* Montpelier, Vermont.

Viles, Chance
2017   "Shutesbury Votes for Budget Hike, School Board Post." 08 May. *Recorder.com.* www.recorder.com/shutesbury-residents-have-say-at-town-meeting-9739320.

Vosk, Stephanie and George Brennan
2008   "Mashpee Tribe Faces Membership Feud." 2 November. *Cape Cod Times.* www.capecodtimes.com/article/20081102/NEWS/811020329.

Waksman, Peter
1999   "A Survey of Stone Piles in Acton, Massachusetts." *New England Antiquities Research Association Journal* 33(1):2-9.
2008   "A Quick Summary of Fred Meli's Talk at the NEARA Spring 2008 Conference." 01 May. *Rock Piles.* rockpiles.blogspot.com/2008/05/quick-summary-of-fred-melis-talk-at.html.
2009   "Native American Tribal Historic Preservation Officers Speak About Ceremonial Stone Structures." 24 October. *Rock Piles.* rockpiles.blogspot.com/2009/10/native-american-tribal-historic.html.
2011   "The First Rock Pile Site Acknowledged by the Indians." 28 February. *Rock Piles.* rockpiles.blogspot.com/2011/02/.
2012   "A Context for Studying Rock Piles in Massachusetts." *Bulletin of the Massachusetts Archaeological Society* 73(2):68-74.
2017a "The Logic of Publicizing Rock Pile Sites." 29 January. *Rock Piles.* rockpiles.blogspot.com/2017/01/the-logic-of-publicising-rock-pile-sites.html.
2017b "Photos from Our Hidden Landscapes." 29 October. *Rock Piles.* rockpiles.blogspot.com/2017/10/photos-from-our-hidden-landscapes.html.
2018a "Indigenous Landscape – Creating a New Mythology." 01

October. *Rock Piles*. rockpiles.blogspot.com/2018/10/indige-nous-landscape-creating-new.html.

2018b "Year in Review - 2018." 31 December. *Rock Piles*. rockpiles.blogspot.com/2018/12/year-in-review-2018.html.

2019 "A Split in the Rock Pile Community." 12 May. *Rock Piles*. rockpiles.blogspot.com/2019/05/a-split-in-rock-pile-commu-nity.html.

2020a "My Little Argument with NEARA and the Goal of Site Protection." 11 May. *Rock Piles*. rockpiles.blogspot.com/2020/05/my-little-argument-with-neara-and-goal.html.

2020b "What did the Indians Know?" 17 October. *Rock Piles*. rockpiles.blogspot.com/2020/10/what-did-indians-know.html.

Walk Free Foundation

2018 "Global Slavery Index 2018." Walk Free Foundation, available from www.globalslaveryindex.org.

Walwer, Gregory F.

2015 "Stone Piles: A Tale of Two Towns." *Bulletin of the Archaeological Society of Connecticut* 77: 111-121.

Walwer, Gregory F. and Dorothy N. Walwer

2005 "Phase II Documentary Archaeological Survey of Stone Features at The Ridges at Deer Lake Housing Development Property in the Town of Killingworth, Connecticut." Manu-script filed with the State Historic Preservation Office, Hart-ford, Connecticut.

2018 "Phase I Intensive Archaeological Survey of the Cedar Forest Estates Subdivision in the Town of Smithfield, Rhode Island." Archaeological Consulting Services, Guilford, Connecticut.

Watts, Galen

2018 "'Cultural Marxism' Explained and Re-Evaluated." 23 June. *Quillette*. quillette.com/2018/06/23/cultural-marxism-ex-plained-and-re-evaluated/.

Watson, Raymond "Two Hawks"

2015 Curriculum vitae. As attached to a letter from Providence Mayor Jorge O. Elorza to the Honorable Members of the Providence City Council on January 26, announcing Watson's re-appointment to the city's Human Relations Commission.

2017 "Hemoc Xelup's NAAIP is a Fraud! FANA Warns people and Organizations in Indian Country." 17 September. *YouTube.com*. www.youtube.com/watch?v=4MBabc0OKPU&fea-ture=share.

2019 "Blackface is Unacceptable in Virginia and RI – Raymond Two Hawks Watson." 3 February. *GoLocalProv.com*. www.golocal-prov.com/news/blackface-is-unacceptable-in-virginia-and-ri-raymond-two-hawks-watson.

Webster, Noah
1790 *Collection of Essays and Fugitive Writings on Moral, Historical, Political, and Literary Subjects.* I. Thomas and E.T. Adams, Boston.

Weiss, Elizabeth and James W. Springer
2020 *Repatriation and Erasing the Past.* University of Florida Press.

Weiss, Matthew V. and Charity M. Weiss
2017 "Stones and Their Places: An Application of Landscape Theory to Ceremonial Stone Landscapes of West Virginia." Paper presented at the Institute for American Indian Studies (IAIS) 12th Annual Native American Archaeology Round Table, October 28, Washington, Connecticut. www.academia.edu/34993300/Stones_and_Their_Places_An_Application_of_Landscape_Theory_to_Ceremonial_Stone_Landscapes_of_West_Virginia.

Wellner, Alison Stein
2005 "Working Together." *American Archaeology* (Spring): 33-38.

Wendell Historical Commission
2018 "Cultural Resource Emergency Concern in Wendell State Forest." static1.squarespace.com/static/5a230104914e6b-1c9b2dfddb/t/5b7de89521c67c7f4f5d4292/1534978203963/Wendell+SF+cultural+resource+emergency+report+4-9-18sm.pdf.

Wessels, Tom
1997 *Reading the Forested Landscape: A Natural History of New England.* The Countryman Press, New York.

White, H.D.
1849 "A Few Hints for the Farmer." Pg. 4. 27 September. *Green-Mountain Freeman.* Montpelier, Vermont.

Widdowson, Frances and Albert Howard
2008 *Disrobing the Aboriginal Industry: The Deception Behind Indigenous Cultural Preservation.* McGill-Queen's University Press.

Williams, Thomas Chatterton
2019 *Self-Portrait in Black and White: Unlearning Race.* W.W. Norton & Company.

Williams, Walter
 2019 "Reparation$." 26 June. *Jewish World Review.*
  jewishworldreview.com/cols/williams062619.php3.

Wilson, F. J.
 1892 "Abandoned Farms. The Cause of this Evil in New England,
  and the Remedy Therefor." *American Farmer* 73(16): 10.

Wilson, Harold F.
 1935 "The Rise and Decline of the Sheep Industry in Northern New
  England." *Agricultural History* 9(1):12-40.

Wilson, John S.
 1990 "We've Got Thousands of These! What Makes an Historic
  Farmstead Significant?" *Historical Archaeology* 24(2): 23-33.

Winokoor, Charles
 2017 "Taunton Council Votes Down Motion to Take Official Stand
  Against Casino Racist Claims." 9 May. *Taunton Gazette.*
  https://www.tauntongazette.com/news/20170509/taunton-
  council-votes-down-motion-to-take-official-stand-against-ca-
  sino-racism-claims.

Winslow, Edward
 1910 "Winslow's Relation [1624]." In *Chronicles of the Pilgrim
  Fathers,* edited by John Masefield, pp. 267-367. E.P. Dutton,
  New York.

Wood, Peter
 2006 *A Bee in the Mouth: Anger in America Now.* Encounter Books,
  New York.

Woods Hole Historical Collection
 n.d. "James W. Mavor, Jr. Collection Biographical Note." Woods
  Hole Museum. woodsholemuseum.org/oldpages/archive/
  MavorJamesW.pdf.

**Zhadanov, Sergey I., Matthew C. Dulik, Michael Markley, George
W. Jennings, Jill B. Gaieski, George Elias, Theodore G. Schurr, and
Genographic Project Consortium.**
 2010 "Genetic Heritage and Native Identity of the Seaconke
  Wampanoag Tribe." *American Journal of Physical Anthropology*
  142(4):579-89.

Zinn, Howard
 1980 *A People's History of the United States.* Harper & Row, New
  York.

Zubatov, Alexander
 2018 "Just Because Anti-Semites Talk About 'Cultural Marxism'

Doesn't Mean It Isn't Real." 29 November. *Tabletmag.com.*
www.tabletmag.com/sections/news/articles/just-because-anti-
semites-talk-about-cultural-marxism-doesnt-mean-it-isnt-re-
al.